THE ROMANCE *of the* ROMANOFFS

Copyright © 2018 Read Books Ltd.
This book is copyright and may not be
reproduced or copied in any way without
the express permission of the publisher in writing

British Library Cataloguing-in-Publication Data
A catalogue record for this book is available from
the British Library

The Tsar Nicholas II

THE ROMANCE
of the
ROMANOFFS

BY
JOSEPH McCABE
AUTHOR OF
"THE TYRANNY OF SHAMS," "THE SOUL OF EUROPE," ETC.

ILLUSTRATED

PREFACE

THE history of Russia has attracted many writers and inspired many volumes during the last twenty years, yet its most romantic and most interesting feature has not been fully appreciated.

Thirteen years ago, when the long struggle of the Russian democrats culminated in a bloody revolution, I had occasion to translate into English an essay written by a learned professor who belonged to what was called "the Russophile School." It was a silken apology for murder. The Russian soul, the writer said, was oriental, not western. The true line of separation of east and west was, not the great ridge of mountains which raised its inert barrier from the Caspian Sea to the frozen ocean, but the western limit of the land of the Slavs. In their character the Slavs were an eastern race, fitted only for autocratic rule, indifferent to those ideas of democracy and progress which stirred to its muddy depths the life of western Europe. They loved the "Little Father." They clung, with all the fervour of their mild and peaceful souls, to their old-world Church. They had the placid wisdom of the east, the health that came of living close to mother-earth,

PREFACE

the tranquillity of ignorance. Was not the Tsar justified in protecting his people from the feverish illusions which agitated western Europe and America?

Thus, in very graceful and impressive language, wrote the "sound" professors, the clients of the aristocracy, the more learned of the silk-draped priests. The Russia which they interpreted to us, the Russia of the boundless horizon, could not read their works. It was almost wholly illiterate. It could not belie them. Indeed, if one could have interrogated some earth-bound peasant among those hundred and twenty millions, he would have heard with dull astonishment that he had *any* philosophy of life. His cattle lived by instinct: *his* path was traced by the priest and the official.

But the American onlooker found one fatal defect in the Russophile theory. These agents of the autocracy contended that the soul of Russia rejected western ideas; yet they were spending millions of roubles every year, they were destroying hundreds of fine-minded men and women every year, they were packing the large jails of Russia until they reeked with typhus and other deadly maladies, in an effort to keep those ideas away from the Russian soul. While Russophile professors were penning their plausible theories of the Russian character, the autocracy which they defended was being shaken by as brave and grim a revolution as

PREFACE

any that has upset thrones in modern Europe. Moscow, the shrine of this supposed beautiful docility, was red with the blood of its children. In the jails and police-cells of Russia about 200,000 men and women, boys and girls, quivered under the lash or sank upon fever-beds, and almost as many more dragged out a living death in the melancholy wastes of Siberia. They wanted democracy and progress; and their introduction of those ideas to the peasantry had awakened so ready and fervent a response that it had been necessary to seal their lips with blood.

We looked back along the history of Russia, and we found that the struggle was nearly a century old. The ghastly route to Siberia had been opened eighty years before. Russia had felt the revolutionary wave which swept over Europe during the thirties of the nineteenth century, and the Tsar of those days had fought not less savagely than the rulers of Austria, Spain, and Portugal for his autocracy. Every democratic advance that has since been won in western Europe has provoked a corresponding effort to advance in Russia, and that effort has always been truculently suppressed. Nearly every other country in Europe has had the courage to educate its people and enable them to study its institutions with open mind. Russia remains illiterate to the extent of seventy-five per cent, and its rulers have ever discouraged or re-

PREFACE

stricted education. The autocracy rested, not upon the affection, but upon the ignorance, of its people.

When we regard the whole history of that autocracy we begin to understand the tragedy of Russia. We dimly but surely perceive, in the dawn of European history, that amongst the families which wandered through the forests of Europe none were more democratic than, few were as democratic as, the early Slavs. We find this great family spread over an area so immense that it is further encouraged to cling to democratic, even communistic, life, and avoid the making of princes or kings. We then find the inevitable military chiefs, not born of the Slav people, intruding and creating princedoms: we find an oriental autocracy fastening itself, violently and parasitically, upon the helpless nation: we find the evil example and the tincture of foreign blood continuing the development until Princes of Moscow become Tsars of all the Russias, and convert a title dipped in blood into a title to rule by the grace of God and the affection of the people. And we find that Moscovite dynasty, from which the Romanoffs issued, playing such pranks before high heaven as few dynasties have played, until the old Slav spirit awakens at the call of the world and makes an end of it.

That is the romance of the Romanoffs, of Russia and its rulers, which I propose to tell. This is not a history of Russia, but the history of its autocracy

PREFACE

as an episode: of its real origin, its long-drawn brutality, its picturesque corruption, its sordid machinery of government, its selfish determination to keep Russia from the growing light, its terrible final struggle and defeat. To a democratic people there can be no more congenial study than this exposure of the crime and failure of an autocracy. To any who find romance in such behaviour as kings and nobles were permitted to flaunt in the eyes of their people in earlier ages the story of the Romanoffs must be exceptionally attractive.

J. M.

CONTENTS

CHAPTER		PAGE
I	THE PRIMITIVE DEMOCRACY OF THE SLAV	1
II	THE DESCENT TO AUTOCRACY	17
III	THE MOSCOVITES BECOME TSARS	37
IV	THE RISE OF THE ROMANOFFS	61
V	THE EARLY ROMANOFFS	82
VI	A ROMANOFF PRINCESS	101
VII	THE GREAT PETER	126
VIII	CATHERINE THE LITTLE	161
IX	ROMANCE UPON ROMANCE	179
X	THE GAY AND PIOUS ELIZABETH	206
XI	CATHERINE THE GREAT	228
XII	IN THE DAYS OF NAPOLEON	258
XIII	THE FIGHT AGAINST LIBERALISM	284
XIV	THE TRAGEDY OF ALEXANDER II	306
XV	ENTER POBIEDONOSTSEFF	338
XVI	THE LAST OF THE ROMANOFFS	337

ILLUSTRATIONS

	FACING PAGE
The Tsar Nicholas II . . . . . *Frontispiece*	
Vladimir, Grande Duke of Kieff, 980–1015 From an Ancient Banner	10
Tatars of the Mongol Period	28
Costume of Boyars in the Seventeenth Century	44
The Patriarch Philaret, father of Mikhail Romanoff, the first Tsar of the New Dynasty. Seventeenth Century . . .	68
Ivan the Terrible, by Antokolsky . . .	86
View of Destroyed Tower of Nicholas, Arsenal, etc., in the Kremlin, A.D. 1812 . From a Contemporary Drawing	108
Peter the Great	134
Room of the Tsar Mikhailovitch, Moscow .	182
Paul the First	214
Catherine II	240

ILLUSTRATIONS

	FACING PAGE
The Red Square, Church of St. Basil and Redeemer Gate, Moscow	266
Winter Palace, Petrograd	290
Cathedral Erected in Petrograd in Memory of Alexander II	312
Tauride Palace, Petrograd, Meeting Place of the Duma	348
Session Chamber of the Duma, Tauride Palace, Petrograd	348
The Tsarina Alexandra	366

THE ROMANCE *of the* ROMANOFFS

THE ROMANCE OF THE ROMANOFFS

CHAPTER I

THE PRIMITIVE DEMOCRACY OF THE SLAV

A LITTLE south of the centre of Europe rises the great curve of the Carpathian mountains. The sprawling bulk of this long chain, rising in places until its crown shines with snow and ice, formed a natural barrier to the spread of Roman civilisation. It enfolded and protected the plains of Hungary and the green valley of the Danube, and it seemed to set a limit to every decent ambition. Beyond it men saw a vast and dreary plain filled with wild peoples whom the Romans and Greeks called "Scythians." It was, in effect, in those days, almost the dividing line of Europe and Asia. One branch of the great European race had gone down into Greece and, becoming civilised, remained there. Another branch had found the blue waters and sunny skies in Italy. A third, the vast horde of the Teutons, was moving heavily and slowly southward in the west.

But about the eastern feet of the Carpathians was a little northern people, the Slavs, which may one day fill the earth's chronicle when Teuton has followed Greek and Roman into the inevitable tomb of warriors. Where these Slavs came from, and what was their precise kinship to the other northerners and to the Asiatic peoples, we do not confidently know. Some tens of thousands of years before the Christian Era the last spell of the Ice-Age had locked the north of Europe. It seems that a branch of the human family followed the retreating ice-sheet and, in the bracing winds which blew off the frozen regions, shed its weaklings and became the vigorous "northern race." From this came the successive waves of Greeks and Romans, Goths and Vandals, English and Norman and German. From these northern forests seem also to have come the Slavs, who split at the barrier of the Carpathians into two great streams: Bohemians and Serbs to the west, and Russians (as they were later called) to the east.

We have not much information about this people which settled across the limit of civilisation. To the Romans they were part of the medley of barbarism which got a rude living out of the bleak north. A few later Greek writers had some acquaintance with them, and an early Russian monk, Nestor, gathered their traditions into a chronicle, and described them as they were before the development

PRIMITIVE SLAV DEMOCRACY

of autocracy obliterated their native features. From these sources we learn that the Slavs were singularly democratic for a people at their stage of evolution.

We know to-day the real origin of kingships and princedoms, which was hidden from our fathers by legends of "divine right." The right of a man to rule his fellows came of his possession of a stronger arm or a wiser head, or a combination of the two: a plausible enough theory until kings began to insist on leaving the power to their sons, whether or no they left them the strong arm and the wise head. As a rule the hunt and the battle gave the strong man his opportunity, and in every other nation at the level of the Slavs we find chiefs, who dispense justice and direct warfare, and exact a reward proportionate to their services.

It is a common and surprised observation of the early writers who notice the Slavs that they had no chiefs. The monk Nestor, who wrote in their midst at the beginning of the twelfth century, says that they had "chiefs," but would not tolerate "tyranny." The primitive life of the Slavs had then been modified, as we shall see, but the reports may be reconciled. The Slavs had no hereditary families of chiefs, no rulers of tribes who exacted tribute. Nestor gives a very different character to the various tribes of the Slav family. Being a monk, he is unable to give any of them a good character in their pagan days, but we may make a genial allowance for this natural prejudice. Perhaps some of the tribes, who were in closer touch with the fierce Finns and Scythians, had chiefs. Warfare is the great king-maker. Clearly the primitive and normal condition of a Slav community was exceptionally democratic.

The one definite institution of those early days that is known to us is the village-council; the institution that, being most deeply rooted in the heart of the Slav, has survived all autocracies by divine right and is familiar to-day to the whole world as the *Mir*. In ancient Slavdom the family was not the basis of the state. It was the state, or there was no state. An enlarged family—for the Slavs were a social and peaceful folk, and the young, founding a new family, clung to the home until it grew too small and some must wander afield—with cousins and children and grand-children, was the unit. The father had patriarchal power in his little colony, and when he departed the next oldest and wisest, a brother generally, took up the mild sway. Such families grew into villages or settlements in a few generations: not too large, for they lived on the land, yet compact, for there were plenty of human wolves east of the Carpathians. The Finns and other Asiatic tribes then filled, or roamed over, the vast area we now call Russia, and their code did not forbid the plunder of peaceful argriculturists. New

PRIMITIVE SLAV DEMOCRACY

colonies would be founded near the old and form villages. Out of this grew the *Mir,* the council in which the heads of the various households met to discuss and decide their common affairs.

No doubt some kind of chairman, some sage elder, would be chosen to preside, but it is clear from later practice and early comment that the council only acted upon a unanimous decision. That form of democracy had inconveniences, and, when Russia begins to have chroniclers, we find that unanimity was often secured, in a struggle, by pitching the minority into the river. That, at all events, was the original Slav custom. In theory even a majority could not tyrannise over a minority, much less a minority over a majority.

There would be frequent calls for these village-councils, as the land, on which most of them worked, was held in common. The head of a family owned only his house and enclosure, and was entitled to the harvest of his own labour. Then there were the rights of hunting in the forest and fishing in the rivers, the constant need to send out new colonies into the eastern wilderness, and especially the need to protect these new colonies from the wandering Asiatics. Flanked by the Carpathians, up which they could not spread, the tribes had to push steadily eastward, and the land was full of Asiatics, for the most part swift and ruthless horsemen. Co-operative defence was as necessary as co-operative counsel. The elders of many neighbouring villages met together in a larger council. There was a rough organisation of villages into a canton or *Volost*. Again there would probably be a president, and some think that a temporary chief or leader might be appointed in an emergency. But the Slavs had no hereditary rulers, no heads of the various tribes.

It also helped to sustain their democratic and communistic life that they had no priests. When priests later come upon the scene we shall find them very easily becoming the instruments of autocracy. We shall find, as is usual, the autocrat enriching the clergy, and the clergy discovering very impressive legends upon which he may establish his title to rule. In the pagan days of the Slavs there were no priests. The religion was the kind of primitive interpretation of nature which we always find at that level of mental development. The fire of the sun, the roar of the storm, the mysterious fertility of the earth, and the awful solemnity of the forest filled the child-like mind with wonder and dread. These things were felt to have life, a greater life than the puny and limited life of man; and the Slavs learned to bow down to the mighty spirits of the sun and the river and the wind and the earth. In particular they mourned the death of the sun, and celebrated joyously its annual re-birth and restoration to full glory. But they had no priests.

PRIMITIVE SLAV DEMOCRACY

The heads of the family or the village performed the invocations and the sacrifices.

We must remember that even in these primitive and patriarchal arrangements there was the germ of autocracy. The eldest male was an autocrat. So absolute was his power that it is said that, when he died, wife and servants and horse had to follow him into the nether world. There seems here to be some confusion between different tribes, and there is evidence that, as among the Teutons, woman was generally respected; although there were ancient marriage-rites which suggest that at one time brides were stolen, and there was some practice of polygamy. However that may have been, the father of the household was an autocrat. We may plead only that he does not seem to have had, as in ancient Rome, power of life and death over his mate.

Such was the Slav people when we first discover them about the feet of the Carpathians. We have next to see how they became the Russian people, and how contact with civilisation and the growth of commerce modified their primitive communism.

The towering masses of the mountains checked the western expansion of the growing tribes. The Danube and the outposts of the Roman Empire—the fathers of the Rumans—shut them from the south. They were, as their number increased, bound to travel eastward, and their pioneers would dis-

THE ROMANCE OF THE ROMANOFFS

cover that the central part of this mighty waste of eastern Europe was a particularly fertile region. From the foot of the Carpathians the land spreads in one of the largest plains of the world until it begins to rise toward the Ural mountains. Between the forests and bleak deserts of the north and the arid prairies of the south there are about a hundred and fifty million acres of "black earth," as rich and fertile as any to be found, and south of these a hundred and fifty million acres of ordinary arable land. At the beginning of the Christian Era this great area would be for the most part forest and morass, chequered by vast spaces of grassy plain, furrowed by broad rivers. The advancing colonies of the Slavs would discover the fertility of the soil and clear the ground for their corn and flax. The rivers gave them abundant fish. The forests swarmed with animals which afforded fur and meat, and the innumerable wild bees gave them stores of honey and wax for the long winters. Timber for the vapour-bath, which the Slav family seems already to have held in affection, lay on every side.

We find the Slavs especially spreading over this fertile heart of Russia about the eighth century of the present era. The land had long been held by the Finns and other Asiatic tribes when, in the third century, the Goths from the north fell upon them and drove them eastward. In the next century began that more formidable invasion from

PRIMITIVE SLAV DEMOCRACY

Asia which flung the Finns westward once more, and cast the Teutons upon the crumbling barrier of the Roman Empire. In the seventh century a new semi-civilised race, the Khazars, created an empire in south-eastern Russia, and drove the Asiatic Finns definitely to the north. It was at the close of these great movements that the Slavs moved rapidly over the fertile regions, between the land of the Finns and the southern kingdom of the Khazars. By the end of the eighth century the various Slav tribes had overrun the central part of western Russia.

The chief change which this migration caused in the life of the Slavs was the development of commerce. The great rivers of the land at once became the highways. Fishers as well as tillers of the soil, the Slavs would spread along the river-valleys, and the junctions of the rivers would naturally become the chief stations for what intercourse there was between the scattered villages. It is probable that in those days, when four-fifths of Russia was marsh and forest, the rivers were deeper than they are to-day. In our time they are for the most part shallow throughout the summer. Only in the spring, when the melting snows and rains flush the broad channels, can large boats ascend them; and in the winter their frozen waters make good passage for the sledge. They became the high-roads of the new commonwealth, as the site of the older cities indicates when one glances at the map.

THE ROMANCE OF THE ROMANOFFS

The Slavs had at that time probably little or no commerce. Some exchange, in kind, of fish, fur, honey, or corn might take place, but the resources were much the same for each village. In a short time after the settlement, however, a busy commercial system was inaugurated. Further north than the Finns were the Scandinavians, whose skill in metal-working was early developed. The Slavs traded with them for swords and spears and axes.

To the south, beyond the land of the Khazars, was the chief representative of civilisation in the west, the Byzantine (or Constantinopolitan) Empire. The northern tribes had now shattered Roman civilisation. The solid roads, the ample schools, the courts of law and municipal institutions established by the Romans in southern Europe were in complete decay, and four-fifths of the city of Rome was a charred and desolate wilderness. But the city which Constantine had founded on the Bosphorus, on the site of ancient Byzantium, lay out of the path of most of the barbarians, and the glory of Constantinople penetrated feebly into the distant forests of Russia. Its soldiers give us our first direct knowledge of the Slavs. Its merchants crossed the Black Sea, ascended the rivers of Russia, and spread before the eager eyes of the Slavs the silks and damasks and velvets, the shining metal-work and imitation-jewels, of the great "Tsargrad," or City of the Emperors. For these the Slavs could

VLADIMIR, GRANDE DUKE OF KIEFF, 980-1015
From an Ancient Banner

PRIMITIVE SLAV DEMOCRACY

offer choice furs, for an enormous variety of fur-clad animals roamed their forests, as well as honey for the table and wax for the myriad tapers of the Byzantine churches.

This busy commerce increased the importance of the settlements at the junction of the rivers. The evenness of the Russian plains, the great depth of soil or clay or glacial rubbish which uniformly covers the level strata below, make stone scarce in the greater part of the country then occupied by the Slavs. The ordinary village was a cluster of rude huts made of timber, with roofs of straw and mud. The towns also were of timber, and the accumulation of merchandise in them for traffic or fairs attracted the Asiatic marauders and increased the need of defence. The *Véché,* or democratic council of the district, grew in importance. Stockades of timber were erected. The Slavs, preferring peace as an agricultural people always does, were compelled to acquire some skill in the art of war.

Up to this point, the ninth century, the democracy of the Slavs was unaltered. The villagers were still free and independent men, while the peasantry over the rest of Europe were slaves or serfs. They regulated their own affairs in their *Mir,* recognised no central government, and paid tribute to neither chiefs nor priests. There was plenty of timber to heat their stoves during the long winter, and in the summer the song and dance cheered the leisure from

THE ROMANCE OF THE ROMANOFFS

their labours. The plot of corn and the nests of the wild bees fed them; the plot of flax clothed them; and the winter harvest of furs, taken to the nearest town or fair, gave them many a tawdry luxury from the great cities of the south. Even in the towns they had still no money or currency. It was not until long afterwards that they cut disks of leather to serve the purpose of coinage. And even in the largest settlements or towns, such as Novgorod in the north and Kieff in the south, the democratic council, with unanimous decision, ruled their little affairs.

The defect of a primitive democracy of this nature soon became apparent. When the less peaceful neighbours who surrounded them on every side made an attack in force the isolated towns or communities could not defend themselves. The Khazars of the south overspread the nearest Slav districts and virtually enslaved them. The Scandinavian pirates of the Baltic pushed southward from the coast and wrung tribute from them. Either they must establish a compact military organisation, which their loose social texture did not easily permit, or they must hire defenders. They chose the latter course, not knowing, as we do, the ultimate price of engaging military chiefs.

The Scandinavians or Norsemen were as little pacific as any people of Europe, and their large frames and mighty weapons made of them formid-

PRIMITIVE SLAV DEMOCRACY

able warriors. The Slavs were well acquainted with them. Somehow they had found the way across Russia to Constantinople, where their services were richly paid. From the southern shores of the Baltic they descended the northern rivers, and, crossing short stretches of country from river to river, they sailed down the broad waterways to the Black Sea. In the ninth century the Slavs were familiar with the tall, blue-eyed, blond-haired giants, with heavy spears and formidable axes. The Greeks of the south, who called them Varangians, clothed them in rich armour and made of them a special imperial guard. The Slavs called them *Rus,* or "sea-farers" (if not "pirates"), a name they seem to have borrowed from the Finns.

This, at least, is what modern scholars make of the ancient legend, given in Nestor, that the men of Rus were foreign warriors invited by the Slavs to come and settle and undertake military service. The story runs that the Slavs of the north, wearied by invasion and pillage, invited these soldiers to defend them and share their goods. Some historians suspect that the legend may be invented by the vanity of the Slavs, who did not care to confess that the northerners had subdued them, but it is not unlikely that they were invited to defend the Slavs as they were invited to defend the Emperors of Constantinople. They had already shown the Slavs that those who did not pay voluntarily might have to pay involuntarily. As the democratic institutions of the Slavs survived most strongly in the city where the Norsemen first settled, Novgorod, it does not seem as if they settled in virtue of conquest. In western Europe the northerners, wherever they settled, established the feudal system, which never existed in Russia.

The story handed down in Russia—as the land of the Slavs soon came to be called—was that three brothers, Rurik, Sineus, and Truvor, answered the call of the Slavs, and, with their kinsmen and followers, settled on the Baltic coast. This is assigned to the year 862. From those seats they cannot have defended, or raised taxes from, much of Russia, but when Sineus and Truvor died Rurik went to settle in Novgorod. That city, about a hundred and twenty miles south of Petrograd, was the chief town in the northern part of the route from north to south. Rurik seems to have built a stone fort overlooking the timber settlement and been content with a kind of tribute for his military services. Novgorod remained until centuries afterwards a jealously democratic community.

The chief Slav town in the south was Kieff, and to this two of the unruly officers of Rurik's troop, Askold and Dir, led a company of the northerners. As is well known, these northern barbarians, once their barriers were broken down, wandered from end to end of Europe, and even to Carthage and

PRIMITIVE SLAV DEMOCRACY

Alexandria, terrifying the natives everywhere with their gigantic frames, their immense axes and swords, their guttural grunts, and their infinite capacity for liquor. The Slavs of Kieff, voluntarily or involuntarily, received the warriors, and a fresh colony of men of Rus was planted. They seem to have infected even some of the Slavs with their piratical spirit, for we read of them leading an expedition down the river and across the Black Sea against Constantinople itself.

The next step was to unite the towns of Novgorod and Kieff, and bring the remainder of the Slavs under the vague lordship of the Norsemen. This was done by Rurik's brother and successor, Oleg. The Teutonic rule of hereditary succession came in with the northerners, and the men of Novgorod seem to have had no further choice. Oleg assumed command, and he marched his troop against the smaller body of his countrymen in the south. Askold and Dir had, he said, acted without orders, and had usurped a lordship which belonged to his brother. Kieff had no more choice than Novgorod. Oleg found it a finer town than the settlement among the marshes of the north. He set up there his court of brawling, drunken warriors, and gradually induced all the tribes of the Slavs to pay him tribute and furnish soldiers. He was so successful that one year he embarked his men on two thousand boats, led them against the imperial city, and forced the Greeks themselves to add to his treasury.

The land of Rus was in those days not the spacious Russia of our time. It spread little eastward beyond Novgorod and Kieff, and it was bounded by the Khazars to the south and the Finns and Lithuanians to the north. But it was now Russia, a group of Slav tribes dominated by a military caste. It was, however, not yet a nation, certainly not a monarchy. Tax-gathering and defence were the sole duties of the military chief, and as the Slavs had demanded the one they were not unprepared for the other. But the germ of autocracy was now planted in the soil, and the terrible events of the next few centuries would foster its baleful development.

CHAPTER II

THE DESCENT TO AUTOCRACY

IT is sometimes said that the Slav people lost its democratic institutions because it was too pacific to defend them. It is true that an agricultural people would tend to be more pacific than hunting tribes like the Asiatics who surrounded them, but the native peacefulness of the Slav has probably been exaggerated. The early Russians seem to have been as much addicted to hunting and fishing as to tilling the soil, and the long winter, when all agricultural work was suspended for six months, would encourage the men to hunt the furry animals which abounded. Certain it is that both the monk Nestor and the Greek Emperor Maurice represent the primitive Slav as far from meek, and the chronicle informs us of constant and even deadly quarrelling.

The truth is that the democracy of the Slavs was too little developed. It was nearer akin to Anarchism than to Socialism, and the mind of the race was not as yet sufficiently advanced to grasp the political exigencies of the new situation. There was no national consciousness, and there could be no national defence and administration, because there was no nation; and a body of disconnected communities, scattered over a wide area, was in those days bound to succumb to marauders.

Russian historians of the official school eagerly point out that the situation plainly called for a monarchic institution, and that the monarchs rendered great service in welding the scattered communities into a nation. That they did unite the people and make the great Russia of to-day is obvious. It is equally obvious that, with rare exceptions, they did this in their own interest, and that in all cases they exacted a reward which made serfs of the independent Slavs, sowed corruption amongst the rising middle class, and laid upon all an intolerable burden.

The period of the Norse warrior-chiefs and their descendants lasted about three centuries, and it fully exposes the fallacy of the monarchic principle. From being military servants the Norsemen rapidly became, as is customary, princes and parasites. As long as they discharged their duty, binding the communities and securing for them the necessary peace against external foes, this departure from the primitive democracy might be regarded as merely a regrettable necessity. But the sheep soon found that the protecting dog was first-cousin of the wolf. The principle of hereditary succession

THE DESCENT TO AUTOCRACY

and the practice of providing for all sons and relatives soon led to a worse confusion than ever, and the distracted and weakened country was prepared for a foreign invasion. The long and sanguinary history of the descendants of Rurik may be briefly sketched before we see how the autocratic Mongols beat a path for the autocratic Tsars.

Oleg, who had united the Slav tribes under his ill-defined rule, was murdered in the year 945. To the north of Kieff a tribe known as the Drevlians ("tree-folk") wandered in the forests and paid a reluctant and uncertain tribute in furs. When Oleg tried to enforce his tax upon these, they captured him and tied him to two young trees in such fashion that, when the bent trees were released, Oleg's body was torn asunder. Oleg's widow, Olga, was a handsome Valkyrie of the masterful northern type, and she sent her armies to scatter the thunders of Thor among the wild foresters. It is said that she afterwards visited the Greek capital and was won to the Christian religion. She lives as St. Olga in the calendar of the Russian Church. Her successor involved the Russians in long and terrible wars with Constantinople, to enforce his ambitious claim to Bulgaria, and at his death the fierce feuds and murders of his three sons plunged the country into a condition of bloody anarchy.

From this sordid strife of the shepherds whom the Slavs had hired to protect them there emerged in 972, over the corpses of his brothers, the blond beast St. Vladimir, the founder of Christianity in Russia. To what extent the lusty and lustful Prince Vladimir was, as the priestly chronicles maintain, transformed into a saint during his life we need not stay to consider. He seems to have been converted as superficially as his prototype, the Emperor Constantine. He was married to a beautiful nun who had been torn from a convent during one of the raids upon the Greek Empire, and whom he had taken from his murdered brother; and thousands of concubines relieved the comparative tedium of her companionship. The monastic chronicle tells us, in trite language, that he at length wearied of sin and sought more substantial spiritual aid than the paganism of his fathers could afford. Judaism, Mohammedanism, and Christianity now offered their rival assurances to such a promising penitent, and it is said that Vladimir, with the broadmindedness of a modern Japanese, sent his servants to inquire into the merits of the three religions. The rich ritual of the Greek Christians at Constantinople prevailed over the more sober practices of the Mohammedans and the less consoling assurances of the religion of the Old Testament, and Vladimir became a Christian and a saint.

But the chronicles also recount that Vladimir, whose principality of Russia was now so important

THE DESCENT TO AUTOCRACY

that it could sustain wars with the Greeks, sought a matrimonial alliance with the royal house of Constantinople, and the prosy imagination of our time finds here a safer clue to the development. The Emperors Basil and Constantine replied that the hand of their sister Anne would be bestowed upon the experienced barbarian if he would consent to baptism; and Greek priests, who were apt also to be courtiers, were sent to expound to him the new religion. Vladimir readily consented to pay so small a price for so great an honour and advantage. He threw into the river the idols of the Russian gods —these carven figures had been introduced since the settlement in Russia—and lent his energy and truculence to the extirpation of paganism. His people were driven in troops into the rivers, the Greek priests pronounced over them the sacred formula, and in a very short time the nature-gods of the old Slavs and Norsemen were turned into devils and the cross of Christ glittered above gilded domes in the wooden settlements of the land. Vladimir was so generous to the new clergy that he died in the odour of sanctity.

But the sins of Vladimir's pagan manhood lived after him. Seven sons, by various legitimate mothers, claimed the succession to his dominions, and there ensued such bloody anarchy as the handsome Teutonic princes, no matter what gods they worshipped, knew how to create. As usual the fitter to survive in such a world—the more lusty and less scrupulous—emerged from the struggle, and Prince Iaroslaf, one of the heroes of early Russian history, reunited the various regions under his rule.

Iaroslaf has been compared, not quite ineptly, to Charlemagne. From Novgorod, which his father had left him, he cut his way to Kieff, and definitely made the southern city the metropolis of the country. Kieff was enriched and adorned with a splendour which, in the mind of the Russians, rivalled that of Constantinople. The southern rivers now bore thousands of Greek artists and architects, musicians and scholars, priests and courtiers, to the new capital of barbarism. Four hundred churches soon shone like gilt mushrooms in the summer sun, and the grateful clergy discovered that a monarchy which rested on a divine foundation in Constantinople could hardly have an inferior basis in Kieff. Iaroslaf, it is true, was not a monarch in title. Russia had no constitution or political organisation. It was still semi-barbaric in culture and judicial procedure. The duel, the ordeal, and the payment of blood-money still flourished, and literacy existed only in the form of feeble lamps here and there in the vast darkness. It must be remembered that Constantinople itself was, with all its splendour of gold and mosaics and jewels and silks, half barbaric in its moral complexion. The most sordid and brutal crimes disgraced its palace-life on the

THE DESCENT TO AUTOCRACY

shores of the Sea of Marmora, and the most revolting penalties of vice and crime were publicly inflicted. The discovery by modern apologists that there was a glow-worm here and there does not relieve the terrible gloom of the Dark Ages.

In such an age, amidst so scattered and helpless a people, Iaroslaf needed no kingly title to enable him to act as monarch. To sustain the new splendour of Kieff and his court—his sister and daughters married into the royal families of Poland, Norway, France, and Hungary—a larger tribute from the people was needed, and it was not meekly solicited. Russian historians of the old school have dilated upon the magnificence with which Iaroslaf invested his capital and the measure of prestige which Russia gained in the eyes of the world. They do not point out that this concentration of light at Kieff and the court darkened the life of the Russian people. For the first time we now encounter the odious name for a child of the soil *moujik*. Foreigners who lightly repeat that name to-day are unaware that it is in origin a term of disdain. It means "mannikin." The warriors in glittering armour or shining silks who gathered about the court were the prince's "men." The vast mass of the people, whose labour ultimately paid for this magnificence, were "mannikins."

The burden fell most heavily upon the scattered peasantry. Not only were the "legitimate" taxes

THE ROMANCE OF THE ROMANOFFS

wrung from them, but the military leaders exacted tribute to support their own splendour and pleasure. The feudal system, which now prevailed over the remainder of Europe, was not introduced. The land was still the possession of the people, and military chiefs remained about the court instead of raising, as they did where stone abounded, massive provincial castles from which they might enslave the peasantry and even defy the ruler. But in their excursions the soldiers behaved as wantonly as feudal barons of the west, and the people sank under the burden. Slavery still flourished in Christendom, and many a Slav found his way to the distant market at Constantinople. Moreover, under the degenerate Greek influence there was introduced the practice of flogging and torture which the rough chivalry of the northerners had hitherto avoided.

To say that the unity of faith, the protection against invaders, and the introduction of art and a small amount of mediocre culture compensate for these evils is an historical mockery. The death of Iaroslaf at once revealed the insecurity and selfishness of the regime he had established. It was followed by two hundred years of civil warfare and murderous confusion. Eighty-three struggles which seem worthy of the name of wars devastated Russia during those two centuries, and over the enfeebled frontiers the waiting tribes repeatedly poured while the guardians of the Russian people

THE DESCENT TO AUTOCRACY

slew each other for their petty principalities. Sons, legitimate and illegitimate, abounded in that world of blond warriors, and the successful chief provided for each out of his dominion. Titles were disputed, or the old title of the longer sword was boldly advanced. A dozen large principalities were carved out of the princedom of Iaroslaf, and fragments of these were constantly detached by heredity and restored by war.

It is not my intention to follow the grisly chronicles over this prolonged anarchy and select for admiration the heroic butcheries of some strong-armed soldier. For our purpose it suffices to notice that the mass of the Russian people were, as a rule, the passive and suffering spectators of this brutal pandemonium. During the summers they sowed and gathered their corn and flax, and the long winters occupied them with the making of clothes and the quest of fur. The Mir was still the centre of every village. But a tithe of its produce had now to go to sustain this costly petty monarchy, a tithe to support the whitened monasteries and gold-domed churches, and a tithe to repair the damage when the tornado of civil war or some fierce band of Asiatics had passed over their district. There were, we shall see, provinces of Russia where the larger intelligence of the townsmen saw that the proper thing to do was to form a strong republic, armed in its own defence. These still hated "tyranny" and sustained the old tradition of the race. But the greater part of the Russian people were not sufficiently developed to perceive this, or were too scattered to achieve it, and they sank under the military power they had invited to serve them.

A few pages borrowed from the story of this dark period of anarchy will suffice to explain how Russia was prepared for the later schemes of the Moscovites. Kieff remained "the mother of Russian cities," and it was natural that, as its princes founded petty princedoms here and there for their descendants, the more ambitious of these should invent a title to the rule of the metropolis itself or found rival cities. One of the chief of these new principalities was Suzdal, on the Volga and the Oka. Here, at the extremity of the Russia of the time, a large dominion was created out of the marshes and forests, and braced by incessant conflicts with the neighbouring Finns. George Dolgoruki, who, after failing to get Kieff, had founded this principality, regarded it as in an especial sense his own creation and possession, and his monarchic sentiment was strengthened.

But the democratic tradition was not wholly obliterated, and the military caste itself—the *boyars,* or captains of the troops—formed some check upon the will of the prince. George's successor, therefore, Andrew Bogolyubski, an astute and ambitious man, made a new capital of a small town

THE DESCENT TO AUTOCRACY

or village called Vladimir. Andrew possessed the supposed miraculous painting of the face of Christ, which had once been the great treasure of Constantinople, and he professed that this gave him some special measure of divine guidance. He pitched his camp near the village of Vladimir, and shortly afterward the people of Suzdal heard with consternation that he had been divinely directed to convert the little settlement into his capital. Andrew had the great advantage of being extremely pious and generous to the clergy, as nearly every great Russian adventurer has been. The priests warmly supported him, and Vladimir soon grew into a city.

Kieff still had an immeasurably greater splendour, and was in closer touch with Constantinople. Andrew raised a large army and led it south against the metropolis. A three days' siege was followed by three days of such pillage that Kieff lost forever its supremacy. Even the churches and monasteries were looted, and the golden treasures of both palace and cathedral were carried off to enrich the aspiring city of Vladimir. Flushed with this and other triumphs Andrew then turned his arms against the republic of Novgorod, where the old democratic spirit was best preserved, and, after fierce fighting, compelled it to accept a prince of his own nomination. He extended his rule in other directions, setting a conspicuous example of autocracy and ambition to the Princes of Moscow who would later issue from his blood. But Russia was not yet reduced to the state of servility which Andrew's design of supremacy required. In 1174 his powerful boyars rebelled and assassinated him, and the oppressed people rose in turn and vented their democratic sentiment in the pillage and slaughter of the rich.

This is but one outstanding figure amidst the host of brutal soldiers or scheming princes who fill the chronicle of the time with blood. It is a wearisome repetition of the same process. A strong or unscrupulous man unites a large part of Russia under his sway, then a group of less strong, but not less ambitious, sons and grandsons fight for the spoil over the helpless bodies of the peasantry. Those who succeed must reward their boyars and the clergy, and the land of Russia passes more and more into the hands of large proprietors and is worked by slaves. "If you want the honey, you must kill the bees," was the characteristic remark of one of these descendants of Rurik, as he despatched his victims; and the little restraint which their new faith imposed upon them may be gathered from the flippant retort of another princeling, who was accused of breaking an oath solemnly made over a cross: "It was only a little cross."

There were, as I said, northern parts where the democratic evolution proceeded healthily. Novgo-

TATARS OF THE MONGOL PERIOD

THE DESCENT TO AUTOCRACY

rod, a large northern city of a hundred thousand souls, rising in the centre of a beautiful plain fringed by forests, had become a republic with wide territory and three hundred thousand subjects beyond the rude defences of the city. There is a legend that it had rebelled even against Rurik, the first Scandinavian adventurer. It accepted, of its own choice, what had come to be called princes, but it endorsed or rejected them, and curtailed their powers, with a good deal of civic pride and independence. "Come and rule us yourself or else we will choose a prince," the citizens said to a Grand Prince of Kieff who ordered them to receive his nominee. To another Grand Prince, who would send his son to govern them, a later generation of citizens replied: "Send him—if he has a head to spare." They had even an independent Church and elected their archbishop. The old democratic *Véché*, or council of citizens, was the central institution of the city, and the great bell summoned all to the market-square whenever some business of importance called for a decision. The neighbouring republics of Pskoff and Viatka were hardly less faithful to the democratic tradition. While these territories were the farthest from Constantinople, they were nearest to Germany and the Baltic, and they were enriched by the commerce which was then beginning to civilise the northern cities.

Even Novgorod, we saw, felt the heavy hand of

THE ROMANCE OF THE ROMANOFFS

Andrew of Vladimir, and the remainder of Russia steadily lost its vitality under the drain of civil war. Upon this distracted and enfeebled population there now fell an autocratic ruler of the most arbitrary character. The year 1237 is, in the chronicles, one of calamities and portents. The fires which so often devoured the timber settlements of the Slavs were more numerous and destructive than ever. Drought and famine made haggard faces over large regions, and from the sky a terrifying eclipse and other portents seemed to mock their prayers for deliverance. As the dreadful year passed a new evil broke upon them. Into the southern principalities poured crowds of fugitives from the east, who told that immense hordes of ferocious and inhuman horsemen were covering the land and completing its desolation. Toward the close of the year the first wave of the Tatars shook the southern frontiers of the Slavs.

Asia had, as well as Europe, its adventurers, and the baleful dream of conquest had lit the imagination of a Tatar chief, Dchingis Khan, amidst the dreary wastes of Siberia. Gathering about him the rough tribes of his race, a swarm of hardy shepherds who knew not what a house, much less a city, was, he led them against the civilisation of the south. His men lived in the saddle, and each was a master in the use of the bow, the sabre, and the lance. Camels and buffaloes bore their (at first) scanty pos-

THE DESCENT TO AUTOCRACY

sessions, and they moved with all the speed of devouring nomads. The villages of Manchuria, the tame and placid cities of China, and all the wide spaces of central Asia were successively overrun and forced to pay tribute. From the civilised Chinese the wonderful and profoundly ignorant barbarian quickly learned the art of gathering taxes and enjoying luxury, and he moved further west in a vague design of conquering the earth.

This strange and terrifying horde, a cloud of fiercely yelling centaurs with troops of animals which no Russian had ever seen, first fell upon the southern Russians in 1224. Their method was to press the peasantry into their service and attempt to disarm the towns with hollow assurances of friendship, but, in whatever way the town was taken, there followed a merciless slaughter and a thorough pillage. The Russians, alarmed by the reports of the outlying tribes, sent out a great army to meet the Mongols on the steppes, and were crushingly defeated. The Mongols had, however, retired to Asia, where their dominion was not solidly established, and it was a vaster army, under a new Khan, that appeared in the south of Russia in 1237.

From 1237 to 1240 the Khan Batu led his army of 600,000 men, with appalling destruction, across the various principalities of Russia. Weakened by their feuds, severed by their selfish rivalries, the various provinces fell one by one under the feet of the merciless invaders. Rape, murder, fire, and pillage were the invariable sequels of success. The Russians appealed to the nations of the nearer west to help them to dam this Asiatic flood, but the Latin Christians were not minded to stir themselves for semi-barbarians who did not respect the Pope. When the Khan passed over the prostrate body of Russia and advanced still further, in his determination to conquer an earth of which he knew less than a child in a modern infant-school, the Poles and Hungarians at length spread their barrier of steel across his path. But the check did not now profit Russia. Batu retired upon Russia, built a city, Sarai, on the banks of the Volga (beyond the limits of the principalities), and began a life of organised parasitism upon the unfortunate people. The comparative unity brought about by their Norse defenders had prepared the way for the Khan. The Khan was to prepare the way for the Moscovite.

Again we may ignore the crowded details, the rise and fall and eternal feuds of petty princes, of the Russian chronicle. What matters is that the entire country which was then known as Russia was overspread by a network of tax-gatherers, and the people learned to tremble at the commands of a distant autocrat. At Sarai the Mongols established a court of barbaric magnificence, and this in

THE DESCENT TO AUTOCRACY

time declared itself independent of the Tatar Empire in Asia and sought the nourishment of its luxury in Russia. The western sovereignty came to be known throughout Europe as the Golden Horde, and the western nations heard with indifference the cynical extravagance and the occasional brutality with which it treated schismatic Slavs.

No prince could now don his tattered dignity in Russia without the august permission of the semi-civilised ruler on the Volga, and a system was soon evolved which enabled the courtiers and concubines of the Khan to share the good fortune of their lord. In the constant disputes about succession claimants to the various Slav principalities made the perilous journey to Sarai, and the richness of the presents they brought sufficed to illumine the obscurity of their titles. Occasionally a prince whose loyalty to the Mongols was suspected was summoned to Sarai, and not a few who could not pass the humiliating tests left their bones among the Mohammedan Tatars. To those who bent their backs or tendered the cup with servile respect the Khan was gracious. They returned with power to extort the taxes for the Tatars and a large additional sum for themselves. If their people or rival princes were restive, a troop of the dreaded Tatar horse was put at their disposal, and the lash and the sabre cowed every attempt at revolt. The spying and flogging with which the servants of the Khan protected their mas-

THE ROMANCE OF THE ROMANOFFS

ter's interests were copied by the Slav-Norse princes. The Byzantine civilisation had itself introduced many devices of autocratic barbarism, for the jails of Constantinople, especially the dungeons of the superb imperial palace, witnessed ghastly tortures and mutilations. The cruelty of the Asiatic completed this machinery of the later Tsars; and the Princes of Moscow were the readiest of all to be the tax-gatherers of the Khan and the pupils of his unscrupulous ministers.

The scattered Slavs had, after the three or four years of terror, returned from the forests to their burned villages and their plundered towns. The gold and silver had gone from their churches: the inmates of their nunneries were the playthings of the Asiatic officers: their democracy was a mockery. Their industry soon healed the torn face of the country, but lands and lives now belonged to the foreign master. One-tenth of all their produce must be paid in taxes, and they might at any time be summoned to do military service. Kieff was in large part a ruin; Suzdal, Moscow, Riazan, and other cities were despoiled. Even Novgorod and Pskoff had, after a bloody resistance, to present their fleece to the shearer.

The miserable condition of the Slavs was further darkened by the behaviour of their Christian neighbours on the west. The Swedes, pleading that the men of Novgorod hindered the conversion to the

THE DESCENT TO AUTOCRACY

true faith of the remaining pagans of the north, induced the Pope to declare a holy crusade, with the customary spiritual and temporal advantages, against Russia, and a zealous army advanced against Novgorod. It was shattered, but the Catholic zeal of the west was not extinguished. The Knights of the Sword, the German order which enforced baptism as truculently as the early Mohammedans had enforced the Koran, next appeared on the Russian frontier, and took Pskoff. The Teutonic adventurers were not less formidable in white mantle and red cross than they had been in the dress of the pagan Norsemen, and were hardly less ferocious, but they had to retreat before the stalwart Novgorodians. In the fourteenth century, however, the united Lithuanians and Poles crossed into Russia and added to the miseries of the people. Only half a dozen of the Russian principalities could hold out against the invaders. The Tatars were now in decay, and the red spears of the Lithuanian knights were even seen as far south as the Black Sea.

It is to this demoralisation of the Russians rather than to any direct Tatar influence that we must turn our attention. There was little mingling of Mongol and Slav blood, beyond the occasional marriage of a Tatar princess by some sycophantic prince, and the enslavement of Russian women in the spacious harems of the Asiatics. "Scratch a Russian and you will find a Tatar" is an untruth. Few races in the civilised world are purer in blood than the Russian Slavs. Nor did the Khans modify the Russian culture more than the levying of tribute demanded. With the clergy they were on friendly terms, knowing their power over the ignorant peasants, and they suppressed neither the *Mir* of the village nor the *Véché* of the town, as long as it furnished the collective tribute. On the other hand, they entirely broke the original spirit of independence; they organised the country for purposes of extortion, and disorganised it for purposes of self-defence; they helped to convert the brutal and masterful Norseman into a calculating and coldly selfish prince; and they encouraged the subjection of women which the teaching of the Byzantian priests and monks had begun.

CHAPTER III

THE MOSCOVITES BECOME TSARS

THE name Moscow has up to the present entered so little into the chronicle that we must retrace our steps and briefly consider its origin. Three successive types of rulers prepared the way for the Romanoff dynasty: the Norsemen, the Tatars, and the Princes of Moscow, or the Moscovites. We have now to see how the third class rose upon the ruins of the Tatar dominion, maintained the evil machinery of subjection which it had constructed, and brought "all the Russias" under a new despotism.

In the year 1147 the Prince of Suzdal, George Dolgoruki, found a village, the site of which is now covered by the opulent Kreml, on the banks of the Moscowa, and is said to have conceived an affection for it. His patronage cannot have extended far, since we find that it remains an obscure village, or small town, for more than a century. It then passed, with a few other towns, to a son of the heroic Alexander Nevski, who (by sharp practice —a fit beginning of the fortune of the Moscovites) enlarged his little principality and bequeathed it to an even less scrupulous brother.

George Danielovitch (1303-25) laid claim to the principality of Tver and took very powerful arguments to enforce his claim, in the shape of handsome presents, to the Mongol court at Sarai. He got his title, a sister of the Khan for wife, and a Mongol army; but he did not get the principality, and the Khan, scenting a larger bargain, summoned both claimants to Sarai. There George ended the argument by having his rival assassinated. He in turn was assassinated, and a terrible feud subsisted for half a century between Moscow and Tver. Ivan, the successor of George, secured another Mongol army to reduce Tver, induced the Khan to remove his rival to another world, and entered upon a series of annexations and purchases which made Moscow the centre of a fairly large dominion, the seat of an archbishop, and a prosperous soil for churches and monasteries; for the piety of all these lords of Moscow was even more conspicuous than their craft and insidious truculence.

This malodorous tradition was sustained by the later princes. There was Simeon the Proud (1341-53) who, at the death of his father Ivan, found the largest bribe for the Mongols and ousted his competitors. At least he held in some check the lawlessness which was bleeding Russia, and it is one of those painful dilemmas of the historian that the

THE MOSCOVITES BECOME TSARS

valuable service rendered by the crafty Simeon was entirely neglected by his pious and gentle brother and successor, Ivan II. But Dmitri Ivanovitch, the son and successor of Ivan, returned to the sturdy lines of princely tradition. He defied and defeated the Tatars, and in the hour of triumph cried to Russia: "Their hour is past." But the cry was premature. A rival Russian prince arranged a coalition against Dmitri of the Catholic Lithuanians, and the Mohammedan Tatars, and the great army of Dmitri once more cut to pieces its opponents. In the meantime, however, the famous Tatar general, Timur, had come from Asia and fallen upon the "usurpers" of the Golden Horde. Dmitri unwisely refused the friendship which Timur offered him, and before long the fierce Mongols set flame to the splendid buildings of his capital and littered the streets with the corpses of its children.

Dmitri recovered and handed down a fair principality to his son Vassili (1389-1425), who shrewdly preserved his territory by a friendly alliance with the Tatars on the one hand and a matrimonial alliance with the Lithuanians on the other. His son, Vassili the Blond, was equally submissive to the Tatars and friendly with the Lithuanians. Then, in 1462, there came to the throne Ivan III, the first of the two great makers of imperial Russia.

At the time when Ivan III ascended the throne

THE ROMANCE OF THE ROMANOFFS

the principality of Moscow was a small and feeble territory menaced by the Lithuanian empire to the west and the Mongol empire to the east. Most of the other Russian principalities had either won a precarious independence or were subject to Lithuania. The republics of Novgorod and Pskoff alternately lost and recovered their freedom, and wavered between the Lithuanian and the Mongol alliance. Riazan and Tver remained independent and regarded with jealous eyes the growth of Moscow. This was the Russia of the fifteenth century, a mere fragment of the country which bears that name to-day.

Nor was this lack of unity the only reproach which we may bring against the princes who had torn the land in their selfish struggles for supremacy. Round the whitened monasteries and gilded shrines the feuds of the princes had gone on without intermission for so many centuries that the blood ran thin in the veins of Russia. It had neither the vitality nor the organisation required to meet its external foes, and every few years some hostile army scattered the customary desolation over the country. On every side, also, were troops of free lances and brigands, who constantly swooped upon the miserable peasantry. It is the claim of the orthodox historians that the Moscovite princes we have now to describe rescued Russia from this degradation, and we must examine

THE MOSCOVITES BECOME TSARS

their methods, their motives, and their attainments.

Ivan III is, in the existing portraits, a lean-faced, sombre-looking man, with large melancholy eyes and the patriarchal beard which the Slavs still preserved. These portraits probably accentuate the ostentatious piety of the man, and give us no idea of the cold ferocity which could light his heavy features. It is said that women were known to faint when they met his eye. Certain it is that Ivan united all the craft and calculating cruelty of the degenerate Greeks with professions of humility and peacefulness which provoke our disgust. Conspirators against his terrible rule were burned alive in cages, and the horrible Byzantine practice of cutting out a prisoner's eyes was more than once employed. Even priests, for whom he affected a humble veneration, were brutally flogged when they departed from the customary subservience of the clergy and took the part of the people. In war he was a coward. All the impulsive and savage bravery of the Norseman had in him degenerated into the mean and shifty hypocrisy of a dishonest huckster.

Ivan ascended the petty throne of Moscow in the year 1462. The city of Moscow was at that time still little more than a large cluster of mud-huts, with a few streets of merchants, about the princely palace and the rich shrines. Ivan looked to his revenues and before long was confronted with the firm refusal of the citizens of Novgorod to pay the tribute he demanded. The Grand Prince proceeded with his habitual craft. Instead of setting out to enforce his demands, he formulated a complaint that the Russian people of Novgorod were oppressed by a wealthy faction, and that this faction contemplated an alliance with the heretics of Poland. We may assume that there was some truth in the charges. Novgorod, still democratic and independent, still proud of the popular parliament on its market-place, was full of factions. In such a city a mutual hostility of rich and poor was inevitable, and Ivan's agents seem to have encouraged the aggrieved workers to appeal to him against what were represented to be the oligarchs. The wealthier and more powerful faction was led by a woman named Marfa, and may very well have contemplated an alliance with Poland against the ambitions of Moscow.

In 1470 Ivan sent against the city a strong Mongol and Moscovite army, and the ruin which it spread over the lands of Novgorod, as it approached, induced the citizens to compromise. But the Grand Prince wanted more than tribute, and his agents continued to foster the grievances of the popular party and encourage appeals to Moscow. When the time was ripe Ivan wrought the republican spirit of Novgorod to a fury by describing him-

THE MOSCOVITES BECOME TSARS

self, in his official documents, as "sovereign" of that city. The educated citizens saw in this the doom of their liberty, and, acting in the violent mood of the time, they put to death the supporters of Moscow. The story runs that the clergy and boyars of Moscow now gathered round their humane and reluctant ruler, and demanded that he should make war upon Novgorod. Certainly Ivan III did not love the hazards of war, especially as it was still the custom for a Russian prince to lead his troops. But we may measure his humanity by the sequel.

The conscience of the Grand Prince was reconciled by conceiving the campaign as a "holy war" against the allies of the Pope, and a formidable army took the road north. The partial resistance of the distracted republic was overcome, and Ivan set about the extirpation of its spirit of independence. The democratic nobles were transplanted to other soil. The commercial prosperity, which Novgorod had developed in its relations with the cities of north Germany, was systematically destroyed. The stores of merchandise and other treasures were transferred to Moscow. The shadow of the popular council, the *Véché,* remained—Ivan's son would complete the work—but a very severe blow had been struck by the Moscovite at what remained of Slav democracy.

The dependent republic of Pskoff submitted to Moscow, and was permitted to retain its institutions. The principality of Viatka was next recovered, from the Tatars, and added to the dominion of Moscow. The victorious troops, indeed, went on to annex a large part of more northern Russia, and the first thin slice of Asiatic territory fell under the rule of the Slav. At a later date the principality of Tver was drawn into the growing empire. Its prince afforded a specious pretext by allying himself with the unholy followers of the Roman Pontiff, the Lithuanians, and religious zeal again edged the swords of the troops.

It will be gathered that the power of the Mongols had now sunk too low to arrest the progress of Moscow. On an earlier page we have seen how Timur had come from Asia and chastised the Khans who had dared to set up an independent sovereignty in Europe. For some reason Timur did not overrun Russia as his predecessor had done. The clerical traditions of Russia attribute the escape to one of the miracles which seem to have been so frequent in that age, but the superior attractions of the new Ottoman Empire in the south, which was then displacing Greece and taking over its treasures, may be regarded as a more satisfactory explanation.

Timur had reduced the strength of the Golden Horde, and the dissensions which followed further enfeebled it. Here was an opportunity after the heart of Ivan III. Dispossessed Tatar princes

Costume of Boyars in the Seventeenth Century

THE MOSCOVITES BECOME TSARS

fled to his court, and he sent them back with their animosities inflamed, while he made the customary presents to the ruling Khan. In 1478 either Ivan or his advisers felt that the time had come to end the Tatar yoke, and Ivan nervously found himself at the head of 150,000 men making for the land of the dreaded Mongol. The issue is one of the most laughable in history. The two large armies encamped in sight of each other for days and dared each other to come on. Priests and officers spurred Ivan to the attack, and his rare fits of confidence, or professions of confidence, alternated with long periods of what we must regard as cowardice. Possibly the intensely superstitious prince thought that one of those miracles of which the clergy spoke so freely would spare him the hazard of war. A miracle, indeed, appeared, and it is difficult for the profane historian to penetrate its mysterious working. Both armies at length, and simultaneously, struck their camps and retreated hastily to their respective homes! The Tatar had sunk as low as the Moscovite.

Ivan's troops, which did not share the timidity of their high commander, next reduced Bulgaria, and the death of his brothers enabled Ivan to add still further, and with less title, to his dominions. His brother Andrew was, in 1493, accused of the usual perfidy and corresponding with the Polish-Lithuanian kingdom. He was thrown into prison, and there he conveniently died. Ivan summoned his bishops and monks and, as the tears trickled down his gaunt face and grey beard, confessed that he had sinned in sanctioning the cruel treatment of his brother. But he added Andrew's territory, and that of two other brothers, to his large dominion.

In the following year the lover of peace attacked the joint kingdom of Lithuania and Poland, which had so long afflicted Russia. Ivan had married his daughter to the Polish king, and had strictly stipulated that she should have entire freedom to practise the true religion amongst the adherents of the Pope. In 1494 Ivan found that this agreement was grossly disregarded, and his beloved daughter ran some peril of her soul. Later Russian historians have learned from the daughter's letters that she had no complaint except against the interested intrigues of Ivan himself. However, a holy war was proclaimed, and a good deal of western Russia was wrested from the Poles and added to the Moscovite dominion.

Such were the methods by which Ivan III doubled the patrimony of his fathers, and accumulated the wealth and power by which his more famous grandson would create the great Russia of the Romanoffs. It remains to see how Ivan organised his dominion, strengthened the autocracy, and raised the culture and splendour of his capital.

Ivan was by nature autocratic. He did not make

THE MOSCOVITES BECOME TSARS

counsellors of his boyars, as had been the custom, and they were compelled to learn the art of silence in presence of their master. But it was Ivan's wife who directed this disposition and created a Court in harmony with it. The Turks had taken Constantinople and had driven the remnants of half a dozen rival Greek royal families, and all that remained of Greek culture, into Italy. Amongst the fugitives was the clever and ambitious niece of the last emperor, Sophia Palæologus. The Pope, who saw in this heavy chastisement of the Greek schism a ray of hope of the reunion of Christendom, fathered the homeless princess and sought for her a useful marriage. Ivan accepted her and the Papal dowry. They were married early in his reign (in 1472), and her forceful ambition was behind many of the schemes of conquest we have reviewed. It was especially she and the clergy who forced upon the prince his inglorious campaign against the Tatars.

But we may see her influence especially in the growing splendour and despotism of the Moscovite court. Bred in the sacred palace by the Bosphorus, where there still lingered, until the Turk came, some remains of the most imposing court of the old world, she was made impatient by the thin coat of gilt which covered the Russian barbarism. Accustomed to a city of marble palaces, with walls of mosaic or porphyry, with bronze gates guarded by hundreds of silk-clad servants, and gold and silver

THE ROMANCE OF THE ROMANOFFS

vessels so heavy that they had to be lifted on to the tables by mechanical devices, she knew how to use the increasing wealth of her husband's kingdom. He was now the successor of Constantine and the Roman Emperors. The two-headed eagle, which had been the blatant emblem of Greek vanity, passed with the hand of Sophia to Moscow, and was emblazoned on the banners and plate of the new dynasty. Ivan did not take the title of "Tsar." His grandson would complete his work.

Sophia invited to her court Greek scholars and Italian architects and engineers, and the splendour of Moscow soon became so famous that its prince corresponded with Popes and Sultans, Kings of Sweden, Denmark, Hungary, and Austria, and even with the Grand Mogul of India. Italy was at that time in the flush of the Renaissance, and much of its colour, and of the less manly art of the Byzantinians, was brought to Moscow. Whatever one may think of the religious quarrel, it can hardly be doubted that the civilisation of Russia would have gained by submission to Rome. The Papacy was then enjoying that period of artistic license which provoked the Reformation, and probably Russia would have joined the Reformers. By its severance from Rome it maintained a barrier against the west, where civilisation was making rapid progress, and prolonged the inferior culture and conservative influence of the late Greek em-

THE MOSCOVITES BECOME TSARS

pire. The glory of the new Russia was but a coat of paint upon barbarism.

In the court the oppressive servility and childish pageantry of the Byzantine palace were encouraged. Golden mechanical lions barked before a golden throne, as they had done at Constantinople, and filled the visitor with mingled admiration and disdain. A very numerous guard of nobles, in high white fur caps and long caftans of white satin, with heavy silver axes on their shoulders, protected the sacred person of the monarch, and crowds of courtiers in cloth of gold or bright silk, with costly necklaces round their necks, vied with each other in flattery of speech and humility of demeanour. Yet these glittering aristocrats still carried a spoon in their jewelled girdles, for knives and forks were not yet substituted for fingers at a Russian feast.

The wives of the boyars were not less splendid. The combined influence of Mongol princes and Byzantinian monks had, as I said, lowered the condition of the Slav women. The *terem,* or women's quarters of the house, was screened as carefully as the *gynecæum* had been in ancient Athens or in Constantinople. The Russians had not indeed introduced that later Greek security for the behaviour of their women, the eunuch, and the frailer protection of religion did not prevent disorders; but the women were, as a rule, carefully guarded at home and abroad, while their husbands claimed the free use of slaves and courtesans. In public the wives of the boyars—or, as we may now call them, nobles—presented a curious spectacle. They painted as liberally as the Greeks had done. Thick coats of vivid red and white covered their faces, necks, and even hands; and their eyelashes, and even teeth at times, were dyed. In obedience to the ascetic teaching of the monks great masses of scarlet or gold cloth, silk, satin, and velvet, concealed, or preserved for the admiration of their husbands, the opulent lines of their figures; for a full habit of body was religiously cultivated.

Round this glittering court, with its Gargantuan banquets and its daily intoxication, spread the wooden city of Moscow, whose hundred thousand inhabitants lived, for the most part, in squalor and grossness. Beyond were the broad provinces of Russia which bore the burden of this barbaric splendour. The mass of the people had at an earlier date, we saw, become *moujiks,* or "mannikins." Others called them "stinkers." Now, by one of the most curious freaks of Russian development, they were known as "the Christians"; as if the quintessence of the Christian doctrine, as it was expounded by the Russian priests, was obedience to a lord and master. Their women had the hardest lot; the priests were content to urge the peasant or artisan, who, like his betters, drank heavily, not to beat his wife with a staff shod with iron or one of a dan-

THE MOSCOVITES BECOME TSARS

gerous weight. Drink was one of the few luxuries left, for the priests and monks gave fiery warnings against the song and dance and games that had formerly lightened the life of the people. Drinking heavily themselves, they could not, as a rule, rigorously forbid intoxication.

Such was the Russia created by Ivan and his Greek wife, with the aid of the Greek-minded clergy, and bequeathed to their second son Vassili. That prince, zealously educated by his mother, sustained the policy of enlarging and coercing his dominions. The republic of Pskoff had, we saw, retained its democratic forms. Vassili held a court at Novgorod, and thither he summoned the chief men of the neighbouring republic to do homage. Too weak to rebel, yet aware that the monarch sought to swallow the last remnant of the primitive democracy, the citizens appealed eloquently to the sense of honour which the Moscovite might be assumed to have. It was useless, and the republic was dismantled. Amidst the tears of the citizens and the laments of the patriotic poets Vassili removed the great bell to Novgorod and suppressed the *Véché,* or democratic council. The commercial life of Pskoff was ruined, and three hundred docile families from Moscow were substituted for three hundred who had clung to independence and were now sent into exile.

Riazan was the next victim. The familiar crime

of corresponding with heretics—with the Khan of the Crimea—was charged against its prince, and the fertile province was added to the Moscow principality. Vassili recovered territory also from the Tatars and the Lithuanians. Russia expanded rapidly, and the splendour and autocracy of the court proportionately increased. There was now only one court for the innumerable descendants of the earlier princes and boyars, and the sternness of the competition for rewards made the nobles more and more sycophantic. Even less than his father did Vassili ask the counsel of his boyars.

The death of Vassili in 1533 led to a romantic and important interlude. Vassili's first wife had been thrust into a convent on the ground that she could not furnish an heir to the brilliant throne. Whether or no it is true that she disturbed the solitude of the cloister with the pangs of motherhood, it seems clear that the chief motive for the divorce was that Vassili had fallen in love with the very pretty and capable daughter of a Lithuanian refugee, Helena Glinski. Helena gave birth to two sons, but the eldest was only three years old at the time of his father's death. The mother vigorously grasped the regency and held power from the furious boyars. Only the Master of Horse, Prince Telepnieff, was allowed to share her despotism, as he shared her affection. The nobles split into factions, and they presently found that the easy-going princess could

THE MOSCOVITES BECOME TSARS

use the most truculent machinery of despotism. When the heads of a few of them had fallen, they poisoned Helena and her lover, and there followed a sordid scramble for power and plunder.

Now of the two children of Helena one was the boy who would live, even in the history of Russia, as "Ivan the Terrible." Ingenious historians have found a milder meaning for this epithet, or discovered that Ivan underwent some strange degeneration in his later years. But the boy who was brought up amidst dogs and grooms, who for sheer pleasure cast his dogs from the walls of his palace and watched them writhe, who stabbed his favourite jester for the most trifling fault, is the same Ivan who in later years soaked petitioners in brandy and set fire to them. His impulses were barbaric, and the unhappy features of his education had stimulated rather than curbed them. He was eight years old at the time his mother was murdered, but he was clever, observant, and self-conscious. He saw the boyars plunder the palace, which was now his, and fleece the long-suffering country. He noticed that any servant to whom he became attached was removed or murdered. He read much, and he grew up rapidly in his solitary world.

And during the Christmas festivities of 1543 Ivan, then thirteen years old, summoned his boyars before him and let loose upon them an unexpected storm of reproach. Andrew Chiuski, the most powerful of them, he handed over at once to his groom-attendants—one wonders how far they had inspired this precocious display—and the great noble was soon dispatched. One account runs that by Ivan's orders he was torn to pieces by the hounds: others say that the grooms acted without orders. Other nobles were banished. The short golden age of the boyars was over. The shadow of a sterner autocracy than ever began to creep over the court.

Ivan had himself crowned in January, 1547, and he chose the title, which now first appears, of "Tsar of all the Russias." Shortly afterwards he announced that he would marry, and his servants arranged the kind of matrimonial parade which had been customary at Constantinople when a prince was to wed. A preliminary survey was made of the daughters of all the nobles of the kingdom, and fifteen hundred of the most healthy and beautiful of them were brought to Moscow and crowded into the palace. A medical examination ensured that they were virtuous enough to wed a prince who was already expert in every variety of vice, and Ivan made the round of the trembling maids. He chose the lovely daughter of a small noble named Roman, a man of either Prussian (Slav—as the old Prussians were) or Lithuanian extraction. Anastasia Romanovna became the first Tsarina and the founder of the fortune of the Romanoff family. It was in the same year that Ivan had some deputies,

THE MOSCOVITES BECOME TSARS

who came from Pskoff to set out the grievances of the town, soaked in brandy and set afire.

The boyars were still powerful. In the same year, 1547, a fire destroyed a great part of Moscow, and the nobles charged it to the account of the Tsar's maternal relatives. The homeless people heard with horror that the Glinskis had stewed human hearts and watered the streets with the magic brew, and they fell upon the Glinski palaces. Even the young Tsar wavered for a moment, and the boyars gained ground. Three years later, however, he summoned a great assembly of all orders of the people—except "the Christians," who counted no longer—in the Red Square in front of the Kreml and impeached the boyars. Reforms were introduced in the holding of land and the administration of justice, and an arrangement was made for the presentation of complaints.

Ivan was still young, and the insolence of the boyars continued. In 1553 he was dangerously ill, and he was aware that they plotted to put a cousin of his upon the throne instead of reserving it for his infant son. Ivan was, like his grandfather, not a man of much personal courage, and he continued nervously to tolerate the opposition and corruption of the nobles. In 1560 he impeached and disgraced their leaders, Sylvester and Adacheff. His wife Anastasia had died, and he suspected poison. A state of intolerable friction and danger now set in,

THE ROMANCE OF THE ROMANOFFS

and in the middle of the winter of 1564 all Moscow was alarmed to see a great imperial cortège leave the palace and retire to the country. Ivan had packed on waggons his plate and treasures, his furniture and sacred ikons; and his court and followers went with him on his strange adventure. The correspondence which followed ended in a curious compromise. Ivan virtually divided Russia into two parts. The greater part of it was to be ruled by the boyars, the remainder by himself and his court.

But the young Tsar had reserved the right to punish treason, and on his return to Moscow he created the machinery by which he could do so. He formed a special guard of a thousand picked boyars and sons of boyars, and the dog's head which he gave them as emblem indicated his disposition. A reign of terror followed. Thousands of nobles and their followers were slain with every circumstance of brutality. Such legends grew out of the red terror that we handle them with some reserve, but we have a document in which Ivan coldly commends to the prayers of the Church 3,470 victims—nobles and priests, men, women, and children—of his new policy. Prince Vladimir (the cousin whom the nobles would have substituted for his son) and his mother were killed; and there is no grave reason to doubt the story that they were murdered in Ivan's presence, and that he then had their maids stripped,

THE MOSCOVITES BECOME TSARS

whipped through the streets, and shot or cut down as they ran. Naked exposure and scourging were common incidents of the terror.

In 1570 a man reported that Novgorod contemplated going over to Poland. A letter to that effect would, he said, be found hidden behind a picture in a certain monastery. Ivan's servants found the letter where the man had put it, and the Tsar and his troops moved grimly to Novgorod. Priests and monks were brutally flogged, so that many of them died, and then the citizens were brought, in batches of a hundred, before the Tsar. Some were roasted over slow fires in the great square, where once the *Véché* had been held: others were driven in sledges, the children tied to their mothers, down an incline into the icy river, where soldiers with pikes saw that none escaped death. The horror lasted five weeks, and so vaguely terrible was the city's recollection of it that the number of victims is variously stated as 500, 3,000, 60,000, and even 700,000. The Archbishop of the city is said to have been sewn in a bear-skin and flung to the dogs, but many of the stories of the time—of Ivan stabbing babes and raping mothers, of his soldiers using white-hot lances, and so on—may be figments of the horrified imagination.

Ivan, we must remember, was not a burly monster, cruel from his own indifference to suffering. He was rather a nervous, calculating man, shrinking behind soldiers chosen for their brutality, coldly following a policy of terror. When he had sacked the shops and palaces, and ravaged the whole territory of Novgorod, he turned upon Pskoff. It is recorded to his credit that he murdered none in that innocent city, but he relieved it of its wealth and banished many of the leading citizens. He entered Moscow with all the pomp of a great Roman conqueror, and soon set up his bloody tribunal in the capital. Hundreds were executed, and the most barbarous torture was inflicted even upon women.

That was in 1570, and from that time onward Ivan ruled his empire by the knout and the knife. His end was as inglorious as his reign. Anastasia had given him two sons, Ivan and Feodor. The three legitimate wives and various illegitimate partners whom he took after Anastasia's death do not seem to have much enlarged his family, and Prince Ivan grew up in confident expectation of the throne. He was on such good terms with his father that one tradition speaks of them as exchanging mistresses. In 1581, however, the Tsar was annoyed with his son's wife, and, with his customary lack of restraint, he struck her with the iron-shod staff which he usually carried. She was pregnant, and the blow was fatal. His son expostulated, and the Tsar again used his staff, or spear, and inflicted a fatal wound. For a time he professed acute remorse. He shed floods of tears and declared that he was un-

THE MOSCOVITES BECOME TSARS

worthy of the throne. His supporters, lay and clerical, did not share his momentary estimate of himself, and he then, it seems, entered upon a period of worse debauch than ever. We cannot very confidently pierce the darkness which falls over the palace after 1581, but it seems to have rivalled in vice the Golden House of Nero. In 1584 Ivan died.

Russian historians are apt to claim that Ivan was a great man marred by a cruel disposition and an environment which fostered it. No one will doubt either the savagery of his disposition or the barbarity and peculiar pressure of his environment, but his constructive work hardly entitles him to be called great. His domestic reforms seem to have been made out of antipathy to the boyars, and we should probably not be far wrong in attributing his other services to Russia mainly to a selfish motive. He broke the remaining power of the Finns and Mongols, slew or sold into slavery whole tribes of them, and made Russian provinces of their territory. He conquered Astrakhan and its territory, and extended the rule of Russia in the direction of Persia. He, after a long struggle, beat the Livonian Knights, and secured respectful peace from Poland and Sweden.

The greatest part of his policy was his endeavour to bring Russia into contact with the west. From Livonia to Hungary a line of fanatical Catholic powers shut out Russia from intercourse with the advancing civilisation of the west. Ivan could hardly realise the historical law that isolation means stagnation, but he did see clearly that everything new and valuable—such as muskets and cannon—came from the west. Early in his reign, in 1553, some English merchants sailed round by the Protestant north to Russia, and Ivan became passionately eager for an alliance with England. There is good ground to believe that his envoys begged for him the hand of Queen Elizabeth herself! Her contemptuous refusal, softened by diplomacy, angered him for a time, but in later life he asked at least the hand of her cousin, Mary Hastings. He had just taken on his sixth consort, and neither Mary nor Elizabeth liked the prospect. The English court, which wanted the profit of trade with Russia, was embarrassed, but as it was in the same year that the Tsar killed his son and entered upon his last sombre phase the difficulty did not remain long.

We have now seen how the Moscovites had made the new Russia—the autocratic and imperial Russia which succeeded the democratic and smaller country of the Slavs. How much "the genius of the Slav people" had to do with the creation of that autocracy the reader will now understand. We have also seen the children of a certain Roman, the Romanoffs, enter the chronicle, and we have next to see how they mount the imperial throne and found a lengthy dynasty.

CHAPTER IV

THE RISE OF THE ROMANOFFS

THE second son of Ivan the Terrible, who now became the Tsar Feodor, was a piquant contrast to his father and brother. Not wives and mistresses, but the ornate services of the Church or long private devotions, occupied his hours. He was as meek as his father had been truculent, and the nobles began to raise their heads once more. His uncle, Nikita Romanoff, brother of the first Tsarina, naturally held the first place in his confidence and relieved him of the profane task of governing his dominions.

But the pious Feodor had married, and his wife Irene had a masterful and ambitious brother, Boris Godunoff. The Godunoffs are said to have descended from a Tatar chief, who had embraced Christianity and settled in Moscow. Irene was devoted to her brother, and she used her influence over the feeble-minded Tsar to promote him. Before long the palace was split into two factions, and the familiar struggle for power and wealth set in. Nikita Romanoff was a man of ability, but he had a more astute rival. Boris Godunoff secured two measures which greatly increased his support in Moscow and the country.

The first measure won for him the gratitude of the clergy. The Russian Church was still in effect the Greek Church. Its supreme head was the Patriarch of Constantinople, who sustained his tattered dignity among the Mohammedans. Boris induced this man to create a Patriarch of Moscow, and he thus won the increasing favour of the clergy. His other measure was one of great and terrible significance for the poor "Christians." The expansion of Russia had created large new estates, and the great land-owners continually attracted peasants away from the smaller estates. But the small landowners, who formed the yeomanry or cavalry of the Empire, were not a body to be despised, either in the interest of the country or of an aspiring politician. It is said that in 1592 Boris played for their support by issuing an imperial decree which forbade the peasants to go from one estate to another. Some Russian historians deny this. If the document is genuine, they say, it meant only that Boris legally fixed a practice which had gradually arisen, on account of the mischief of these peasant-migrations. However that may be, there is no doubt that Boris Godunoff legally established serfdom in Russia at a time when it was being abandoned elsewhere. The peasants grumbled and suffered, but they now had upon their backs an autocracy that treated their wishes with entire contempt.

As the reign of Feodor (1584-1598) wore on, and no son appeared, Boris pushed his ambition to greater lengths. The heir to the throne would now be the young Prince Dmitri, the son of Ivan the Terrible's seventh wife. Early in the reign of Feodor the nobles had compelled Dmitri's ambitious mother to take her infant son and her relatives to a remote provincial estate, and from that exile the mother and her kin nervously studied the failing health of Tsar Feodor and the condition of his wife. The subjection of women in Russia does not seem to have extinguished their ambition, and there was at the court itself the usual party, out of power, which espoused the hope of a possible dynasty. The court seethed once more with sordid passion.

In 1591 the Dmitri faction at court was shattered by the announcement that the young prince was dead. Boris ordered an inquiry, and as a result he announced that, owing to the carelessness of his mother in supervising him, Dmitri had committed suicide. With becoming zeal the virtual Regent forced the mother to enter a nunnery and consigned her relatives to various prisons. Moscow at large, reflecting that the tragedy removed an important obstacle from Boris's path to the throne, preferred to believe that his servants had murdered the prince. That is the general opinion of historians, but there are some who maintain that the child was not murdered at all, and that the adventurer who will presently enter the story was really Dmitri.

For the present, at all events, the way was cleared, and the death of Feodor in 1598 left the throne vacant. The nobles and people offered their allegiance to the Tsarina, but Irene, suddenly discovering a remarkable distrust of her powers and dislike of the world, fled to a nunnery. Boris had, with equal modesty, retired to the same nunnery, but his supporters worked for him, and presently the convent was sought by an impressive procession of the clergy (headed by the obsequious patriarchs), the boyars, and the people of Moscow, offering the crown to Boris. He declined an invitation which seemed to him to come from too small a section, and the general council of the Empire was then convoked, and it repeated the offer. After a further mockery of resistance he accepted and became Tsar Boris.

I have said that Boris Godunoff was as able a man to fill the autocracy as could have been found at that time, and he endeavoured to complete the plans of Ivan the Terrible. He kept in check Sweden and Poland, consolidated the gains in Asia, and maintained close and profitable relations with Queen Elizabeth. He encouraged Russian students to go to western countries for the completion of their education. But we are concerned

THE RISE OF THE ROMANOFFS

with the rise of the Romanoffs and may summarise other matters.

Three years after the accession of Boris a dreadful famine spread over the land. It lasted three years, and so great was the destitution that in later years horrible stories were whispered of parents devouring their own children. Streams of the suffering country-folk poured into Moscow, and, as its own provisions were soon exhausted, the streets of the capital were filled with pale and emaciated ghosts. It is said that hundreds of thousands died in Moscow alone, and throughout the land the superstitious people spoke of the sin of Boris Godunoff in murdering the heir to the throne. The nobles themselves stirred, and Boris put into operation the usual machinery. The Romanoff family seemed to be an especial source of danger, and the chief representative of that family, Feodor Romanoff, was thrust into a monastery and buried under the monkish title of Philaret. His wife was compelled to enter a nunnery and assume the name of Marfa.

The scattered feeling of discontent at length gathered round the person of a singular adventurer. In the summer of 1604 the news spread through Russia that Dmitri, the third son of Ivan the Terrible, was not dead, but was approaching Moscow with a Polish army to oust the usurper and put an end to their miseries. Gregory Otrepieff, who is generally believed to have been "the false Dmitri," had been a roving monk who had turned brigand with a band of Cossacks. From the southern steppes he had gone to Poland, and there, it was announced, he had, believing himself to be at the point of death, revealed to a Jesuit confessor the secret of his birth and shown the priest a jewelled cross which proved his identity. The Jesuits were still in their melodramatic phase of secret conspiracy for the Church, and may well have invented, or embroidered, the story. They pressed Dmitri upon the Catholic king and nobles of Poland, and in October he crossed the frontier of Russia with an irregular force. Would the Jesuits add to their many triumphs the submission of Russia to the Vatican after so many centuries of resistance?

Otrepieff's force was defeated, but there was a good deal of treachery, and presently a large body of the Cossacks came to join the army of their former companion. At this juncture, in 1605, Boris died, and priests, soldiers, and people declared that they were convinced of the genuineness of the adventurer. The late Tsar's wife and son were murdered with the usual barbarity. The people of Moscow lustily received the monk-brigand, when he came for his coronation, and even the widow of Ivan IV publicly fell upon his neck and identified him. Her relatives were, of course, promoted to wealth and honour, and even the Romanoffs returned from

THE RISE OF THE ROMANOFFS

the monastic shades to the sunlight of prosperity. Monk Philaret was made a Metropolitan, or Archbishop.

But the rise to power was not so speedy as the fall from it, and both give us some measure of the ignorance and barbarism of the times. Otrepieff was a clever and accomplished man, but he either lacked, or disdained to use in so credulous a world, the art of tact. He brought a Polish wife whose suite laughed at the uncouth ways of the Russians. He himself too openly railed at the backwardness of the country, surrounded himself with foreigners, and acted with scandalous independence. He was plainly, as his adventures would indicate, a sceptic, and he snapped his fingers at the Pope and the Jesuits the moment they had secured the throne for him; but he was no more respectful to the clergy and religious forms of Russia. He disdained monks and ikons, asked no blessing on his table, and refused to follow any of the court-traditions. And within a month of his entrance into the Kreml the adventurer lay dead upon the stones of its courtyard. People, amazed at their own credulity, now exclaimed that he was a sorcerer, and the spell had to be broken by blowing the ashes of his burned corpse from the mouth of a cannon.

The succession to the throne had now been interrupted, and a ruler had to be chosen. Vassili Chuiski, a military noble of distinguished family, a

THE ROMANCE OF THE ROMANOFFS

bald myopic man of little energy, secured the suffrages of Moscow and mounted the throne. But while the sluggishness of communication enabled Moscow thus to choose a sovereign for the entire country, it left the provinces in such a state of confusion and unsettlement that any rebel could find support there. Another Dmitri arose, and was accepted. People recollected that the real Dmitri had, like a true Russian, worn a beard, while Otrepieff had had none. The new claimant had a beard. A regiment of nobles in one province, an army of disaffected peasants and brigands in another, raised the standard of the new adventurer and united their forces within sight of Moscow. There the nobles quarrelled with and deserted their baser comrades, and the new claimant ended on a gallows.

But the name "Dmitri" was now a phrase under which any kind of rebellion might find shelter. A number of men who claimed that they were sons or grandsons of Ivan the Terrible appeared, and the known morals of that monarch did not make the number implausible. A "third false Dmitri," a very poor type of adventurer, was fabricated, and before long the rebels again set up within sight of Moscow the court of "the real monarch." The new impostor went so far as to claim that he was not merely the Prince, but the first "false Dmitri" also, having escaped assassination, and he sent tender messages to his "wife" Maryna (who had married

THE PATRIARCH PHILARET, FATHER OF MIKHAIL ROMANOFF, THE FIRST TSAR OF THE NEW DYNASTY. SEVENTEENTH CENTURY

THE RISE OF THE ROMANOFFS

Otrepieff) and her father. In later years they maintained that the impostor had, after killing their servants, torn them from their home and brought them to Moscow, but such trickery was common. Maryna's father, still thirsting for a crown for his daughter and a share of its magnificence for himself, brought his daughter to Moscow and bade her open her arms to her recovered "husband." "I would die first," she said, after seeing the worthless adventurer; but the father persisted, and soon the "genuine" Tsar and Tsarina held court outside Moscow, while Chuiski and his friends nervously kept the city.

The situation was complicated by the insidious behaviour of the king of Poland. King Sigismund continued with a hypocritical pretence of justice to support the claimant, while he negotiated a surer way of getting the crown. He claimed the Russian throne for his own son Ladislas, and sent an army against Moscow. The terrified boyars now compelled the useless Chuiski to resign and formed a council, including one of the Romanoffs, Ivan Nikititch, to direct the affairs of the distracted country. This small group of boyars accepted Ladislas. But it became clear that Sigismund and his Jesuits put forward Ladislas only as a pretext to seize the throne, and a terrible agitation seized the people. Their historic faith was in danger. The shadow of the Pope fell upon their very walls. The small

Polish army had to be conducted into the city during the night. The people awoke to find Popery in their midst, and soldiers and the nobles who supported Poland, including the Romanoffs, had to shelter in the Kreml.

The impostor was at length driven away from Moscow, and in December the news came that he had been slain by the Tatars. But this removal of one element of strife now only embittered the people further against the Poles. King Sigismund was taking Russian towns in the east: the Swedes were busy in the north. Russia had returned to as grave and costly a confusion as it had ever witnessed, and the long-suffering peasants looked up with dull eyes from their plough to hear the latest news of their masters, or fled before the unrestrained bands of brigands. In Moscow itself a row between the people and the Polish soldiers led to days of murder and burning of houses, and the skirmish was turned into regular warfare by the arrival of an army of Cossacks. The Poles and a number of Moscow nobles, including the wife and son of Archbishop Philaret, who had gone to plead with the Polish king and been held prisoner by him, were closely besieged in the Kreml.

It was a butcher of Nijni-Novgorod who raised at length a national standard and rallied the best elements of the country. His forceful and sincere personality bound together his townsmen in a

THE RISE OF THE ROMANOFFS

league of effort and sacrifice, and in the late summer of 1612 a large and solemn army, headed by the priests and monks and sacred pictures, came within sight of the golden domes of the metropolis. The townsfolk eagerly joined them, and the few hundred Poles who remained in the Kreml were summoned to surrender. Worn with famine, though they had begun to eat the flesh of their slain comrades, and had made soup of the old parchments in the Archives, the brave troops at first stubbornly refused to yield without an order from their king. They surrendered on October 26th, and a company of living ghosts emerged from the sacred enclosure. Amongst them was Ivan Nikititch, of the Romanoff family, and Philaret's wife Marfa; and with Marfa, his large eyes wondering at the scenes of horror, was her son Michael who was destined to be the first Romanoff ruler.

A provisional government was formed, and a summons to a great popular assembly was sent over the country. A number of loosely chosen representatives—except of the peasants, who no longer counted—came to Moscow, and the task of choosing a monarch was confronted. The nobles were generally in favour of Ladislas of Poland, but the bitter anti-Roman and anti-Polish feeling restrained these. They must have a Russian monarch, and men naturally asked if they had not still amongst them some man of royal blood. From

Philaret, whose embassy had won him some prestige, but whose clerical condition debarred him from the throne, attention was soon drawn to his son.

The mother, Marfa, had left Moscow after issuing from the Kreml, and had gone to a country estate at Kastroma. There were, however, other Romanoffs in the assembly, and Philaret himself (who, however, is said to have urged the election of a boyar) maintained contact with it from his exile. Most zealous for the boy—for Michael was only seventeen years old—was a crafty old fox who had married a niece of Philaret, and might reasonably expect some reward. To the nobles he pointed out that the youth and feebleness of Michael would leave them a larger power. To the clergy he observed that to have the father of the Tsar a Metropolitan of their Church held out a large prospect of power for them. In short, the nobles were induced to realise that blood was the thing that mattered, while the clergy and monks were guided by supernatural visions in which the boy appeared as "God's chosen one." Michael was elected on February 21st. Three weeks later a solemn procession approached the monastery at Kastroma in which Marfa guarded her precious son. She wept at the prospect of Michael assuming so dangerous a dignity—tears are second only to blood in the chronicles of Moscow—and for several days maintained a most virtuous resistance.

THE RISE OF THE ROMANOFFS

And on May 2nd Marfa and Michael entered the Kreml once more, the chosen rulers of Russia.

There can be little doubt that the hesitation of the nobles, who really had no prominent candidate before their eyes, was chiefly overborne in favour of the Romanoffs by a consideration of the youth of Michael. Marfa was not one of the strong women who abound in the Russian chronicles. We shall soon see her return to the convent from which the national agitation had drawn her. Philaret was a prisoner in the hands of the Poles, and none could surmise when he would return. We see in the election little of the national spirit which had cleared Moscow, yet the country groaned for the creative genius of a statesman and the virility of a strong soldier. The ravages of war had terribly enfeebled it; its industrial life was in decay; its hereditary enemies threatened it on every front.

Michael was a feeble youth whose eyes still looked dully upon the strange scenes he had witnessed. He passed at once into the hands of his mother and her relatives, the Saltykoffs, and the court hummed once more with petty intrigue for money and offices. Marfa appropriated the hereditary treasure of the Tsarina and, knowing something of the history of Russia, formed about her a body of spies and supporters. The older nobles resisted the upstarts, and fierce quarrels for precedence and appointments occurred even in the presence of the Tsar. At times the knout was laid upon too offensive shoulders, but several years passed in these selfish recriminations.

There were, however, urgent affairs to be settled, and by raising the taxation to one fourth of the individual's income sufficient money was gathered, and escaped the fingers of the nobles, to raise an army. So great had been the disorder of the previous twenty years that Moscow itself had lost a third of its population, and the impoverished merchants writhed under the tax. But the Cossacks were threatening. The romantic Maryna, who will be remembered as the wife of the first and companion of the second false Dmitri, had given birth to a son, and she transferred her versatile affection to the Cossack leader, Zarutski, and relied upon him to secure the crown for her little Ivan. Zarutski swept triumphantly from town to town, while other brigands emptied villages, and the Swedes and Poles pursued their accustomed inroads. The new army scattered the Cossacks, impaled their leader, and hanged the little Ivan—an infant of three years—in order effectually to settle the brood of pretenders. Maryna ended her curious career in prison, and southern Russia was restored to comparative calm.

The councillors of Marfa now turned toward the Swedes and Poles. A direct struggle with such adversaries was impossible, and Russian envoys made

THE RISE OF THE ROMANOFFS

the round of Europe seeking either money and men to meet them or mediation to disarm them. At the western courts the Moscovites did not convey a favourable impression of their country. Their gross manners and dirty ways affronted even the English and Dutch of the early seventeenth century, nor were the silver articles of the table or the maids on the streets quite safe from their ready hands. But England and Holland had, besides the moderate advantage of hating Rome, a keen desire to trade with Russia and the East, and they endeavoured to secure peace. Poland scornfully refused to treat with "the son of a Pope" who had usurped the throne of their Ladislas. In 1617, however, Gastavus Adolphus, of Sweden, was bought off by a large indemnity and a few towns, and Russia was able to oppose a stronger defence to Poland. King Sigismund now offered a truce, and at a conference it was arranged that he should renounce the claim to the Russian crown, but keep Smolensk and other cities.

The peace was followed by an exchange of prisoners, and in the summer of 1619 the Archbishop Philaret hastened to secure the power which awaited him. It happened that the patriarchal throne of Moscow was vacant, and Philaret occupied it. That he was a priest *malgré lui,* and enjoyed the more luxurious and comforting tastes of a profane layman, did not much matter in that world. Far more

THE ROMANCE OF THE ROMANOFFS

religious prelates than Philaret drank heavily and habitually. The patriarchate was the highest power he could nominally and legally hold, and he was not wanting either in energy or ambition. For a patriarch, however, to have a wife about the court was scarcely seemly, and he "persuaded" Marfa to return to her convent. He felt also that it was expedient to remove some of her friends, and in order to do this with a show of justice he reopened a very curious case that had been settled in his absence.

In the year 1616 Michael had decided to wed a young woman of obscure family named Maria Ivanovna Khlopoff. Her name was, in accordance with custom, changed to Anastasia; her espousals were celebrated; the day of the sacred ceremony which would make her Tsarina was within her delighted view. Then the luckless Maria fell ill, which no bride of a Tsar must dare to do. The doctors examined her and pronounced her "unfit to serve the delight of the Tsar," and the unhappy maiden and her relatives were suddenly dispatched to Siberia. Philaret, who knew with what anxiety the existing favourites at a Russian court regarded the coming of a crowd of relatives with a Tsar's bride, and how frequently the chosen maid met with accidents before the wedding-day, looked into the affair when he returned. Her confessor admitted that she was innocent—it now transpired

THE RISE OF THE ROMANOFFS

that a certain indiscretion in eating fruit was the full extent of her fault—and she was recalled from Siberia and permitted to settle, with a small pension, at Nijni-Novgorod.

It appears that Philaret had hope of securing a more distinguished Tsarina. During the next few years he approached the courts of Denmark and Sweden, but without success. The king of Denmark bluntly remarked that the air of Moscow was not good for the chosen brides of Tsars. So Philaret returned to the affair of Maria Khlopoff, and was now convinced that the jealous Saltykoffs (Marfa's people) had fabricated the charge. He fell upon them with great severity, and drove several into exile. Marfa, however, succeeded in saving the remainder of the family, and also in preventing the return to court of Maria. To cut the story short, yet fitly introduce the next generation of palace-squabblers, we may say that in 1624 Michael married Princess Maria Dolgoruki; and, as she died soon afterwards, he married a woman of undistinguished family, Eudoxia Strecknieff. The new Tsarina provided a son, Alexis, and the precious dynasty of the Romanoffs was saved from a premature extinction.

Philaret had ability, and we need not quarrel with the way in which he took the power from the hands of his feeble and incompetent son. That he was a Wolsey or a Richelieu, as some historians conceive him, is far too flattering an exaggeration. The Cossacks, the Poles, and the Swedes were disarmed while he was still absent, and when the Poles renewed the war in 1632 Philaret's army was badly beaten, and he could think of nothing better than to have its generals executed. He had friendly relations with France and England, because both wanted to enter, through Russia, into a profitable commerce with Persia; which was refused. The Turks, of course, barred the Mediterranean route to the east. The Sultan offered Philaret an alliance against the Poles, but he was at that time unprepared for a big war. On the whole it was a balance of interests rather than statesmanship which gave Russia some years of peace.

Internally Philaret did more active service. The question had already arisen whether Russia should be Europeanised. The colony of foreign merchants which now grew just outside the walls of Moscow exhibited a higher culture. The western armies were constantly superior to the Russian in equipment. The envoys to France, England, and Holland spoke of refinements which made the luxury of Moscow seem tawdry. On the other hand were the inevitable croakers who protested that Russian trade, Russian religion, or even the Russian State, would not survive an invasion of western ideas. Philaret boldly adopted the progressive view and summoned foreign teachers to Moscow. Astronomers brought their marvellous instruments to astonish or scare the populace; mathematicians and literary men opened schools in the metropolis. Against one western discovery, tobacco, the Russians remained obdurate; while the man who was caught surreptitiously taking snuff, as the westerners did, had his nose cut off.

The religious controversy also contributed to the sharpening of the wits of the nation. The Jesuits still lingered heroically on the fringe of the Empire and sought to bring it under the rule of the Papacy. Even a new pretender was tried—a son of Maryna who had escaped murder, they said—but the man, a commonplace peasant, was not chosen with their usual skill, and little harm was done. In the Russian provinces which were subject to Poland, however, they worked with such effect that the Church was rent by a great schism. Some of the Russian prelates were for union with Rome. The struggle had an echo in Russia, and some education for controversial purposes was inaugurated. We must, however, not exaggerate the effect on the Russian mind of this controversy. It is estimated by Russian historians that at that time not one person in a thousand, at the most, could read, and even in the city-circles in which the points at issue were debated the clash of ideas must have been of the crudest conceivable nature.

Philaret, who sincerely endeavoured to introduce

THE ROMANCE OF THE ROMANOFFS

some western culture into this dense jungle of ignorance and superstition, died in 1633. Michael continued for twelve years to sustain feebly the plans of his father, and the period may be described as one of slow recovery. An amusing episode of Michael's last year will give some idea of the condition even of the court.

In 1641 Prince Valdemar of Denmark came to Russia on behalf of his father. The court decided that it would like him to wed the Princess Irene, and, when Valdemar was deaf to hints and returned to Copenhagen, a deputation was sent to consult with his father. King Christian favoured the proposal, but Valdemar had seen Moscow and was not attracted. When one of the envoys fervently pledged his head as a guarantee that all would be well, the young prince asked: "What should I do with your head?" At the beginning of 1645, however, he submitted so far to the pressure as to go to Moscow, and a quaint struggle followed. For five months the prince fought against the marriage. In vain were the person and virtues of Irene impressed upon him. He was assured that she never got drunk, as other Russian ladies did, and her personal attractions, which seem to have been feeble, were eloquently exaggerated. Valdemar found the pretext that his evangelical faith was in grave danger if he joined the Russian court, and he proposed to return to Denmark. He was virtually a

THE RISE OF THE ROMANOFFS

prisoner in the Kreml, and on one occasion he created a scandal by drawing the sword and threatening to cut his way out. In July Michael died, and his successor allowed the Danish prince to return home.

CHAPTER V

THE EARLY ROMANOFFS

THE feeble Michael had, we saw, provided an heir to the golden throne, and, owing to the comparative length of his reign, his son Alexis had reached a mature age when his turn came to rule. The portraits of all the Tsars have been so thickly overlaid with rhetorical paint that we have some difficulty in discerning their true historical features. Alexis seems to have been a ruler of generally excellent intentions and very moderate ability. He was at the time of his accession a youth of sixteen: a tall, handsome youth, physically stronger than his father and fond of hunting, but nervous and irritable. It needed no keenness of vision to see that Russia was in a deplorable condition. The nobles and officials were as corrupt as ever; the fiscal system and administration of justice were atrocious; the merchants struggled feebly against foreign competition, and the serfs were crushed to the ground under their burdens. Alexis assuredly resented this corruption and incompetence, and sus-

THE EARLY ROMANOFFS

tained the small efforts of his father and grandfather to improve the country.

The Tsar's mother died soon after his accession, and the customary place of chief favourite and virtual ruler fell to Boris Ivanovitch Morozoff, who had for the preceding three years had charge of the prince's education. Morozoff had the ambition and moral indelicacy which were common to his time and class, and he and his friends grew rich. But there was one cloud on the horizon of their prosperity. Alexis must soon marry, and behind the bride, whoever she might be, Morozoff and his friends saw the usual crowd of greedy relatives hastening to Moscow and clamouring for wealth and power. Morozoff cleverly conceived his plans to avoid this danger.

In the early part of the year 1647 the thrilling message went through the Empire that the young Tsar would choose a bride, and every noble or commoner who had, or thought that he had, a youthful daughter with the required degree of health, beauty, and virtue, made application to the officials. A swarm of officers spread over the Empire and conducted the preliminary examination. Then some two hundred picked beauties, rotund and blushing, were drafted to the imperial palace and packed into what might seem to be a large harem. At night, when the palpitating maids had retired to bed, the Tsar and his medical attendant went from bed to bed and inspected the very wakeful beauties. The golden rose fell on this occasion to Euphemia Voievolojski, the daughter of a noble who was in poor circumstances. But the unexpected honour was too much for the obscure provincial girl. She fainted from joy and agitation, and the party of Morozoff, who were apprehensive of the coming of rivals, put a grave interpretation upon her weakness. She must be epileptic, and entirely unfit to rear a brood of little Romanoffs; and poor Euphemia and her relatives, who for a moment had had golden visions, were dispatched to Siberia.

Morozoff had another plan for marrying the Tsar. An obscure man of the boyar class named Miloslavski had two pretty daughters, and Morozoff designed to wed one and make a Tsarina of the other. Whether he was already in love with Anna Miloslavski, or whether he merely felt it prudent to annex her and her relatives when the Tsar married her sister, is not apparent. It is enough that Alexis married Maria, and ten days afterwards Morozoff wedded her sister Anna, and neatly secured the linking of the ambition of Miloslavski with his own. Legend afterwards said that the two girls had, not long before, sold mushrooms in the public market at Moscow. Certainly their father had been poor and insignificant, and just as certainly he and his relatives at once began to heap up wealth by every corrupt device known in the tradition of the Moscovite court. Other Miloslavskis came to court, and a fresh brood of parasites fastened upon the veins of the country.

The Tsar was a good-humoured, indulgent man. Good-humour, which really meant an indolent and short-sighted habit of extracting whatever pleasure the actual circumstances afforded, was at that time, and remained until the present crisis, the chief characteristic of Russia. The democratic peasant of the primitive tribe had relieved his labours with the song and the dance. The serf now had little joy in life, but, while the song and dance were banned, a new and potent element of gaiety had been introduced: brandy. Everybody drank, and nearly everybody drank copiously. Alexis himself was sober in habit, though even he liked to intoxicate others at his table, but drunkenness was the daily rule. The Patriarch of Moscow got drunk, the priests and monks got drunk, and the people—as far as their means went—followed the example of their lords and pastors. Vast quantities of wine, hydromel, and especially brandy were consumed, and pepper was mixed with the brandy to improve its sting. Babies drank neat brandy. Wives lay drunk, side by side with their husbands, in a state of alarming *deshabille,* in the sleighs and coaches which ran noisily along the street. The few who resisted were, as a jest, compelled to drink. Even nuns and delicate young girls had more than once the option of emptying a flagon of brandy or enduring a whipping. Women at times prostituted themselves, and men sold their clothes, in order to get the precious *vodka*.

Russian life generally did not rise much above this level. The people were, as I said, so illiterate and ignorant that scarcely one in a thousand could read. Superstition throve in proportion to the ignorance, and vice and brutality were not far behind. Women were atrociously treated. The women of the richer class contrived, as we shall see, to creep through the restrictions imposed upon them and share the license of their lords, but in the great mass of the people the mother had a generally deplorable position. Wives were often whipped or beaten until the blood flowed, and many a brutal husband rubbed salt into the wounds. At times a frantic wife killed her husband, and in such cases the law exacted an awful penalty. In other cases bloodshed was too common an event to be severely punished. Moscow was distinguished among European cities for violence and bloodshed.

Vice and coarseness were still common enough all over Europe, but it is the almost unanimous opinion of the foreign visitors to Russia at the time, who wrote their impressions, that vice was particularly free at Moscow. Unnatural vice was a matter of jest. When the theatre became popular, as it

IVAN THE TERRIBLE, BY ANTOKOLSKY

presently did, the vice was coarsely suggested on the stage. Word and gesture everywhere were licentious. As the immense majority of the Russian families, which were usually large, huddled over the stove in one room, day and night, during the six months' winter, the atmosphere that the children breathed may be left to the imagination. Except amongst the wealthier nobles, who were being modified at this time by foreign culture and refinement, manners were indescribably gross. On all this the mass of the clergy had, and purported to have, no influence. The greater part of the monks were as gross as the monks of Europe had been generally before the Reformation, and the false standards of the better monks—who laid a fierce anathema upon chess or the dance or Sunday-work and a blessing upon ignorance—made their influence small and ineffective. Kiss the ikons and be docile, was the general philosophy they recommended.

That the early Romanoffs made a few improvements in this chaotic and half-barbarous world is not saying very much to their credit. But beyond a vague perception that more foreign light must be imported they had no plan or statesmanship, and they proceeded piece-meal, under pressure. The foreign merchants who were introduced or permitted to enter kept industry and trade in their own hands, and did little for the native development of

Russia. The avarice and corruption of the court and officials thought only of extortion, never of wise development. The people, even of Moscow, sank under taxation and injustice, and a certain measure of independence grew out of their very misery.

One day in the summer of 1648 the Tsar and the Patriarch were returning to the palace from some ceremony when a frantic group of the people approached with cries of grievances. They were, as usual, driven off; but the distress was acute and soon an angry and dangerous throng of soldiers, artisans, and small merchants and shop-keepers besieged the Kreml and demanded the justice of the Tsar upon the bloodsuckers. Either in fear or in anger—for Alexis was apt to boil over when the misdeeds of some noble "son of a bitch" (as the Emperor put it) were brought to his notice—the Tsar handed over to the mob two of the most hated officials, and they were savagely murdered. The Clerk of the Council, who was held particularly responsible for the salt-tax, which restricted the supply of salt-fish, was assassinated on a dung-hill. The whetted appetite then turned against Morozoff's palace, but it was ingeniously protected from destruction by the Tsar's sending to the mob an assurance that it was his own property. Morozoff himself was hidden in a monastery until the fury of the storm spent itself, but the Tsar had to promise to punish him, and to appoint a reform-commission. The autocrat shed a flood of facile Moscovite tears as he protested that the people's grievances should be remedied; and his servants discreetly scattered money amongst the soldiers, who formed the more dangerous part of the mob. The fires which now threatened the entire city were extinguished, and the people slowly and sullenly returned to discipline.

The insurrection had spread to the provinces, and the former republics of Pskoff and Novgorod showed that their spirit of independence was not extinct. Pskoff, in fact, inaugurated a genuine rebellion and had to be reduced by the imperial troops, after a siege. Novgorod plundered the stores of its foreign merchants and murdered more than one supporter of the corrupt autocracy. When the Archbishop Nikon (of whom we shall see more) attempted to defend the cause of the Tsar (as he was careful to write to that monarch), his palace was invaded and he sank under a rain of stones which nearly ended his life. Only the sworn promise of a reform of the Empire put an end to the bloody insurrection.

It was under these circumstances, and with the added evil of an economic system which failed yearly and a constant danger from the Poles, that the second Romanoff began the reform of his kingdom. Morozoff was condemned to a luxurious internment in a monastery, from which he contrived for a long time to watch his interests and influence the Tsar, and the sturdy Archbishop of Novgorod began to enjoy favour. A commission of inquiry was appointed, and many reforms of the taxes, the administration of justice, and the court were brought about.

In 1652 the Patriarch of Moscow died, and Nikon, who had steadily advanced, was appointed to fill his place. For the next six years Nikon was chief favourite and councillor, and his story is so characteristic of the time that it must be briefly told. He was the son of a provincial peasant: a man of robust constitution and conscience, and of no small ambition. His success as a ruler of monks had won for him the archbishopric of Novgorod, and he knew how to capture the nervous and superstitious monarch. He claimed visions, and his shrewdness was at least supported by a vigorous will. Before long the Tsar was little more than an instrument of his will, and an abject spiritual pupil. He would protest with tears that he was unworthy to wear the crown, and it was only by reliance upon the Patriarch's strong counsel that he was dissuaded from abdicating.

The Tsar, like his predecessors, loved the elaborate ritual of the Church, and Nikon interested him in the work of ecclesiastical reform. The Slav translation of the Bible was very corrupt, and the

THE EARLY ROMANOFFS

corrupt texts and ancient superstitious usages were to be rooted out. While Poles and Swedes and Turks threatened—while the country rotted in ignorance and economic folly—an immense zeal was concentrated upon the purification of the text of the Scriptures and upon such grave issues as the shaving of the beard, and the number of fingers that one must use in making the sign of the cross. The court was purified of "heretics" and the forces of the Empire were put at the Patriarch's disposal for the purification of the entire country. Easygoing Russia had as yet not recognised its many heresies. Provided that one repudiated the Pope one was esteemed orthodox; and indeed most of the priests and monks were too densely ignorant to examine a man's orthodoxy.

It was now seen that a vast amount of heresy existed in Russia, and every weird phase of dissent was truculently persecuted. Whole colonies of monks were infected, and in places their monasteries sustained for several years the attacks of imperial troops. Nikon was astute as well as ambitious. He would invite some ragged popular fanatic of Moscow to drink wine at his table, and would make great nobles tremble before his power. He acquired enormous wealth, made an impressive display of pomp and luxury, and contrived to indulge the heavy sensuality which then belonged to all classes. Russia had become an autocracy. Nikon would make it a theocracy.

But in such a court a man must have the truculence of Ivan the Terrible or Peter the Great to hold such a power, and the undercurrents of intrigue began in 1657 to weaken the Patriarch's position. Old believers, dissenters, and discontented nobles concentrated their hatred upon him. It was in the summer of 1658 that he began to perceive the effect. A foreign prince was to be entertained, and Nikon was not invited to the banquet. He complained, and was insulted; and he next perceived that Alexis was absent from *his* functions. He resolved to try a desperate remedy. Summoning his clergy and the people, he solemnly and tearfully laid his sacred vestments upon the altar and declared that enemies compelled him to abandon his high office. He retired to the New Jerusalem monastery near Moscow to await the summons of the Tsar to return to office, but no summons came.

For several years Nikon fiercely fought his clerical and lay opponents from the monastery. "Brigand, pagan, stinking dog," he howled at his enemies; and they retorted that he was a "mad wolf." In 1664 two high oriental prelates, the Patriarchs of Alexandria and Antioch, visited Moscow, and it was felt that they might be induced to end the scandal by condemning Nikon's reforms. But Nikon was undoubtedly right, and the Tsar had to

THE EARLY ROMANOFFS

end it in his own way. The Patriarch was degraded and imprisoned for life in a distant monastery. The issue is a sad page of ecclesiastical history. The ageing Nikon lit up the monastery with debauch. Not only did his large consumption of brandy immoderately increase, but he loved to have women, especially young women, brought into the monastery and stupefied with drink. At night his cell took on a Rabelaisian aspect; and he died in an odour of sulphur, and was solemnly buried with all the honours of a patriarch, in the year 1681.

By this time another interesting revolution had taken place at the court. Power had passed to the Miloslavskis, the family of the Tsarina, and they followed the familiar tradition. It may at least be said that under their lead, and that of the boyar Nastchokin, a measure of reform was carried out, and the country was strengthened against its enemies. The Cossacks of the south were still under the dominion of Poland, and, after many years of oppression and revolt, they appealed to Moscow for help and protection. In 1654 the Tsar declared war upon Poland and wrested a good deal of Russian territory from it. The Swedes also were at war with Poland, and in the north the ambition of Russia clashed with that of Sweden. Alexis made peace with Poland and entered upon an unsuccessful war with Sweden. It ended indecisively, and the Poles returned to the attack and inflicted severe defeats upon the Russians. The war later ended in a costly compromise.

The economic condition of the country was such that the new drain caused frightful distress, and the people of Moscow stirred once more. Copper roubles had had to be coined, and poverty became deeper. One summer day in 1662 the Tsar was at chapel in his country mansion, a few miles from Moscow, when he was told that a crowd from Moscow beset the palace and clamoured to be heard. His officers had dared to tear down a placard on which they had exposed their grievances. The pious Tsar vigorously refused to leave his devotions for so profane a cause, but he was overruled, and he confronted the mob. He would, he said, proceed to Moscow at the close of the service and make an inquiry. He must come at once, with them, they answered; and a few of the bolder climbed the balcony and pulled at his cloak. He was, however, permitted to return and finish his devotions after he had taken a solemn oath to inquire into their grievances. When he came down to carry out his promise, he found that a larger and more violent crowd surrounded the palace. Two regiments of the militia were summoned and, as the vast crowd still jeered and flourished weapons, the order was given, and thousands of the people were shot. Hundreds of others were afterwards exiled, and the growing spirit of popular independence was, apparently, stifled.

Favourite succeeded favourite at court. Nastchokin and the Miloslavskis gave way to a new and remarkable noble named Artaman Matveeff. Nikon had, as I said, disposed the Tsar in favour of progress, of a kind, and Matveeff was for still larger and more comprehensive progress. The industrious and gifted son of a small official, he had become one of the most accomplished and refined of the progressive party. His wife was a Scottish woman of the Hamilton family. Like so many other-foreigners, many of the Scots who were driven from their country by Cromwell found their way to Moscow and settled in trade there. The foreign colony outside the walls grew, and its comparative refinement and culture impressed the imagination of many of the Russians. Matveeff married the refugee, and his home had a western complexion. The Scottish lady would not be confined behind curtains. The furniture was of the more elegant western kind. A library, and even a chemical laboratory, formed part of the establishment.

Matveeff seems to have won the attention of the Tsar in the course of some employment about the court, and he went on to secure his friendship. He was promoted to the office of chief minister, and the Tsar liked to visit him in his stimulating home. We may presume that it was in the foreign quar-

THE ROMANCE OF THE ROMANOFFS

ter, where the neat brick villas, surrounded by flower-gardens and shrubs, were in vivid contrast to the dull and slovenly aspect of the clusters of wooden Russian houses. A new romance of the court was born of this intercourse.

Matveeff adopted a beautiful orphan girl named Natalia Naryshkin, whose father had been a captain of the militia. The Tsar, whose wife had died in 1667, without (as we shall see) leaving a very promising heir to the throne amongst her numerous children, was much struck with the charm of Natalia, as she waited at table. Legend says that he at once offered to "find her a husband." He at all events decided to marry her, and told Matveeff. But the courtier was too prudent to provide a wife for the Tsar in this personal fashion. He persuaded Alexis to issue the customary summons to a competition of health and beauty, and some hundreds were lodged in the palace and gravely inspected. There seems to have been some danger of Natalia losing her fortune, or else the comedy was carried out very thoroughly. Another maiden was selected, and the opponents of Matveeff pressed her charms. But it was decided that her hands were too thin for a model of Russian beauty, and the intrigue was defeated. The Tsar duly discovered the grace and gifts of the pretty brunette Natalia—which he was not supposed to have seen in any re-

THE EARLY ROMANOFFS

spectable Russian house—and in January, 1671, she was raised to the throne.

The young girl had no conception of the opposition which her entrance into the court would cause. Not only were the brother and other relatives of the late Tsarina entrenched in lucrative positions, but several of her children survived, and a grim silent struggle for the succession grew up about the ageing monarch. Every act of the new mistress was invidiously discussed. She declined to be secluded in women's quarters; she refused to have closed curtains to her litter when she went abroad; she despised paint and the tawdry display which Russian women usually made. A Russian envoy who had visited Italy brought news of a magical form of entertainment known as a theatre, in which painted scenes of castles and landscapes were put together and disappeared, and life was remarkably imitated. Natalia and Matveeff set up a theatre, and, although they did not venture beyond biblical plays, the monks and reactionaries and envious made a great outcry. She brought into the world, on May 20th, 1672, a wonderfully vigorous boy—the future Peter the Great—and malicious tongues whispered that such a child was assuredly not the son of Tsar Alexis, whose earlier sons had been feeble. Two daughters followed in the next three years, and the silent struggle became more tragic. Which of the two families—that of the first or the second Tsarina—would secure the succession? The Tsar himself brooded over the difficult problem; and in the midst of his brooding, in 1676, he died, and left the settlement to the court.

Maria Miloslavski had had thirteen children, and of these two sons and six daughters were alive when the Tsar died. The younger son, Ivan, was a weak-witted boy whom none could seriously regard as a future ruler of Russia. The two eldest sons had died. There remained Prince Feodor, and the Miloslavskis had little trouble in securing his accession. A charge of magic and other evil practices was trumped up against Matveeff, and he was flogged and sent to Siberia. Natalia and her three children were still at court, and she made a spirited stand against the grown-up daughters of her predecessor and the three aunts who lived at court with them. Her brother Ivan was banished, and she seemed to be in danger of losing all hope, when a fresh court-revolution modified and complicated the struggle.

The young Tsar, Feodor, was an invalid. Few expected him to live long, and the prospect gave edge to the keen rivalry for power. But a former tutor of Feodor's elder brother now crept into favour and cut out the Miloslavskis. This man and his brother were admirers of Poland, and, in order to prepare the way for Polish influence, they induced the sickly Tsar to wed a young and undis-

THE EARLY ROMANOFFS

tinguished woman of Polish extraction named Agatha Grouchstska. Polish nobles and officers flocked to the court, and an entirely new prospect was opened when, in July, 1681, a child was born. Natalia and her children were now living in a village not far from Moscow. The Miloslavskis had been disposed to make a nun of her, but they were now fighting desperately for their own power. Agatha, to their relief, died in childbirth, and the baby died a few weeks later. The resolute friends of Poland made a last effort. They induced the dying Tsar to wed a relative of his dead wife. But death made an end of the mockery. Feodor died, in his twenty-first year, a few weeks after his marriage, and the intriguing Poles were swept out of court.

Before the Miloslavskis had time to marshal their forces, the friends and relatives of Natalia, the Naryshkin, got together the boyars and persuaded them that the boy Peter was now the only possible heir to the throne. The elder prince, Ivan, son of the first wife of Alexis, was, as I said, an obvious imbecile. Peter, on the other hand, was a sturdy and intelligent boy who promised to become a vigorous man. Before the day was out on which Feodor died Natalia was summoned to Moscow by the news that her son was Tsar, and she herself soon rejoiced in the titles of Tsaritsa and Regent. Her brother was recalled, and a speedy messenger was sent to bring back her friend and patron, Matveeff,

THE ROMANCE OF THE ROMANOFFS

from Siberia. It was on April 27th, 1682, that Feodor died and Natalia returned to power. On May 11th Matveeff arrived from Siberia, and received the respect of the troops. The new regime seemed to be solidly established. And four days later Moscow was shaken by one of the most sanguinary revolutions that we find in its chronicles, and the Miloslavskis returned to power. The story of that revolution introduces us to one of the strangest princesses of the Romanoff house, who was to rule Russia for the next seven years.

CHAPTER VI

A ROMANOFF PRINCESS

THE surviving family of Maria Miloslavski and Tsar Alexis consisted of six sturdy daughters and one purblind, weak-pated boy. On the approved principles of Russian, especially imperial, education, these daughters ought to have been reconciled to the modest position to which the inferiority of their sex condemned them, and, as their brother was plainly incapable of ruling, they ought to have passed into convents or been distributed amongst the households of wealthy courtiers. But there was at least one daughter, Sophia, who had not the least intention of submitting to the priestly theory. If her fifteen-year old brother could make no effort for the throne, she would make it for him. She would fight the hated Anastasia.

Visitors to the court have left us very different impressions of this remarkable princess, but we have little difficulty in removing the thick coat of flattery and obtaining a satisfactory glimpse of her. She was twenty-five years old at the death of Feodor: a short, very stout, and very vigorous young woman, her face covered to some extent with a fine hair which gave her an even more masculine appearance. Probably she had led the usual enclosed life during her father's reign, but in the time of her invalid brother she had had more freedom. She especially made the acquaintance of Vassili Gallitzin, a very clever and accomplished prince, of European culture, who overlooked her entire lack of personal charm and—either then or at a later date—became her lover. In her apartments she formed a literary circle, and through her visitors she got into touch with remote elements of Moscow society.

One of these sections of the population of Moscow which a conspirator would naturally explore was the military force known as the *streltsui*: a privileged corporation of soldiers who handed on the office from father to son and gave themselves airs of importance. We have no direct proof that Sophia got into communication with this body, but the historical facts, and the later action and expressions of Peter the Great, seem to put it beyond question. The streltsui were mutinous at the time of the death of Feodor, because their pay was, as usual, in arrears. They were reduced to silence by the application of the knout, publicly, to the shoulders of their officers, but they remained sullen and inflammable. It is said that the agents of Sophia and her uncle went amongst them distributing money and whispering poisonous libels. The late

A ROMANOFF PRINCESS

Emperor, it was suggested to them, had died of poison.

When Matveeff returned from Siberia they greeted him with apparent respect, and the court settled to its usual prosperous life. Four days later, however, the Kreml awoke to find a grave and ominous movement afoot. Twenty regiments of the streltsui had seized their arms and were irregularly massed in front of the Kreml. The sleeves of their red shirts were rolled up, as if for butchery, and a close observer would have found that they reeked with vodka. Behind them was the rabble of the town. The bells were calling shrilly from the steeples. Drums were beaten, and cannon rumbled toward the palace. The servants of the court learned that some one had spread amongst them a report that Princes Ivan and Peter had been strangled, and a brother of Natalia had seized the crown. Natalia hastened to show the princes at the top of the red staircase, to the crowd, and for a moment it seemed to be baulked. Matveeff and the Patriarch prudently addressed the men, and they were about to disperse.

It is said that Prince Dolgoruki, one of the group of courtiers about the Tsarina, then made offensive and arrogant remarks to the soldiers, and the whole mass of inflammable material took flame. The prince was soon flung from the head of the steps and caught on the spears of the soldiers below.

Matveeff was cut to pieces, and the murderers searched the palace for Natalia's brother. After murdering one or two wrong men, they found him in the chapel and dispatched him. Another brother was torn from Natalia's arms and cut to pieces. Three younger brothers escaped from Moscow. For three days the friends and relatives of the Tsarina were sought and butchered: dragged by the hair through the streets, knouted to death, flung from windows upon the spears, roasted with red-hot spears, cut to pieces, and so on. One does not like to dwell upon the horrors, but there will come presently a page in the life of Peter the Great that requires explanation. Peter, then nine years old, trembled by the side of his mother in the Kreml while her friends and relatives were barbarously slain on every side—by the streltsui. It is said that Sophia at length interceded and arrested the butchery; and that she gave ten roubles each to the streltsui.

A week later the emboldened soldiers came again and demanded that the idiot Ivan should be associated with Peter in the Tsardom. Most of the boyars were opposed to so ridiculous and unprecedented a change, but the Patriarch and other ministers were conveniently at hand, and it was done. In a few more days there was a fresh riot. Ivan, being the elder, must have precedence of Peter; and so it was appointed. Some historians find it not unnatural that after this display of zeal for her brother Sophia should provide a feast for the streltsui, and with her own plump hand pour out their wine. Perhaps it was just as natural that the streltsui should next return with a demand that Sophia be appointed Regent for the young Tsars. The nobles now saw how the wind sat, and they obeyed. A double throne was ordered of the Dutch merchants and, when it came, Sophia had a hole, decently veiled, cut into the back, so that she could listen to the audiences. She occupied the place of the Tsarina and, with the aid of her lover Gallitzin, ruled the Empire. Gallitzin was married, but, at Sophia's suggestion, it is said, he "persuaded" his wife to enter a convent, which left him free to marry again. Apparently the virago would wed him and share the throne with him.

But the streltsui were old-fashioned believers, and were in no mind to see the traditions of Russian decency thus violated. Their murmurs were strengthened by those of other malcontents. Sophia was more punctilious about ritual and doctrine than conduct, and, like Nikon, she laid a heavy hand upon dissenters. One of their leaders at Moscow was executed. The rumble in the city grew louder, and Sophia, affecting at least to believe that the streltsui now threatened her life, fled with her court to the large and fortified monastery at Troitsa, eighteen miles from Moscow. She prudently took with her Ivan and Peter, and she issued a frantic summons to the country to protect her and them. Tens of thousands of boyars and soldiers streamed to Troitsa, and the streltsui became apprehensive. Their leader, Khovanski, and his son were invited to come and confer with Sophia at Troitsa, and they unsuspectingly went. They were arrested on the way and put to death; and the streltsui, cowed by her strength, came, with ropes round their necks, to Troitsa, to ask and obtain forgiveness.

But the discontent was not eased at Moscow, and the policy upon which Sophia and Gallitzin now concentrated their resources fed the murmurs. All Europe was alarmed at the continuous menace of the Turks, and in 1686 Gallitzin led south a large army for the purpose of chastising them and their Tatar allies, and regaining territory for Russia. The costly army, terribly reduced in the southern wilderness, was forced to return without having even sighted the Turks, and the complaints and satire of Moscow were loud. Sophia and Gallitzin endeavoured to cover the disgrace by sending to Siberia an inoffensive general and loading the soldiers with honours. It was, however, necessary to redeem the failure, and in 1689 a second grand army was entrusted to Gallitzin. His nerve may have been shaken when, as he was starting, he found a coffin, placed by unknown hands, on his doorstep; and he can scarcely have been unaware that it was generally believed that during his absence Sophia consoled herself with the attentions of his colleague Shakloviti. He failed once more, and all Sophia's pretence of triumph could not hide his disgrace. She walked in triumphal procession, distributed brandy, and heaped honours upon the "victors."

Men now spoke of her with contempt. It was rumoured that she had a melodramatic plot of marrying Ivan and—since he would have no children—providing his wife with a lover. When this woman bore a son, Peter could be thrust aside as not in the line of succession; and, when Peter was excluded from the situation, the illegitimacy of the child might be discovered, and Sophia and Gallitzin might rule in peace. The plot was so ludicrous that she can scarcely have entertained it, but it served to fan the growing resentment of her rule.

That rule was, however, now threatened by Peter himself. During these years the boy had grown up sturdily, with his mother, in a village a few miles from Moscow. On important occasions he would be driven into Moscow, to sit beside his goggle-eyed half-brother on the golden throne, but he detested the Kreml and loved the free, open-air life of the village. His mother, Natalia, seems to have belied entirely the excellence of her early years and scandalously neglected his education. He learned to read, and he read a great and confusing assortment of books of history and adventure. He learned to write, but the lesson stopped at so rudimentary a stage that he always had great difficulty in spelling. His days were spent amongst grooms, servants, and any boys with whom he pleased to associate. He became a creature of impulse, and in that world in which he grew up the impulses one followed were neither gentle nor decent. The theory that Peter the Great profited by his rude education in contact with nature and real human beings, instead of being reared in the artificial atmosphere of the imperial terem, may point with some pride to his energy, his promptness, his scorn of conventions; but it must embrace also those impulsive outbursts of ferocity and those unchecked debauches which kept his character throughout life little above the level of a savage.

Peter had lately passed his seventeenth birthday when, in 1689, Gallitzin returned from his second failure. The one imperial idea which grew amidst his vices was the thought that he would some day command the military forces of Russia, and his play constantly turned upon soldiering. He formed companies out of his servants and associates. He had a fort built at the village of Preobrajenshote, which he made his chief centre, and a kind of rough, informal court grew up about him. Nobles and boyars joined his military games, his mimic regiments; and they joined also in his nightly revels. He must have heard much disdainful talk

VIEW OF DESTROYED TOWER OF NICHOLAS, ARSENAL, ETC., IN THE KREMLIN, A.D. 1812
From a Contemporary Drawing

about the campaigns of Prince Gallitzin, and no doubt there were ambitious men who urged him to act. The city, he would know, now openly complained. One day a paper was found in one of the squares telling the finder that a valuable paper was hidden behind a picture of the Virgin in a certain church. A crowd sought the miraculous communication, and found a lampoon on the Regent Sophia.

Hence when Sophia would prepare a triumphal return for her lover, and grant honours to the defeated soldiers, Peter refused his imperial consent. When Gallitzin thought it prudent to visit Preobrajenshote, after Sophia had acted on her own account, Peter refused to see him. The two camps began to glower at each other; and men began to pass from the Kreml to the village.

During the night of August 7th, a few weeks after Gallitzin's return, Peter was roused from sleep with the news that his half-sister was gathering troops at the Kreml which were to come and destroy him. It transpired afterwards that there was a troop assembled at the Kreml that night. Sophia declared that the soldiers were to accompany her on a pilgrimage on the morrow, but it seems to be proved that Sophia and her friends discussed the idea of dispatching Peter, and it was, apparently, some of the soldiers themselves who brought the news. Peter was not a youth of courage. He jumped out of bed, got a horse from the stables, and rode hard, in his shirt, for the forest. A few officers and soldiers took his clothes and joined him, and they galloped to the famous monastery at Troitsa. They arrived at six in the morning, and Peter, shuddering with fright, the tears streaming down his blanched cheeks, implored the archimandrite (abbot) to protect him.

During the day Natalia joined her son, bringing the young wife, Eudoxia, whom she had driven him to wed, but whom he had promptly discarded for coarser pleasures. A few regiments of soldiers came, and the monastery-fortress was put into shape for a fight. The majority of the troops had not yet made up their minds which of the royal autocrats they would support, and a period of uncertainty and parleying followed. With Peter there were able nobles like Boris Gallitzin, cousin of Vassili, and they urged him to be bold. He ordered detachments of the various regiments at Moscow to appear before him at Troitsa. Sophia's servants intercepted the orders, and she bade the troops, under penalty of death, to keep to their barracks. But the balance of confidence was on the side of Peter, and as time went on furtive streams of soldiers and nobles passed to Troitsa. A formidable army grew up there.

On the other hand, Moscow was very far from united in favour of Sophia. Her troops melted away. The dissenters, whom she had heavily pun-

A ROMANOFF PRINCESS

ished, gathered boldly about the Kreml and noisily advised her to go into a convent. Vassili Gallitzin wanted to go to Poland, to borrow an army. Whether or no Sophia distrusted her nervous associate, she refused to consent, and Vassili deserted her and retired to his country seat. She sent the Patriarch to Troitsa, and presently learned that the prelate had decided to remain there, a supporter of her detested half-brother. Then she boldly set out for a personal discussion with Peter—she had twice as much courage as he and, at that time, three times as much energy—but troops barred her way and sent her back to Moscow. She threw herself upon the gratitude of the streltsui, and they loudly swore that they would die for her. But in a few days they came to demand that her second favourite, Shakloviti, be surrendered, as a scapegoat, to Troitsa, and, after a frantic and tearful resistance, she was compelled to yield.

She had, for the moment, lost the struggle. Shakloviti was knouted until he confessed that there was a plot against Peter, and he was then beheaded. Vassili Gallitzin, the man of many accomplishments and few capabilities, crawled to the feet of Peter's rude throne and begged forgiveness. He was banished to the frozen north. Other nobles were executed or exiled, and Sophia was at her brother's mercy. She would foresee the hated sentence. Peter permitted her to choose her own convent, and she chose the convent of the Virgin, near Moscow. She may have smiled at his leniency.

But Peter had wanted merely security for his wild life, not the heavy duties and responsibilities of reigning. His simple half-brother Ivan he did not notice, and it is much to his credit—one of the very few things to the credit of his personal character—that as long as the weak-witted man lived Peter left him untouched. It was not the Moscovite way. He let Boris Gallitzin and his mother's relatives squabble for power, as was the custom, and he returned to the almost useless, and partly disgraceful, life he led on the outskirts of Moscow.

Peter was now a well-formed and handsome young giant, more than six feet high, with intelligence enough to know his duty and strength enough to achieve it. To say, as is said, that he was slowly preparing himself for a great task is mendacious flattery. He was enjoying himself, and he cared for naught else. What there is in his later life to entitle this flower of the Romanoff shoot to be called "great" we will consider in the next chapter, but well into his manhood he was merely vicious, impulsive, and selfish. He disliked the pomp and conventions of the court, and avoided them, mainly because he had the taste of a boor, and was happier in squalid rooms where he could spit, and slop brandy, and riot as he willed. His days, especially in the summer, were spent in hard work, because he loved it. He worked at ship-building—there was a large lake at hand—with just the same zest and motive that a boy does, not from any far-sighted vision of a need to cleave a path for Russia to the sea. He drilled and drilled, and gradually formed regiments which would one day be famous, because he had a passion for soldiering and, as I said, a vague imperial idea of one day commanding armies and gaining great victories. And when the work was over, or when the fierce grip of winter arrested all work, he sat down to orgies which few could endure long.

Between the village where he lived and Moscow lay the foreign settlement to which I have occasionally referred, and here Peter got some education. The neat brick villas did not impress his imagination, for he had not even an elementary taste, but he had a mechanical, inquiring mind, and the instruments these foreigners brought into the heart of Russia piqued and stimulated him. Somehow these people beyond the plains could do everything better than the Russians. They could make clocks, watches, astronomical instruments, elaborate tools, superb weapons, magnificent fire-arms. He heard that they could make ships compared with which his boats on the lake were like children's toys. He must get these secrets for Russia. One secret he learned—the making of fireworks—and the whole country reeked and stank with his constant displays.

And they could drink, these English and Scots and Germans of the foreign quarter. Caravans of wine and brandy poured into the quarter, and Peter would come along, black with the smoke of his fireworks or streaming with perspiration from drill or shipbuilding, and sit down to a glorious carouse. His great friend was a Swiss named Lefort, whose capacity for drink was phenomenal. Peter built a small palace, with a huge ballroom, for Lefort, and made it the headquarters of their debauches. It was a general rule that everybody was drunk every night. If a woman refused a pot of brandy Peter would fetch her a clap on the side of the head to which drunkenness was preferable. Decent women kept far away from the two colonies. Peter sober had little self-restraint, but Peter drunk . . .

The shipping idea grew upon him until, in 1693 —he had wasted four years since the retirement of Sophia—he decided to visit Archangel. It is curious to read of such a man asking, like a boy, his mother's permission, and promising not to go upon the water. He, of course, took no notice of his promise when he got there and saw the ocean. A ship he had ordered from Amsterdam was out in the roads and he impulsively started off in a totally unsuitable boat to visit it. He was nearly drowned. When he trod the deck, dressed as a Dutch captain, and saw the great sails belly in the wind above him, he went into transports. He sat for hours drinking hard with the Dutch sailors and listening to stories of their voyages round the world. There was no country like Holland, and he there and then adopted for Russia the Dutch red, white and blue flag, reversing the order of the colours. In January he was summoned back to Moscow with the news that his mother was dying. She died so slowly, and kept him so long from the sea, that he cursed volubly. But he shed copious tears, boy as he was, when she died; and he fled like the wind back to Archangel.

That there was any large profit in this minute study of ships and sailors may be confidently denied. Monarchs and statesmen have built fleets without knowing the difference between port and starboard. Peter was enjoying himself. But in his wild mind there was inevitably growing a recognition of his position and opportunities. He was now more than twenty years old, and intelligent. It was quite time that he recollected that the destiny of Russia was entrusted to him. Of its internal condition he does not seem to have had the glimmer of an idea, but it suited his passion to believe that Russia needed a fleet, and must first have a sea to put the fleet on. The powerful Swedes dominated the Baltic, so he turned south and decided to take Azoff, on the Black Sea, from the Tatars. He may have known that the country was disgusted and scandalised at his idleness, and that Sophia watched eagerly from her convent.

His expedition against Azoff was crudely conceived and a total failure. He saw at least that he and his amateur foreign friends were inadequate, and on his return to Moscow, he sent abroad for skilled men: sailors and shipwrights from Holland and England, soldiers and engineers from Austria and Prussia. Some came, and many of these, when they saw the crowds and the country, returned. All drank copiously. But Peter's mighty energy was roused, and in a remarkably short time he had a sea-going fleet built on the Don, ready to co-operate with his land-attack upon Azoff. He took it, and returned in triumph to Moscow.

The one vague imperial idea in his wild and much-abused brain fed on his success and grew larger. Russia must have a mighty fleet, like Holland and England, and must learn this western art of doing things. He sent fifty officers abroad for education. But he must see these wonderful lands himself—he must know everything himself—and he began the preparations for the famous melodramatic journey which shocked Russia, and scandalised Europe, and undoubtedly brought great profit to him and his country. Boyish in all things, he would go incognito. Russian historians have invented a score of interpretations of every weird action of the hero. He hated pomp and ceremony, it is said; but the truth is that he sulked heavily when he was not recognised. The simple fact is that he had a boyish, impulsive, muddled mind, its great strength and originality marred by a wicked education and by debauch. He would pretend that it was a deputation of Russian envoys, and he made a sort of prince of his friend Lefort, giving him a suite of forty-four gentlemen and servants. He would hide his own figure—he was six feet eight inches in height, and wore disguises that would attract attention at a hundred yards—in the crowd under the modest title of Peter Mikhailoff, a non-commissioned officer of the Preobrajenshote regiment.

The journey was to start in February, after the carnival revels, about which a word may be said later. But a plot against his life was discovered at the last moment, and he delayed to punish it. A former servant of Sophia, named Tsikler, and some of the streltsui were implicated in it. The implication of the Miloslavskis brought on one of those blind rages in which he behaved as one demented. He had the body of Ivan Miloslavski, which had rotted in the grave for twelve years, dug up and brought on a sledge, drawn by twelve hogs, to Preobrajenshote. There it was placed, in an open coffin, under the scaffold on which Tsikler and his chief accomplice were hacked to pieces, so that the blood of the traitors might splash upon what was left of the mouldering remains of Sophia's relative.

Leaving a large army to overawe Moscow, he set out in March, 1697. The journey has been described so often that only a few details concerning his behaviour need be noted here. From Sweden, where his incognito was respected with a cynical correctness which infuriated him, he passed to Germany, where the Elector of Brandenburg was eager to conciliate him. His conduct was rather worse than that of an undergraduate on a holiday, as he did not even know the elements of polite behaviour. The Elector sent his Master of Ceremonies, a grave and learned gentleman, to greet Peter at his lodging, since he refused to be recognised on the ship by the prince sent to receive him. Peter snatched Johann von Besser's powdered wig and flung it away. "Who is this?" he demanded sullenly; and, when the old gentleman's functions were explained to him, he broke out: "Let him bring me a wench, then." Later, when a noble came to announce that the Elector could not call upon him, Peter, drinking heavily and slobbering over his friend Lefort, started angrily to his feet, grasped the noble by the throat, and almost suffocated him. In the street he met a lady of the court and startled her with a gruff

"Halt"; then he curiously examined the watch at her wrist and let her go. One night, when he supped with the Elector, a servant dropped a plate. Peter sprang up, sword in hand, livid with excitement; and he was not pacified until the servant was flogged. They had, in the city, a wheel on which criminals were broken, but they protested, in answer to Peter's wish to see it work, that they were without a criminal. "Let them have one of my men," he said coolly.

His adventures at Koenigsberg would precede him, and he made his way loutishly from court to court until he reached Holland. Every one knows the idyllic picture of Peter the Great serving a long apprenticeship to shipbuilding in the village of Saardam. It is another exploded myth of our childhood. Peter remained there only a week, staying at the village inn (where he seduced the maid), smoking large pipes and drinking large pots with the boatmen. That he used an adze is certain, but there was little romance. His tall, slovenly form, very untidily dressed in Dutch fashion, attracted the stones of the little boys, and he moved on. He appeared in more polite quarters in a brown overcoat with horn buttons, coarse darned socks, and dirty shoes.

Some one suggested that he would see better shipbuilding at London, and he crossed, and bewildered London. He had a fine brown skin and large handsome eyes and thick hair, but, apart from his habitual untidiness of dress, he had a nervous malady which caused a twitching of the limbs and a remarkable habit of grimacing. He constantly took for it a powder made of the flesh and wings of the magpie. At table his habits were atrocious. In fact, he and his servant Menshikoff discovered a little tavern on Tower Hill where he could smoke his pipe and drink peppered brandy as if he were at home. At Deptford, where he lived in Evelyn's house while he studied shipping, he made such filth and damage that Evelyn estimated the repairs at 1,750 dollars. Here, as elsewhere, his morals were notorious. Professor Morfill politely observes in his "History of Russia": "The great monarch was somewhat irregular in these matters, it must be confessed." The phrase would have sent the great monarch into convulsions of horse-laughter. There is grave reason to believe that such irregularities were not his worst vices.

The redeeming feature of his journey was that he learned a vast amount in those few months. Much of his learning was a result of sheer nervous instability and did more harm than good. He studied dentistry—the dentistry of the seventeenth century—and took implements home with him, to the terror of his friends. When his valet one day complained to him that his wife refused to discharge her conjugal duty on the ground of tooth-ache, the

A ROMANOFF PRINCESS

Tsar had the woman brought to him, and he extracted a tooth. He gathered also a box of surgical instruments, and often used them. On one occasion he tapped a poor woman of Moscow, who suffered from dropsy, and caused her death. He pried into everything, rushing from place to place and working with prodigious energy; though it is said that he ended every day of his life intoxicated. What came of it all for the development of Russia we shall see in the next chapter.

The voyage came to an abrupt end at Vienna in the late summer. There had, he heard, been a new revolt of the streltsui. General Shein had put it down, and severely punished the rebels, but Peter decided to return to Moscow. On the day after his return the nobles came respectfully to Preobrajenshote to do homage and share a banquet. Peter, half drunk, called for scissors, and soon the beards of his nobles—the beards which an almost sacred tradition imposed in Russia—were falling upon the floor. Was it a drunken man's joke? Peter did far worse things in liquor. He cut right and left with his sword: he caned an offending servant until he died; he ran his sword through an abbot who offended him; he even one day knocked down and trampled on his intimate friend Lefort. But this was not a jest. The ukase went forth that in future Russians must shave. He was going to westernise Russia.

THE ROMANCE OF THE ROMANOFFS

Some Russian historians, seeking to palliate the horror of what is to follow, apply to it in some measure the idea of reform. The streltsui were in the way of the reform of the army. They were undisciplined, obsolete, incompetent. Their last revolt had given him the right to destroy them, and he would. But there was much more than this. He was convinced that Sophia was at the bottom of the revolt, and he would make a terrible inquiry.

There seems to be little doubt that Sophia had fomented the spirit of revolt and attempted to direct it in her interest. All the Russian world was scandalised at the Tsar's conduct, and she had from her convent watched the spread of the discontent. At last, while Peter was in England, some representatives of the streltsui had come to Moscow to complain of their treatment. After the taking of Azoff Peter had brought his favourite regiments to share his triumph and pleasure at Moscow, and had left the streltsui to rebuild the shattered fortifications in the distant south. With something of their old independence they had sent a few men to Moscow to lay their grievances before the Tsar. There they were astounded and further angered to hear that the Tsar had left Russia months before, and no man knew where he was. There could be no redress for grievances when the Tsar turned his back upon his people and wasted his life amongst the detested foreigners. Sophia's friends and servants pressed the lesson deep. Was it not advisable to think of a new ruler, one who would be considerate to the streltsui?

The men probably saw the great strength of the garrison at Moscow, and they returned to Azoff only with a sullen report of their helplessness. The military authorities then ordered part of the streltsui to the Polish frontier, and this drove the men to fury. They set out on the long march to Moscow, in full mutiny, with the intention, apparently, of exterminating Peter's supporters. But the Tsar had left his best generals, Shein and Patrick Gordon, in command of the troops, and they met the mutineers outside Moscow. After a futile parley the cannon and the cavalry were turned upon the helpless foot-soldiers, hundreds were slain and thousands captured. The revolt was thoroughly suppressed long before Peter reached Vienna.

But the young Tsar was in one of his moods of deliberate ruthlessness. The streltsui had deluged his mother's palace with blood when he was a child; they had commemorated his departure by a plot and had taken advantage of his absence to rebel. These paid servants, these antiquated soldiers, presumed to criticise his plans and fancy themselves as masters of the Russian throne! And behind all their revolts he saw always, barely concealed in the gloom, the figure of his masterful half-sister. He resolved once for all to remove this source of irritation from his Empire.

Immediately after his return fourteen torture-chambers were fitted up in the village of Preobrajenshote, and the captured streltsui were soon suffering all the agonies that Byzantine and Moscovite ingenuity could devise and the fiendish temper of the Tsar could augment. Peter himself hovered round while his victims writhed on human gridirons or had their flesh torn from the bones by the knout. Many of their womenfolk were included in the ghastly torture, which went on night and day for three days. But Peter got no confession of the guilt of his sister, and he decided to act without it. On September 30th a first batch of two hundred of the unhappy rebels, part of them scarred and drawn with torture, were brought up for execution. It is credibly reported that Peter wielded the axe himself and severed five heads. His companions were told to follow his example, and few dared draw back. His infamous servant, Menshikoff, is said to have cut off twenty heads, and the horror of incompetent bungling by amateurs in such matters may be seen in other pages of mediæval history.

In brief, the slaughter extended over several months, and thousands of the streltsui were executed. The ancient corporation was entirely broken and the fragments were included in the new army. In the Red Square at Moscow the heads of the rebels remained on the points of pikes until they rotted into grinning skulls. The wives and children were driven from Moscow. It was decreed that none should give them bread, and they disappeared silently into the plains and forests beyond. How many escaped famine or the wolves no man knows. Russia learned that it had an autocrat: Peter the Great.

And this meant the end of the career of the masculine Sophia. As she shuddered in her convent two hundred of the rebels were brought up and hanged within sight of her windows. Some of them held in their dead hands copies of a petition to her to see their grievances remedied. Then Peter turned upon her. She must lose her rank, have her hair shorn, and pass the rest of her life in strict seclusion as a nun. With the name of "Sister Susanna" the forceful and unscrupulous woman passes out of sight. Although there was no evidence of her guilt, and it is indeed unlikely that she was involved, Peter's wife, Eudokia Lapukhin, was condemned to the same fate. She was at least guilty of refusing to share Peter's tastes, and he had lived little with her. He was free; and from the horrible shambles he turned to the revels of the carnival of 1698 and the more congenial company of the women of his favourite district.

CHAPTER VII

THE GREAT PETER

THE Tsar Peter was near the end of his third decade of life when he broke the power of the streltsui and definitely expelled his sister from the sphere of public life. The fortune and destiny of Russia now lay in his hands, and the heavy discontent of his people, coerced as it was by the appalling punishment of the rebels, invited him to take up the serious duties of kingship. It would be, even if we admitted that the intelligence of a genius was allied with his strange character, too much to expect that such a man would settle down to the study of the constructive problems that confronted him. He was at all times incapable of sustained intellectual concentration, of patiently working out into detailed plans the large ideas which arose in his feverish imagination. Congenital nervous disease might have been corrected by the hard labour in the open air in which he delighted, but the debauch which regularly closed his labour undid its effect. He returned, even after his recent ghastly experience and his tour of Europe, to his disordered ways.

THE GREAT PETER

It will be enough to illustrate the kind of life which he and his companions led by a short account of one of their pastimes. I have said that the expedition to Holland and England, which had in part the object of seeking grave alliances for the Empire in the west, was preceded by the revels of the carnival. These took the form of such pageantry and rioting as one found in most countries of Europe at the time, but there was an incident of the Moscow procession which introduces us to a startling feature of the life of Peter's circle. One of the leading figures of the procession was a drunken old man who was dressed in ludicrous imitation of the Patriarch, the head of the Russian Church, riding on an ox, and accompanied by his spiritual court, an equally drunken and dissolute crowd, on the backs of hogs, bears, and goats. These were Peter's intimate friends, and the entire masquerade was designed by him.

The mock Patriarch was Zotoff, the tutor whom Natalia had given her son in his youth and who had suffered Peter to contract at an early date a love of every kind of dissoluteness. Some time before this year Peter, who led the revels in the foreign quarter and outdid all in boisterous practical jokes, had dubbed the old man—he was now nearly seventy, though he took his wine and brandy with the youngest—"Archbishop of Presburg and Patriarch of the banks of the Iaouza [the neighbouring stream], and the whole of the Kaukaui [a slang name of the wild foreign quarter]." The joke grew upon the heavy taste of the Tsar. He declared himself the Patriarch's "deacon," and his friends were formed into a group of "cardinals," who must hold occasional "conclaves." The ridicule of the Papal Court was doubtless appreciated at Moscow, but even the most thoughtless may have been sobered by the equal burlesque of the head of the Russian Church. Historians again break into a dozen different explanations. Some hold that he was preparing the way for his destruction of the power of the Russian clergy: which is to credit him with a large foresight and deliberateness of action that one finds it impossible to accept. It is more likely that he acted from sheer mockery of religion, adding the Papal details so as partially to disarm or perplex his Russian pietists. We need not suppose that Peter had definite sceptical convictions. There were few definite convictions of any kind in his sodden mind.

Earlier Tsars had humbly walked beside the Patriarch, holding the bridle of his mule, in the great procession on Palm Sunday. Peter substituted for this the procession of his mock Patriarch, an aged toper who must have made a pretty Silenus, and his court. The "cardinals" were, as I said, the hardest drinkers and most dissolute adventurers of Peter's intimate circle. The Frenchman

THE GREAT PETER

(or Genevan) Lefort and the Scot Patrick Gordon were prominent amongst them; and there were other foreigners. They sprang from the lowest ranks of the people or from the highest nobility. Race, religion, or rank counted for nothing in "The Council of the Mad Ones," as the society was (amongst other titles) known. From cunning and policy, and out of his constant itching to test his authority, Peter included also men of high taste and character. When men were forced to take quarts of wine and brandy they were apt to speak their thoughts, and Peter always kept a sober ear.

This was the detail of the carnival-procession of 1697. It was repeated in 1698, at the conclusion of the red horror of the streltsui. A mitre crowned the white locks of the intoxicated Zotoff, who was otherwise dressed as Bacchus, and a crowd of Bacchantes (probably the lady-friends of the cardinals from the foreign quarter) performed the well-known lascivious dance around him. With that freakishness which often gave something akin to the license of insanity to Peter's imagination, he ordered his Bacchantes to bear burning tobacco-leaves. In England he had disposed of the tobacco-monopoly, and he was determined—in spite of the frowns of the clergy—to make his subjects smoke. The "Mad Ones" followed on their fantastic steeds.

It is necessary, if one would pass a comprehensive verdict upon Peter "the great," to tell that this was something far more than a carnival-jest. He maintained the institution all his life, and was ever inventing fresh enormities for it. When a man was, willingly or unwillingly, appointed to the "council," he had to go to the house of the Patriarch, where four stutterers belonging to the large troupe of entertainers in the Tsar's household introduced him. He received his red cardinalitial robes, and went to the "Consistory," or meeting of the cardinals. There they sat on casks before the throne of Zotoff, were served with much wine by men dressed as Roman monks, and went in procession to the "Conclave," which was held in a house prepared as a parody of the Sistine Chapel at Rome during an election of a Pope. They were confined there for three days and nights, and plied constantly with drink by Peter's servants; and Peter himself listened in secret for any hint of treasonable inclination. The kind of language used, and the things done, may be gathered from the extant letters of Peter to his Patriarch. At their normal meetings various women, of whom we will see something presently, were present.

Two incidents will show how Peter sustained to the end of his life the frame of mind which he shows in these things; for it was he who laboriously invented every detail of the riot. In 1714, in the midst of his heavy struggle with Sweden, he de-

THE GREAT PETER

cided that he would marry Zotoff, who was then eighty-four years old, to a lady of noble birth sixty years old. The most elaborate and costly preparations were made for months, and a brilliant pageant was put upon the streets of St. Petersburg. All the nobles, sober or dissolute, had to take part, dressed as savages or bishops, making a hideous discord with every instrument of noise that could be invented. A banquet and mighty drinking bout, prolonged for several days, closed the ceremony.

Zotoff died a few years later, and it was necessary to proceed to the election of an "Archbishop of St. Petersburg in the diocese of drunkards, gluttons, and madmen." The Conclave was held in a mock nunnery, presided over by a lady of noble birth and dissolute habits; and the "cardinals" kissed her breasts as they took the ballot-balls (eggs) from her hands. Later still, within a few years of his death, Peter decided that his new Patriarch must marry Zotoff's widow. After ceremonies which could only partly be described the couple were married, thoroughly intoxicated, and put to bed in a monument in the public square where the populace could enjoy the spectacle in its own indelicate way. In fine, only two years before the Tsar's death, the Patriarch died, and it was necessary to elect another. Peter's idea on this occasion, which was carried out, was to enclose the "cardinals" for twenty-four hours, saturating them all the time with wine and brandy, and then let them choose a spiritual head.

It is not "history" delicately to suppress these things, or merely hint that Peter sought relief from his colossal labours in somewhat boisterous jokes, and then enumerate the deeds by which he earned the title of "the great." These, and his ferocious bursts of rage—his brutal attacks on a man or woman who offended, and his truculent torture and murder of graver offenders—are part of his normal character. He had no feeling of decency or morals; indeed his whole life was a mockery of it. He was wholly devoid of any kind of fine or tender sentiment. Occasionally, with a dull air of generosity, he pardoned an offender; and he set up many philanthropic institutions at Moscow and St. Petersburg. Habitually he was coarse and unrestrained in the last degree. He would in public play with the breasts of noble ladies of the court, and many of his private acts and expressions cannot be described. I am not stressing the fact that Peter was immoral, which is not inconsistent with greatness, even of character. He was, in these and a thousand other things, little, petty, shallow, uncivilised.

It would, however, be not less unjust to dwell upon these matters to the exclusion of those services to his country which have, it is generally understood, made Peter the one great monarch of the Romanoff dynasty. These must be duly consid-

THE GREAT PETER

ered. They fall naturally into two categories: the reforms by which he at least broke some of the ice which locked Russia in its rigid mediævalism, and the wars by which he lessened the power of its hereditary enemies and profitably extended its boundaries.

The habit of writing history from a dynastic point of view is so deep-rooted that many a reputation lingers in our democratic age after the sentiments on which it was originally based have disappeared. This applies in part to Peter's fame as a conqueror. He created an army and a navy, he weakened and thrust back the Swedes, and he regained a large part of southern Russia. These were large and needed services, but—without passing minutely from battlefield to battlefield, which is not the purpose of this study—we must see how far these aims were plainly conceived in a mastermind and with what ability they were achieved.

Peter had spent ten precious years playing at soldiers and making boats in the vicinity of Moscow. The shallowness of the plea that he was seriously preparing for a great task is seen the moment he sets out on his first military adventure. He decided to attack Sweden. Some historians would have us picture the young genius brooding over a map of Russia and considering in which direction he may cut a channel for its commerce (which hardly existed) to the sea and the broad world beyond. That was not his way. His one imperial idea was, as I said, that he would create an army and a navy, and would use them. It was fairly obvious that they must be used against Sweden, but his journey had, in any case, lodged this idea in his mind. It had begun in Sweden, where the King had treated the young boor with the disdain he felt for his person and his power. It ended in Poland, which had succumbed to Sweden and hated it. From Vienna, at the end of his trip, Peter had gone to Rawa and spent a few days with Augustus II of Poland. Augustus was a man after his own heart: a tall, strong man, a great hunter and hard drinker and loose liver. They talked much about Sweden and, with the fervour of intoxicated youth, decided to smite that formidable power.

Sweden was still at the top of the wave which lifted up and cast down one European nation after another, and many powers were jealous of it. Peter and Augustus entered upon a crude diplomatic campaign for the formation of a league against it. The Prussians were too cool and cynical to promise to do more than share the spoils of any victory, but the Danes and Dutch consented. In 1700 Peter secured peace with the Turks in the south and joyously led his grand new army, of 40,000 men, to the siege of Narva. He would, he said, avenge the insults put upon his imperial majesty in Sweden: to which he had gone as a

PETER THE GREAT

THE GREAT PETER

non-commissioned officer of the Preobrajenshote regiment. His artillery made little impression upon the town, and his long carouses left him imperfectly informed on the larger situation. In point of fact the King of Sweden had patched up a peace with Denmark and was hurrying to Narva. On November 17th the Tsar heard that King Charles and his seasoned soldiers were a day's march away from his camp, and—he fled. It is suggested that his officers prevailed upon him not to expose his valuable life to danger. It is claimed that he hurried off to spur on his lagging reinforcements. It is said—by himself—that he did not know of the nearness of the Swedish King. From all which the majority of soldiers and historians conclude that Peter fell into a panic at the first smell of real gunpowder, and fled. His grand new army could do no better, and a Swedish force not one-fourth as large sent the Russians scurrying back to their frontier.

It seems to have been the laughter of Europe which roused the Tsar from the half-hysterical condition into which he fell, and it may be said that from that time forward he became a more vigorous and skilful, and generally courageous, commander. That he ever became a great soldier is emphatically denied by many competent authorities. But he had, we saw, two qualities of value: a colossal nervous energy, and a great promptness

THE ROMANCE OF THE ROMANOFFS

to seek teachers in the more advanced west. He entered upon terrific preparations for a more promising campaign. Brushing aside the clergy, he melted down their bells to make cannon, and he, swinging from place to place with giant strides, spurred his subjects to throw all their energy into the task. That he had a clear and statesmanlike idea of opening "a window upon Europe" may very well be questioned. It is more in accord with his psychology to suppose that his mind did not go much beyond a fierce resolve to beat Sweden. But out of his very need to create an army for this purpose he began to develop his Empire. He needed money, and his merchants must earn more money. He needed metal, and it must be found. He was stung by the opinion of the world that Russia was still barbaric, and he struck fiercely at cherished old traditions. He saw the Church, especially on its monastic side, as a great fat pale fungus sucking the national sap, and he attacked it.

Many of his internal reforms belong to this period. In 1698, we saw, he had fallen, scissors in hand, upon the Russian beard, and desecrated it. A ukase ordered all Russians to shave the chin, and even this change cost a mighty struggle. Ancient texts of Scripture plainly sanctioned the beard: sacred ikons showed that the saints, and even Christ, had always worn beards: and, in fine,

THE GREAT PETER

it was not comfortable to have to face the piercing Russian winds in the winter with a clean-shaven face. Peter fought for years against this symbol of the power of antiquity. Soldiers were put at the doors of churches and instructed to *pull out* the beards of rebels. Heavy fines were imposed.

With this went a reform of the clothing. Long, skirted coats were traditional, and had become sacred; and they were considered warmer in a Russian winter. Peter ordered shorter and more workman-like coats, and patterns were exhibited in the streets to the outraged people. The nobles were, as a rule, not unwilling to dress in western fashion. The poor were allowed a few years in which to wear out their long coats. But it was a long and futile struggle, as pictures of Russian peasants show to-day. Even women were ordered to trail less cloth and, to the boisterous amusement of the crowd, the skirts of the recalcitrant were lifted up in the street by officials and torn or sheared.

The position of woman was a more direct religious concern. The customs which made the Russian woman, especially of the middle and better class, a slave of her menfolk and easy victim of the clergy, had been elaborated and codified by the clergy themselves, though in substance the zealous enclosure of women was, we saw, borrowed alike from Tatars and Greeks. A girl lived in terror behind locked doors, growing fat for the marriage-mart. The way out from her quarters was through the father's room, and, whenever she was suffered to go out, she was heavily veiled. Marriages were arranged by deputies. Even during the ceremony bride and bridegroom were separated by a curtain. The bride went to bed while her new husband was thoroughly intoxicated below—the worse the bargain his relatives had made for him the more carefully he was stupefied with drink—and when he at length reeled into the room, she showed her face for the first time. Usually he did not examine her face closely. If he were sober enough to find that he had a pock-marked, cross-eyed, lean and skinny spouse, he might there and then bully her into a promise to enter a nunnery and leave him free. The marriage was generally consummated before he came to dislike her, but the resource was still open to a resourceful man. The stick was a powerful instrument of persuasion, and it was used generally and brutally. Women drank heavily in their miserable quarters, and remained in the last degree of ignorance and superstition.

Peter's mother, and the example of Sophia, had already raised some defiance of this tradition. Peter himself loathed it and violently assailed it: partly because it was one of the antique practices which made Russia ridiculous and kept it unprogressive, partly because he genuinely wanted the

THE GREAT PETER

women, morals or no morals, to enjoy life as his gay women-friends of the foreign quarter, and later of his court, did. He kicked over the barriers and encouraged women to come out. He ordered a six weeks' interval between betrothal and marriage, and wanted girls to see men before they married them. He gave his daughters a French governess, and urged his nobles to do the same, or send their daughters abroad to be educated. In 1704 he startled and outraged Moscow by having a procession of young ladies on the street, scattering flowers and showing their fresh faces to the world.

Toward the close of his reign (in 1718) he desperately ordered his people to hold periodical receptions, or "drawing-room" entertainments, in their houses from four in the afternoon until ten. It is understood that his recent visit to Paris gave him the idea. Chess and smoking and dancing and drinking—but no cards or dice—were to be provided, and men and women were to mix socially. But social intercourse enforced by the knout is not apt to be genial. They were, as far as the law was obeyed, melancholy entertainments.

To all these reforms the clergy and monks were opposed, and he quickly attacked their power and wealth. In the December of 1699 he flouted the Church-calendar and decreed that henceforward, as in the rest of the civilised world, the year would begin on the First of January. An entire reform of the calendar was beyond even his audacity, and Russia still lingered behind the world. In 1700 he ordered the opening of apothecaries' shops in Moscow, and, although the bulk of the messes sold in such places at the time were not much more efficacious than charms or the prayers of the monks, it was a healthy assault on tradition and the trade of the priests. In the same year he began his direct assault upon the ecclesiastical authorities.

The Patriarch of Moscow died in October, and Peter boldly refused to appoint a successor. It could not be pretended that such an institution was an essential part of the Russian tradition, as the patriarchate of Moscow had been founded only by Boris Godunoff, but the murmurs of the clergy may be imagined. Peter appointed instead a "Superintendent of the Patriarchal Throne," and through this man he got control of the wealth and affairs of the Church. A separate department took control of the monasteries, and the Tsar made a bold attack upon this economic evil. Monasteries and convents were full of men and women who were religious only in name and dress. Frequently they took no vows, and their sole intention was to enjoy the immunities, the well-fed idleness, and the frequent dissoluteness of the religious institutions. As in other lands, centuries of ignorant piety had showered wealth upon an institution which at first had won sympathy by its austerity and now retained it by hypocrisy. Such a condition, when Peter sought for war-purposes every rouble he could get, stirred his wrath, and he had little piety to restrain him. He "regulated" the incomes of the monasteries and convents in such fashion that they became less attractive to economic parasites and sensual hypocrites. As time went on he increased the restrictions of monastic life, and tried to compel the monks to teach or work.

To the dissenters he was, naturally, more lenient than his predecessors, though he took advantage of their nonconformity to secure heavy fines for his treasury; and to foreign heretics he gave complete liberty. Clergy, monks, and dissenters roared their discontent, openly calling him "Antichrist," but Peter was content with an occasional execution or application of the knout to some monk's broad shoulders. In 1721 he at length conceived a plan of Church-government, and created the "Ecclesiastical College," as the supreme clerical authority, which became in time the Holy Synod. His futile efforts to educate Russia out of its morass of superstition and conservatism will be noticed later. For the moment I would recall only how the mighty problems raised by the appalling condition of the country forced themselves upon him in the course of his one clearly conceived design: the destruction of the Swede. When he thus saw an abuse he smote it, angrily and unscientifically. He had not the mood or mind to sit down to the elaboration of a constructive programme. He probably devoted more time, and more cheerfully, to creating the rules and orgies of his "Mad Ones" than to the conception of a system of education.

In 1701 he, after a mighty drinking bout with Augustus, made a fresh treaty with Poland and renewed the war with Sweden. The war went on with varying success until, in 1703, Peter took the marshy region which included the mouth of the river Neva. For some reason—it may have been because it was believed that here Rurik and his brothers had entered Russia—the Tsar fell into the wildest rejoicing, and began almost immediately to form a wooden settlement on the bank of the river. This was the humble foundation of St. Petersburg. It seems to have been at a later date that he conceived the idea of making it the new capital of Russia, and his choice has been very severely criticised. For a metropolis it was too near Sweden, the great hostile power of the time, and not easy of defence. For commercial purposes it was inferior to Riga or Libau, which he afterwards took, and could only with great difficulty and sacrifice be converted at all into a centre of commerce. But Peter loathed Moscow, with its musty air of conservatism and its gilded palaces and churches. He must have a new capital, and a centre of the

THE GREAT PETER

northern region he was gaining. His genius was energy, not insight or foresight. With the labours of—it is said—hundreds of thousands of Swedish prisoners, whose lives were recklessly squandered, he raised the primitive St. Petersburg and embodied in it, as he thought, the new spirit of progress.

He was now creating, with dim large vision of a great future, and his wild Dionysiac nature rejoiced in the labour and in the rewarding feast. In the next year, 1704, he took Narva, after a long and bloody siege; and in his morbid nervous way, with his wretched lack of self-control and chivalrous feeling, he struck the brave Swedish commander across the mouth, for resisting so long, when that general was brought before him, and, with pitiful spite, had the body of the man's wife dug up and thrown into the river. Still he had to fight on for years, with varying fortune. All the time he wrung money out of his country and urged his generally incompetent and despised envoys abroad to get for him money and allies. Poland deserted him and made peace with Sweden; and just at that time trouble arose in the south, among the Cossacks, to divert his attention.

Ivan Mazeppa, the hetman of the Cossacks of Little Russia, or the Ukraine, disliked finding taxes for Peter, and entered into negotiations with the Swedes. The Ukraine was, like most of Russia, full of bitter discontent. There seemed some hope of securing independence. A Cossack chief whose daughter was seduced by Mazeppa fled to Peter and warned him; but Peter's insight failed, as it often did, and he handed the informer to Mazeppa for punishment. Mazeppa continued to correspond with the Swedes and promise co-operation if they invaded Russia. It was the early summer of 1708 before Charles of Sweden entered Russia, and Peter decided to baffle him as Napoleon would be baffled at a later date. The Russians fell back, laying waste the provinces as they retired, and drew the Swedes on to spend a winter in the frozen plains. The details do not concern us. Charles in time found himself threatened with famine. Mazeppa found, when he was at length stung into action, that only two thousand of his Cossacks would follow his adventurous banner; and he packed his gold in two barrels and set out on his hopeless enterprise. And Peter, reaping at last the reward of all his toil, fell upon the Swedes at Poltava and defeated them.

It is true that King Charles was wounded and the Swedish army worn and demoralised; and it is true that Peter, eager to celebrate his victory in the usual way, allowed the Swedes to retire more cheaply than a great commander would have done. But he had redeemed his failures, and had dealt a great blow at Sweden.. Incidentally he had done much to recover, or gain, his personal repute, so badly shaken since he had fled at Narva. In the battle of Poltava he faced the bullets, and got one through his hat and another—rather a disputable one this—on the breast, which broke its force miraculously on his jewelled cross. He was soon back in Moscow arranging a pageant. He posed as Hercules in the procession.

The next few years were spent in feverish dreams of larger armies and imperial expansion, checked periodically by bad diplomacy and poor economics. His generals took Riga for him, however, and overran the Baltic provinces. Then the wily Swede roused on his flank a more terrible enemy than the Cossack. At the beginning of 1711 he heard that the Turks and Tatars were afield, and he hurried south with 45,000 men: also many thousand women and camp-followers, for, when the Tsar would take his Catherine, other officers would have their wives or some equivalent. The result was that the large and unwieldy body soon found itself in a worse situation than that into which the Russians had drawn Charles. An army of Turks and Tatars, four or five times as numerous as the Russians, closed round them on the river Pruth. There was no escape.

From the many accounts of Peter's behaviour on that occasion one seems bound to conclude that he lost his new courage, and fell into a state of maudlin despair. It seems also to be a myth that his

Catherine roused and saved him. His generals fortunately knew the venality of Turkish commanders, and a very heavy bribe—including, apparently, Catherine's jewels—passed to the Grand Vizier's camp. The terms, one would think, were hardly worth so large a bribe. Peter was to evacuate Azoff and all the territory in the south that he had taken from the Turk: he was to give up the Baltic provinces to Sweden, except the district at the mouth of the Neva, for which he passionately pleaded; and he was to pay a very large indemnity. He swaggered back to Moscow and endeavoured to brazen it out.

Again he settled down to stern exertions, to prepare an army and navy and seek allies. In 1717 he went to Paris in search of aid, carefully leaving Catherine behind, though (as we shall see) he had now married her. His conduct was more sober than on the earlier journey, though it was eccentric enough and gave Paris food for talk for many years. When they had at length found Peter a lodging more or less to his taste, he declared that the young king, Louis XV, must come to see him; and, eager as he was to see the sights of Paris, he kept his hotel three days and nights in the hope of forcing the visit. But we need not again enlarge upon his eccentricities. He came away without hope of alliance, and France played with him to the end of his life. Two years later he proposed

THE GREAT PETER

to marry his daughter Elizabeth to Louis XV, having failed to get the grandson of George I. When that project was at last very firmly declined, he asked at least for a prince of the blood, and he was humoured with negotiations until he died. As we shall see, Elizabeth was the illegitimate daughter (legitimised by later marriage) of Peter and a peasant-woman who had been for a time almost common camp-property.

In brief, to make an end of wars, Peter took Finland and beat the Swedes on the Baltic, but he brought the terrible English fleet upon his new vessels. A peace was arranged at Nystadt in 1721, and, for a payment of two million crowns, Peter was suffered to keep his gains on the Baltic. There was a stupendous flow of beer and wine and brandy at St. Petersburg. Peter lit the fireworks with his own hand, and, although the Senate now gravely nominated him "Father of his Country" and "Emperor of all the Russias," he mingled with the crowd, wore a fancy dress, and danced and sang and leaped on to tables like a school-boy.

Peter had, therefore, as a result of twenty years of costly warfare, which embittered his subjects, been permitted to *buy* the fringe of territory which brought his Empire to the shores of the Baltic: the Cossacks of the Don and the Ukraine were, of course, already subject to Russia, and were merely prevented from breaking away. This, and the creation of an army and navy and lowering of the prestige of Sweden, were his accomplishments on that side. His other ventures in the way of expansion were crude and unsuccessful. Several times he made fruitless efforts to reach India and Persia, but was always defeated. In 1721 the governor of Astrakhan sent word that the Turks would forestall his design upon Persia, and in the following May, having peace with Sweden, he led 100,000 men south from Astrakhan. The expedition was poorly organised, and had to return in some disgrace.

In the following year, 1723, he made his last and wildest effort. Two frigates set sail, secretly and hastily, from the port of the capital, and were presently driven back by storms. These two vessels, of poor capacity, had actually been ordered by Peter, in the prime of his age, to take the island of Madagascar, and possibly sail on from there to India! Peter had heard that the Swedes were about to do this, and he had written a letter to "the king of Madagascar," urging him to see that a Russian was better than a Swedish protectorate. Such was the value of the Tsar's famous training in shipbuilding that he insisted that a few useless alterations should be made and the boats should start again, and he fell furiously upon his officers when they pointed out the impossibility.

The internal reforms which he effected were of

THE GREAT PETER

that large, violent, and unsystematic character which one would expect from his nature. I have described some of these, and shown how they were, in great measure, angry and impulsive thrusts at evils which thwarted his plans. Brigandage was still very common, on a large scale, in Russia, and interfered with the industry which was to supply his sinews of war, so Peter attacked it vigorously. Mendicancy had, as everywhere in the Middle Ages, become an opportunity of virtue and a wicked leak of the nation's energy. The lash of Peter's knout fell upon the beggars. Men still killed each other instead of killing Swedes and Turks, and Peter forbade them to carry knives. He fostered and protected home-industries, and sent young men to Holland and Italy to learn trades. He spurred the native production of iron and copper, sent expeditions in search of gold, dug miles of canals, and tried by heavy punishments to break Russian traders of their notorious dishonesty. He pressed reform in agriculture, introduced breeding studs, and slightly alleviated the lot of the serfs, who were now sold like cattle or negroes. He regulated municipal life, dividing the country into administrative areas and created a Senate. Nothing was done thoroughly, and all was done for the purpose of extracting (by a crude fiscal system and thoroughly dishonest officials) more money for the army and navy. Yet these were all valuable innovations, and they entitled Peter, as far as they went, to a name only a little less than "great."

His most beneficent design, and his chief failure, was in the matter of education; general illiteracy was still the rule in Europe. Russia was merely a few degrees worse than other countries in that respect. But social visionaries were appearing here and there, pointing out the connection between ignorance and crime and poverty, and some of them found the ear of Peter. Impulsively, as usual, he declared that he would have universal, compulsory education in Russia. A Ukase of February 28th, 1714, ordered the opening of provincial schools, and Peter rushed to other tasks. Five years later he learned from an official report that one such school had been opened, and it had twenty-six pupils. He returned again and again to the subject, and failed as much from his own lack of patient study as from the general hostility of his subjects. His ideas of schooling were extremely crude, and they stultified themselves in practice. All that we can say is that, as in the case of most of the other reforms, he did bring a few rays of light into the mediæval darkness of Russia, and is for that entitled to grateful recognition.

Had these reforms been associated with a different type of character they might very well, in spite of their grave incompleteness, dispose us to grant the title of "Peter the Great." But if that

THE GREAT PETER

epithet is to measure the stature of the whole man we must strenuously refuse it. The Tsar was energetic, persevering in congenial tasks, even highly endowed in intellect; but his gifts and accomplishments were marred by deep, habitual vices and weaknesses which make it ludicrous to call him a great man. To this aspect we turn again before we consider the closing tragedies of his reign.

I have sufficiently introduced the kind of men who were the intimate friends and coworkers of the Tsar in his youth. Lefort and Gordon both died in 1699, and new favourites arose. Some of these were, like General Sheremetieff, fine and loyal servants of proved worth. Some were, like Romodanovski, nobles of high birth and ability who, in spite of their insufferable haughtiness and despotism, served the Tsar and the State well. But a large number were mere adventurers whom a glib tongue, a large capacity for liquor, or a contemptible obsequiousness commended to the Tsar, and who then plundered the Empire with utter unscrupulousness. Of these Menshikoff was the most prominent, most successful, and most infamous.

Legends grew like mushrooms in the dank soil of Peter's reign, and Menshikoff's origin is, like that of many of his colleagues, very obscure. It seems certain that, either as a boy or a young man, he sold meat-pies on the streets of Moscow; and Peter lets us know that he was an illegitimate child. The wit with which he plied his trade attracted Lefort, who made a valet of him, and then attracted Peter, who appropriated him. Peter gave him a license which many historians interpret in accordance with the morals of the time. He went everywhere with the Tsar and became rich. In 1706, for no public merit, he became a Prince; in 1711 he bought the Duchy of Courland. He was the most corrupt and venal of Peter's corrupt ministers, and was, on various occasions, compelled to disgorge a total sum of two and a half million dollars, yet remained fabulously rich, and as haughty and brutal to his serfs and servants as he was rich. Count Golovin, in later years, found a similar type of man, a boot-black, and pushed him at court as a rival of Menshikoff. He did become Public Prosecutor, but he never dislodged Menshikoff.

After 1700 this man was Peter's chief associate and private minister. The young Tsar, as we saw in the last chapter, built a palace for him in the foreign quarter, and made it the chief scene of his rollicking. Menshikoff had two sisters, Marie and Anne, who, with Daria and Barbara Arsenieff and Anisia Tolstoi, formed the nucleus of the loose young women of the colony. Peter had, at his mother's instance, married Eudoxia Lapukhin, who bore him two children, Alexander (who died young) and Alexis. She was a typical Russian, of a type as different as possible from that of the

THE GREAT PETER

Menshikoff's and Arsenieff's. When his mother, Natalia, died, he scattered Eudoxia's relatives and practically deserted her. He is said to have soaked her brother in spirits of wine and set fire to him. Some historians have a light way of marking these stories "incredible," but very little was incredible in Peter's world. His pious sister-in-law, Prascovia, widow of the Tsar Feodor, one day poured her bottle of brandy over an offending servant, set fire to it, and beat him with her cane on the sore spot.

To finish for the moment with Eudoxia, Peter's first and, apparently, only legitimate wife. In 1698, as we saw, he condemned her to enter a convent, though there was not the least evidence that she was involved in the conspiracy. She struggled hard, but a coach bore her away to Suzdal, where we will resume her strange adventures later.

Lefort had been intimate with a young woman named Anna Mons, the daughter of a German wineseller (or, according to others, jeweller) of the colony. Peter, as in other cases, took over his friend's relict, and set her up, as chief favourite, in a handsome house. In 1703, however, the Saxon envoy was drowned near Moscow, and tender letters from Anna were found in his pocket, it is said. At all events Anna went to prison for ingratitude, but she found the way out and joined the establishment of the Prussian envoy: who, when he presumed to ask of Peter some favour on the ground of his new position, heard her described in terms which may not be translated.

But the list of Peter's amours, curious and interesting as it is, would unduly swell the dimensions of this volume. It is enough to note here that his mistresses, of an hour or a year, were almost all of the most common fleshy type: buxom, sensual, and coarse. One must say seriously, in connection with Peter's character, that it was as much a matter of economy as of taste. And this is the simple key to his association with the woman whom he eventually, legally or illegally, married and made his Tsarina.

The Empress Catherine shall have a chapter to herself, in which we will tell her early story. From orphan-maid in a Lutheran pastor's house at Marienburg she had, in 1702, passed to the Russian camp and been successively promoted until she shared the tent of the General, and then entered the harem of Menshikoff. There Peter had discovered her and annexed her. She was then eighteen and, by all accounts, not a beauty. But she had the large hips and full bosom, the round red lips and cheeks, the rolling sensual eyes, which Peter loved. Candid observers speak of the eyes as insipid and staring, and describe the nose as turned up; but she must have had qualities. Probably she was shrewd, pliant, simple-minded, and rather motherly in his hours of rage and illness. She settled with him in his humble cottage at St. Petersburg and washed his shirts. She bore him two sons, and went with him on his campaigns; and in 1712 he went through the form of marriage with her.

Catherine bore Peter in all eleven children, but the heir to the throne was Prince Alexis, son of his first wife. Eudoxia had had two sons. Alexander had died, and Alexis was, when his mother was enclosed in a convent in 1699, entrusted to the egregious care of Menshikoff for education. One of Menshikoff's first tasks was to teach him to drink brandy, and he acquired a truly Russian capacity for drink. As he matured, he was similarly educated in license of conduct. He was, like his father, nervous and unstable, and he became irritable, moody, and coarse. But there was a singular difference between father and son. Alexis was very pious. Piety, in Russia, was apt to lodge in a special part of the brain, and did not exclude drunken and dissolute habits. Alexis loved Moscow and its churches and rich ritual and legends of the saints. And, naturally, the spreading discontent at Peter's "reforms" and blasphemies found something in the nature of a focus in the court of Alexis. As he grew up, he intensely disliked his father's policy.

Peter roughly summoned him to quit Moscow and prepare, by a military education, for the throne. He quailed and protested that he did not want to be a soldier. Peter sent him to Dresden, and, hearing that his lady-friends were too numerous and notorious, married him to Princess Charlotte of Wolfenbüttel: a gentle, religious, pock-marked young lady, who could not compete with the livelier dames. She died in childbirth, and Alexis continued to drink and riot and admire the religious art of Dresden. Peter again sharply scolded him, and gave him the alternative of becoming either a soldier (and Tsar) or a monk. Alexis whined that he would rather be a monk than a rough and bloody soldier; though he shuddered at the ascetic prospect, and, apparently, intended to escape at his father's death on the ground that he had taken the vows under compulsion. He still dallied.

In 1716, Alexis being now twenty-six years old, the Tsar peremptorily bade him enter the monastery at Tver or join the army. He replied that he was coming to Russia, and he begged to be allowed to bring his latest passion, a young lady named Euphrosyne. After a short delay Peter heard that Alexis and Euphrosyne had fled, and in a terrible rage he sent his agents over Europe in search of his son. They traced him and his lady to an ancient castle in Austria. Alexis had fled to Vienna and hysterically begged the Emperor's protection, and the Emperor had sent him to the obscure castle until he could bring about a reconciliation. When it was known that Russian spies watched the castle, the Emperor ordered the Prince to leave behind all his Russian comrades, who encouraged him in deep drinking, and fly to Naples; and Alexis, taking only one page for whom he passionately pleaded—it was Euphrosyne, in male dress—fled to the south. Naples was then under the Empire.

The Russian agents at the court of Vienna demanded the surrender of Alexis. Dreading the anger of the Tsar, the Emperor sent them on to Naples, and directed his Viceroy that they *must* have an interview with the Prince. The doors were thrown open, and the agents persuaded Alexis, by lying representations, that Peter would forgive him. Their last argument was that Euphrosyne would be taken away from him unless he complied, and the girl—a lusty, thick-lipped peasant-girl, like Catherine, it seems—tearfully begged her royal lover to go. The jade had been bribed by Peter's agents. She was pregnant and was left in Italy, where the price of her treason was quickly spent. Alexis, full of the promise that he had only to ask forgiveness and he could retire to his country-seat and wed his dear Euphrosyne, hurried joyfully to Moscow.

He arrived on the last day of January (1718), and Moscow, ignorant of the arts by which he had been entrapped, beheld him with tragic astonishment. The Tsar was in one of his worst moods. Three days later a court of clerical and lay dignitaries was formed, and father and son met before them. Peter showered invectives on his miserable son, and then, as Alexis flung himself to the ground and asked pardon, promised to forgive him if he would renounce his right to the throne and betray the accomplices of his supposed plot. Every man or woman to whom Alexis had disparaged his father was named, and Peter shuddered with rage. There had been no conspiracy, Alexis said: nothing but vague murmurs. But the torture-chambers soon rang with shrieks, and Russian blood streamed again upon the stones of Moscow.

In his bloodshot fury Peter conceived, or affected, a suspicion that his first wife, Eudoxia, had been in the plot, and a gang of "questioners" went to the convent at Suzdal. Fifty nuns were flogged and questioned, but the innocence of Eudoxia could not be brought under suspicion. Unhappily a curious page of Eudoxia's conventual life, which had ended years before, was brought to light. She had had a lover in the convent. A noble named Gleboff had befriended her, and from friendship they passed to intimacy. Her impassioned love-letters of eight years before were put before the Tsar, and he saw red. Gleboff was horribly tortured and—wrapped in furs, as it was cold, to preserve his vitality and torture a little longer—impaled. It is said, but of this we cannot be sure, that Eudoxia was scourged, naked, by two monks. She was, at all events, confined more strictly from that time.

THE GREAT PETER

Alexis had complied with the conditions, but Peter "the Great" had not done with his son. The vile Euphrosyne was brought to Moscow, and she supplied fresh "evidence." A new court was convoked, and it shrank from the murder that the Tsar plainly contemplated. Alexis was confronted with his faithless lover: he was knouted: and he held to his simple story that he could not be a soldier, and had done no more than criticise. A third court was set up, and it issued sentence of death; and a few days later the Prince's body was exposed to the public gaze, with a story that God had spared the father the blood of his son by visiting Alexis with apoplexy. How the Prince really died no man knows, but few, now or then, would believe the story of natural death. . . . It was June 26th; and on June 29th, we read, a new ship was launched, and Peter joined with his usual robustness in the merrymaking.

In 1719 Catherine's son Peter died, and, on the hereditary principle, the crown should pass to little Peter, son of the dead Alexis and Charlotte of Wolfenbüttel. The Tsar was worried, but took no effective steps to settle the very grave matter of the succession. Catherine, too, was worried, for Peter had a new mistress, a woman of far greater charm than she, and it was well within the sphere of his ingenuity to secure a divorce and wed again. But the romance of Peter Mikhailoff has already,

THE ROMANCE OF THE ROMANOFFS

in spite of condensation, run to such length, and the new romance so largely concerns Catherine, that we may open a new chapter and present that lady properly to the reader before describing the last phase.

CHAPTER VIII

CATHERINE THE LITTLE

THE whims of monarchs have created more romances in the history of women than the fancy of the novelist has ever invented, and the story of Peter's wife and successor is one of the most piquant of these real adventures. Although in the years of her prosperity she did not shrink from the mention of her humble origin, the details of her childhood were never confidently known and are a matter of endless speculation. It is generally believed that she was the daughter of a Livonian peasant, but she makes her first certain appearance as maid-of-all-work in the house of a poor German pastor. Profoundly ignorant, plain of feature, coarse in taste, this woman became in time the sole mistress of the Russian Empire.

At the beginning of the Swedish war, in 1702, General Sheremetieff and the Russian forces besieged Marienburg. The Swedish commander threatened to blow up the fort rather than surrender, and the inhabitants fled to the Russian lines. Amongst them, brandishing his credentials (his

Bible), was the Lutheran pastor of the town, with his wife and children and maid. He was suffered to proceed to Russia, but the maid remained in the camp. She was then seventeen years old, a lusty and vigorous peasant-girl such as soldiers covet. The pastor had eked out his slender income by taking lodgers, and it may or may not be true that Catherine, or Martha, as she is believed to have been named at the time, was too intimate with them, and had been married by the pastor for the protection of her morals. She had no more morals than Peter. In the camp she now gained rapid promotion. At first she washed the shirts and shared the bed and board of a non-commissioned officer; then she had the favour of General Sheremetieff; then the florid taste of Menshikoff was attracted to her, and she was drafted to his household, and harem, at Moscow. There Peter saw and appropriated her.

There is, as I said, little reason to seek some secret of her success. She was of the robust sensual type that Peter preferred. But she must have been at once shrewd and amiable to have kept his affection as long as she did. His letters to her show, besides the link of common coarseness and frank sensuality, a good deal of affection on both sides. Peter took her to the cottage which he built on the banks of the Neva, where her second boy was born. It was a small two-roomed cottage, of rough-hewn trunks of trees, only about fifty feet in frontage and less in depth. In one of the plain rooms, the walls of which were covered with canvas, Peter planned and received visitors. In the other Catherine and he dined, with an occasional intimate friend, and slept. In 1708 he built a larger and rather finer cottage, more neatly furnished, but, as in earlier days, he preferred to let Menshikoff keep a palace in which, with all splendour of gold plate and powdered lackeys and an army of cooks, he could give his banquets. In the cottage with Catherine he ate his large coarse meals, drank his tea and gin and brandy, and smoked great quantities of tobacco. He carried about with him his wooden spoon and bone-handled knife and fork. Catherine darned his woollen socks and washed his shirts—fine clean linen was almost the one luxury he liked—and babies appeared with great regularity. Often when the tramp of his heavy boots told that he was in a mood of fury, when servants and friends fled, for he would hit out with fist or cane or even sword at such times, Catherine took his blood-congested head in her plump hands and ran her fingers through his thick hair; and he gradually sank to sleep on her breast.

She was good to him, he felt, and he must provide for her and the children. But he was now a great monarch, corresponding with all the courts of Europe and visiting many of them. The idea of marrying her must be given long consideration. There were Eudoxia's sons, and there were Catherine's sons. It was a puzzling business, and Peter did not attack a puzzling business when it could wait. In 1706 he seemed to make up his mind. He took the whole company of "the girls"—Catherine, and Anisia Tolstoi, and the two Menshikoffs and two Arsenieffs—to Kieff, summoned Menshikoff, and told him that he must marry Daria Arsenieff and become respectable. Menshikoff was not the man to be restricted by vows of marriage, and he obeyed. But Peter did not, as Catherine expected, follow his friend's example. He was content to make a will in which he assigned her and her four children an imperial legacy of 1,500 dollars!

By 1711 he let it be understood that Catherine was his wife, and he publicly went through the form of marriage with her. Whether there was a valid marriage or no is not clear. Catherine is said to have been married at Marienburg, and Peter's first marriage does not seem to have been annulled by the proper authorities. Russia and Europe would not inquire too closely. Catherine went with him everywhere, except to Paris, and shared his long rides on horseback and his rough camp-life. She never attempted to interfere in affairs of State; but she secretly made large sums of money by get-

CATHERINE THE LITTLE

ting favours or pardon for offenders. She remained very friendly with Menshikoff, who taught her the security of foreign investments.

Peter discovered her trickery, and a cloud came over their relations, but the question of the succession worried him. The new complication was that he was intimate with the charming daughter of Prince Kantemir of Wallachia. The Prince had lost his little principality after Peter's defeat on the Pruth, and had come to St. Petersburg to seek compensation. He knew the relation of the Tsar to his daughter Maria and expected him to divorce Catherine and wed her. It was a very anxious time for all. Alexis died, or was executed, in 1718; Catherine's second son died in 1719; and in 1722 Maria Kantemir, who was then at Astrakhan, expected a child. To the relief of Catherine and her party, and the violent anger of Peter, Maria had a miscarriage and nearly died.

Catherine now got the title of Empress, and in 1724 she was crowned. Still Peter, although his health gave great concern, evaded the problem of the succession, but he allowed Catherine a superb coronation. When she showed him her magnificent robe, which cost 2,000 dollars, he impatiently pushed it aside, but he let her have a crown made which cost nearly a million dollars. And within little over six months she, by her reckless and ungrateful conduct, forfeited whatever right she may have had and barely escaped with her life.

We remember the giddy Anna Mons, Peter's mistress for a time in the foreign settlement at Moscow. Anna's brother William was one of Catherine's chamberlains, and the whole court believed that they were intimate. At length a letter which is said to have proved it fell into Peter's hands. He seems to have felt bitterly the ignominy of publicly discrowning his new Empress, and for a long time he did nothing, beyond torturing a witness or two to extract proof. They thought that he had decided to overlook it, and both Catherine and Mons were at supper with him one night in November. "What time is it?" he suddenly asked, and Catherine replied that it was nine. He grimly took her watch, put it on three hours, and said that, as it was midnight, everybody would go to bed. Mons was arrested and tortured, and, after a few days, beheaded on the ground of corrupt practices. His sister Matrena was knouted and sent to Siberia. Catherine's personal fortune was taken out of her hands for administration, and officials were forbidden in future to take any orders from her.

The iron nerve of the woman in those awful days proves that, in spite of her origin and ways, she had a steady head and strong character. Peter took her for a drive, and passed so close to the scaffold that her dress almost brushed against the body of Mons. She did not flinch. He had the head put into a glass vessel of spirits of wine and placed in her room. She took no notice. When he angrily smashed a costly Venetian glass with his fist, saying that he would so treat her and her relatives, she scolded him for the waste. He still saw Maria Kantemir daily, and he now professed to make a discovery which doubled his fury. He had the Greek doctor who had attended Maria in 1722 "questioned," and Catherine was accused of having procured the miscarriage.

What his precise reasons were for not prosecuting and disowning Catherine we do not know. Some think that he spared her out of affection: some that, as he still sought a French prince for his and her daughter, he shrank from the scandal. His mind was in a maudlin state. Decades of terrific work and constant debauch had brought their inevitable consequence, yet, with periods of enforced sobriety, he still maintained his wild ways. The year 1724 had been one of reckless orgies and much illness, and it was in 1725 that he caused the death of an aged noble by making him sit for hours, naked, on the frozen Neva because he would not join their licentious and childish revels. Peter was still the man who, in 1715, had dissected with his own hands the corpse of his aunt Apraxin to see if she was really a virgin.

THE ROMANCE OF THE ROMANOFFS

In the first month of 1725 he had a superficial reconciliation with Catherine. A few weeks later, however, he caught a fatal chill, and he died within a fortnight. Russia did not mourn. His great and real services were such as only a later age could appreciate. His rugged, vicious, cruel personality was known to all, and the cost of his work had been heavy. One might say that there was in Peter the material of a great man, but the Romanoff dynasty never produced a great man. The material, in this one opportunity, was too deeply vitiated to develop. Peter was an incarnation of the national vices and—except indolence—the weaknesses he ought to have assailed.

The unsubstantiality of most of his work appears in the sequel. Before he was dead there began the traditional squabble for power, the familiar grouping and intriguing of parties. The great majority of the nobles and clergy were in favour of Peter, the young son of Alexis and Charlotte. Catherine was too closely identified with the dying Tsar and all his hated schemes and reforms. But a few great nobles like Prince Menshikoff and Count Tolstoi knew that their fortune was bound up with that of Catherine, and they set to work as soon as the Tsar's illness proved fatal. The troops were discontented, their pay in arrears and their limbs weary from the heavy constructive work to which Peter had put them. Catherine was directed to appeal to them for support and promise ample pay. The higher clergy who held power under Peter's new scheme of Church-government were equally interested in sustaining his work. The palace was full of whispers and secret movements.

The Council met while Peter lay dying, and the spokesmen of the majority confidently proposed his grandson for the throne. Tolstoi attacked them, and proposed Catherine; and after a long and furious debate Catherine was declared Autocrat of all the Russias. They found her weeping at Peter's bedside, and there was a rush to take the oath. Moscow was mutinous for a time, but the army was won by generous treatment, and the country followed. The guards were provided with new uniforms and pay, and it was decreed that in future soldiers must not be employed upon such work as the making of canals. For the mass of the people, too, a great relief was afforded by the reduction, by one third, of the crushing poll-tax which Peter had imposed; and a political amnesty brought back thousands to their homes from the squalid jails or the frozen wastes of the north and of Sibera.

Catherine gladly suffered the power she had obtained to pass into the hands of the nobles who had fought for it. We may, in fact, dismiss her rule, in its personal aspect, with the remark that she did not rule at all. She had the wealth and security which she desired, and her one concern was to retain them through all the quarrels and intrigues of her court, and, if possible, transmit them to one of her daughters. As trouble increased, she retired more and more to the privacy of her luxurious apartments and sought oblivion in intoxication.

A half dozen nobles who had been trained in the school of Peter formed a small aristocratic clique which governed the country and sustained some of the late Tsar's innovations. Of these Menshikoff was, naturally, the most powerful and most prominent, and the haughtiness of the former vender of pies rose so high that it is said to have even inspired him with a hope of attaining the crown. He now acquired wealth without restriction, and promoted rivals to distant employments or punished critics as if he were already the Autocrat. The bribing of the army and the reduction of taxation left the exchequer in a parlous condition. Troops were disbanded, and superfluous officials removed, but the treasury still cried for funds, and the corrupt tax-gatherers were hardly checked.

A good deal of discontent arose, and it found a spokesman in one of the most powerful prelates, the Archbishop of Novgorod. The prelate had supported the election of Catherine, but he had expected her to show her gratitude by reviving the patriarchate and entrusting it to him. Quite possibly some such promise had been made. It was a world of consummate knavery. Theodosius, therefore, when he saw that there was no intention of reviving the patriarchate, discovered, and angrily declared, that it was little less than a scandal to have a woman at the head of the Russian Church. Menshikoff made short work of the hypocritical zealot, whose ways were notorious. It was soon established that Theodosius had appropriated for domestic use the gold and silver vessels of the altar, and had melted down such ornaments as could not be put to profane use. He was disgraced and banished.

A more curious rival of the favourite—a rival even, according to some, in the affection of the dissipated Empress—was Charles Frederick, Duke of Holstein, nephew of Charles XII of Sweden. He was an amiable, mediocre youth who had lost his duchy in the European scramble for fragments of the broken Swedish kingdom, and he had come to the Russian court with a pretension to the Swedish throne itself. Catherine's protection of him gave great offence in England and embarrassed her ministers. George I had no wish to see the question of the old Swedish possessions reopened, and in all the courts of Europe his representatives fought, and defeated, those of Russia. Indeed in the spring of 1706 he sent a fleet to Russia, and the admiral insolently announced that he had come to compel the Russian fleet to keep to its harbours. The English had heard that Catherine was collecting troops for some enterprise in the interest of her favourite. She—or her able minister Ostermann—made a bold reply, and joined the Spanish-Austrian League which confronted England and her allies. Fortunately, the struggle did not reach the strain of war, or the loose and shifty administration of Russia might have suffered.

Charles Frederick remained for the present at the Russian court and was assiduous in attendance upon the Empress. He was made a member of the Privy Council of six which took affairs out of the hands of the listless Catherine, and on May 21st, 1725, he married the Princess Anne. Neither Anne nor Peter had welcomed his offer, but Catherine now urged the match.

The other leading members of the Privy Council, or the oligarchy, were Count Tolstoi and the foreign minister Ostermann. Tolstoi was one of the envoys of Peter who had enticed Alexis from Naples: a polished and supple courtier, an astute diplomatist, and an unscrupulous adventurer, who watched Menshikoff as one sharper watches another. Ostermann was one of the ablest, and certainly the most conscientious of the group; while a fourth of Peter's men, Yaguzhinsky, a man of poor origin who had attracted the late Tsar's esteem by his vivacity and his extraordinary capacity for liquor, was the most bitter and outspoken critic of Menshikoff. Before Peter had been buried many days they quarrelled violently, and Yaguzhinsky, who was drunk, went to the tomb of his late master, during service, and dug with nails and teeth into the lid of the coffin. He was not admitted to the Privy Council, which led to a fresh outburst; and he may have felt some justification when it was known that Menshikoff had invited his fellow-Councillors to a banquet before their first sitting, and all had got so drunk that business was impossible.

Catherine was only forty-two years old, and a woman of robust constitution, but in the second year of her reign her unhealthy habits began to undermine her health and give concern. She, as I said, kept apart, drinking in seclusion. Only Menshikoff and a few others were admitted to the rooms where, her stout and somewhat bloated frame dressed in heavy and tawdry finery, a bunch of orders and little figures of saints dangling on her breast, she sank deeper into the great national failing. She drank great quantities of Tokay. Her legs began to swell. The eternal question of the succession to the throne was reopened, and the violent quarrels and rivalries ran once more to secret intrigues.

There was a growing party in favour of the boy Peter, grandson of the late Tsar. Peter the Great had disliked the son of his rebellious son, and had disdainfully thrust him out of notice. Peter had, in fact, issued a pronouncement in which he claimed that the autocrat had the power to leave his throne to whomsoever he willed. He had, we saw, never carried out this intention and appointed a successor, and the hereditary principle was still strong in the mind of Russia; while the nobles and dignitaries still claimed, in effect, the right to choose between such candidates as the hereditary principle seemed to designate. It was now a question whether the throne should pass to the boy Peter or to one of the young daughters, Anne and Elizabeth, of Catherine and the late Tsar. The Duchess Anne, a tall and stately brunette, but quiet and yielding, was not very popular. The choice seemed to lie between the boy Peter and the Duchess Elizabeth, the younger and sprightlier of Catherine's daughters: a very merry and saucy child with pink cheeks and laughing blue eyes and golden hair, and a forwardness which would very soon lead her into mischief.

Ostermann, who had charge of Peter's education and saw that he and Elizabeth were attached, boldly proposed to marry them (when they came of age—they were yet children) and thus reconcile the factions. But Elizabeth was Peter's aunt, and Menshikoff turned impatiently away from the learned Teutonic arguments by which Ostermann sought to justify his plan. Catherine, of course, wanted the crown to pass to one of her daughters, but the feeling that Peter was the rightful heir grew in strength. Anonymous letters accused Menshikoff and Catherine of usurping power. The majority of the courtiers were looking to Peter. There was at court a powerful body of old-fashioned nobles who had never been reconciled to the innovations, and these were naturally disposed to adopt the son of the pious Alexis, who had died for the sacred traditions of Russia. They might then bring back the late Tsar's first wife, Eudoxia, from her convent and let her religious and conservative influence rule the boy.

Menshikoff at length discovered, and informed Catherine, that the feeling in favour of Peter was irresistible. He had a daughter, Maria, and he had resolved to wed this girl to Peter and thus secure his own position under the new regime. Ostermann, a decent and sober statesman who sought the good of the country, adhered to this plan, and Catherine was compelled by her favourite, and virtual master, to agree to it. Count Tolstoi, however, violently opposed it. He foresaw that Menshikoff would become more powerful than ever, and he dreaded the reappearance of Eudoxia, as he had very strongly supported the late Tsar in persecuting her. The Count led Catherine's daughters to her room and made a stirring appeal for them. The young women fell upon their knees and wept, as only Russians could, imploring their mother's protection against the impending dangers.

But the failing Empress could only murmur that Menshikoff had decided, and she was powerless.

Tolstoi turned to the court and tried to form a party. It had little prestige, though there were always a few in the Russian court who were willing to gamble on the desperate chances of an outsider, and it in turn split on the question which of the sisters ought to be adopted. The struggle became more tense as Catherine's health sank. In April, 1727, she passed into a grave condition, and Menshikoff induced her, though she made a maudlin demonstration in favour of Elizabeth, to sign a will bequeathing the crown to Peter. This did not put an end to intrigue, as it was a question whether the nobles would recognise this right of legacy which had been arbitrarily created by Peter.

Toward the end of April it was thought that the Empress was dying, and Menshikoff, with her will in his possession, carefully guarded her from alien influences. At length her hour, apparently, came, and the whole court was permitted to assemble about her chamber. Through the open door the glazed eye of the former maid and washerwoman fell upon the brilliant throng who waited, with intense strain, the opening of another chapter in the history of the Romanoffs. The Duke of Holstein saw the last chance of his wife's succession ebbing away, and he nervously implored Count Tolstoi to make his way to the dying woman's side and plead for Anne. Tolstoi shook his head. Menshikoff watched the play with rapid pulse, counting the moments before the danger was over. And suddenly his opponents were delivered into his hands. One of Tolstoi's party, Count Devier, was intoxicated, and he began to behave in a way that certainly desecrated the chamber of death. Quick as thought Menshikoff had the rooms cleared and Devier arrested. The ever-ready torture-chamber was opened, and, under the lash of the knout, Devier betrayed Tolstoi and his associates. Tolstoi and his son went to Siberia, and Devier to the shores of the Arctic. And on the same day, May 16th, 1727, Catherine laid down her sceptre and passed away.

Her will—or the document which Menshikoff had composed and she was supposed to have signed—was read to the dignitaries and notabilities. The son of Alexis and Charlotte was named Peter II, and there was little disinclination to take the oath to a grandson of the great monarch. Few, in the agitation of the hour, saw the possibility of a reaction from a son of Alexis, and the few who perceived that possibility thought that they had provided against it. The Privy Council, headed by Menshikoff, was entrusted with the Regency; and Menshikoff would see that his relation to the boy-Emperor would soon become more intimate. In the event of the boy's death the crown must pass to Anne: in case of her death to Elizabeth. Never before had there been so clearly conceived and far-seeing a plan of succession; yet within the next three years there were to be two revolutions, with the usual terrible consequences, at that court of greed and passion.

CHAPTER IX

ROMANCE UPON ROMANCE

PETER II was a fine, handsome lad of eleven summers, the fruit of the unhappy union of the miserable Alexis and hardly less miserable Charlotte of Wolfenbüttel. From such a stock Peter the Great had expected no good. He disliked to think of the boy, and, careful as he generally was about education, he allowed the child to pass to the hands of ignorant and incompetent trainers. Catherine, or Menshikoff, who may have early conceived his plan of the future, altered this state of things at the death of Peter the Great. The conscientious German minister Ostermann was charged with the education of the young prince, and we perceive by his scheme of lessons, which survives, that he was prepared even for the duties of a monarch.

Unhappily, the best scheme of education depends for its result upon the co-operation of the pupil, and Peter was a bad pupil. He liked Ostermann, but he disliked lessons; and the consciousness that he was now a monarch did not dispose his lively imagination to submit to prosy toil. There was a strain of nervous instability in nearly the whole of the Romanoffs at this stage. Peter liked sport and riding and play. His sister Natalia, two years older than he, was a good playmate; even better was Aunt Elizabeth, the younger daughter of the late Empress. Elizabeth was now a very sprightly and pretty young lady of sixteen, the exact opposite of what a Russian princess ought to be on the old standards. She shunned books, but took like a boy to riding and hunting and fencing. Her lively tongue and merry blue eyes attracted young officers; and she was the daughter of Catherine and Peter in such matters.

Menshikoff did not like the intimacy and he carried Peter off to one of his palaces and put trusted servants and the sober Ostermann about him. He also introduced the young Tsar to the charm of his own domestic circle, and he presently announced to the Privy Council that Peter had honoured him by asking the hand of his daughter Maria. The ceremony of betrothal was, in fact, publicly celebrated. Inconvenient or critical people were humanely removed by appointments abroad. Even the Duke of Holstein was induced to return to his native land and take his Duchess with him; and they were treated very generously in the matter of provision. Honours and offices were distributed with such generosity as was consistent with the supreme power and increasing wealth of the for-

ROMANCE UPON ROMANCE

mer premier. Members of old noble families, like the Dolgorukis and Golitzuins, were promoted.

With the aid of Ostermann for foreign affairs Menshikoff ruled the country advantageously. There was, fortunately, no stress at home or abroad, for he had no ability as a statesman, but he passed a number of measures which promoted trade or tranquillity. The Cossacks were more than pacified by the concessions he made to them. Eudoxia was liberated from the rigorous and dismal confinement to which Peter the Great had condemned her; which greatly pleased the orthodox. The tariff was lowered. The ghastly poles and spikes on which it had been customary to fix the heads or limbs of criminals were abolished.

But in the world which the Romanoffs had created, or suffered to develop, the supreme concern was the fortune of the individual. I do not mean, of course, that this selfishness was unknown at the court of Louis XV or of George I, but the sequel will show how far Russia lagged behind even the primitive morality of those elegant courts. There were few who did not look with green eyes upon the princely fortune of the adventurer, and there were some who felt it an outrage upon the nobility. Russia was prosperous; but could a land prosper indefinitely when the national genius was mocked by foreign innovations and the sacred traditions of Moscow were scouted? The nobles gave an idealist complexion to their discontent, and whispers reached the ear of the growing prince.

Menshikoff was imprudent in meeting Peter's first movements of resentment. One day the young Tsar received what appears to have been a personal payment of nine thousand ducats, and he sent it to his sister Natalia. Menshikoff met the messenger and took away the money. Peter, he said, did not yet understand the value of money. Peter sent for him and gave him, to his amazement, an imperial scolding. He might have recognised a bit of his old master in the stamping and raging boy, but he did not take the lesson. Soon afterwards Peter sent to Natalia a fine service of plate which had been presented to him, and Menshikoff tried to make her restore it. The First Minister was then compelled to take to his bed for some weeks. When he recovered, he found that Peter had gone to the palace at Peterhof, some miles away, and was wildly enjoying himself with Natalia and Aunt Elizabeth. Ostermann and the Dolgorukis also were there. Menshikoff, as an offset, demanded the accounts of the palace, and discharged a servant for some item he found; and the boy-Tsar, in a fiery interview, told him to mind his own business.

This was in August. Menshikoff, now seriously concerned, thought that the influence of Ostermann was mischievous, and he got up a violent quarrel

ROOM OF THE TSAR MIKHAILOVITCH, MOSCOW

ROMANCE UPON ROMANCE

with him and threatened to send him to Siberia. From a loyal colleague Ostermann became one more enemy of the First Minister, and the story of his fall ran rapidly. On September 6th Menshikoff went out to Peterhof to pay respectful homage to the Tsar. Peter not only turned his back upon him, but drew the attention of his smiling courtiers to the fact that he did. The minister prepared a festival, and, when the Tsar scouted his invitation, he nervously begged an interview. The answer was a troop of soldiers such as he himself had sent to darken many a home, and he fell to the ground in a swoon.

A few days later the fallen man appeared before the Privy Council and received sentence. He was fined, for conspiracy against the throne, 375,000 dollars, stripped of all his honours and offices, and ordered to retire to the dreary waste of the steppes. But his wife Daria—we remember Peter the Great forcing him to marry that merry lady—appealed passionately against the brutal sentence, and he was suffered to retire, instead, to a beautiful estate he had in the Ukraine. Few wept when, one morning in September, a long caravan bore Menshikoff and his wife and daughter out of the life of Russia. But his enemies were not satisfied. The Dolgorukis, who came to power, trumped up a charge of conspiracy in the following year, and, on the miserable word of tortured witnesses, which

THE ROMANCE OF THE ROMANOFFS

in Russia was still admitted, banished the brokenhearted adventurer to the frozen shores of the Arctic. There for two years, until death set him free and ended one of the great romances of that stirring period, Menshikoff supported by the labour of his own hands his devoted wife and the unlucky girl who had thought to become an Empress.

Ostermann remained the most important and most useful statesman, but the Golitzuins, Dolgorukis, and other families of the old nobility now came to power and they made an effort to drag Russia back to the ruts from which Peter the Great had violently shifted it. They were of what came to be called in the nineteenth century the "Russophile school": narrow-minded conservatives who railed at all innovation and foreign influence, and persuaded themselves that the genius of Russia was different from that of other European nations. St. Petersburg was to them the hated symbol of the new order, and they induced Peter to return to Moscow. He was crowned there on February 25th (1728) with all the archaic ceremonies of Russian tradition, and they took care to impress him with the contrast between the comparatively bright and healthy air of Moscow and the dank climate of the northern metropolis. This court remained at Moscow, and the departments of State were presently transferred to it.

ROMANCE UPON ROMANCE

To complete the transformation from the ideals of Peter the Great to those of Alexis the aged Eudoxia was appointed Regent, and a court of the old type gathered about her. Ostermann was alarmed, and the reactionaries tried to remove him. Peter, fortunately for Russia, would not hear of the dismissal of his old director, but he allowed the conservative nobles to act much as they pleased and he was encouraged by them to spend his time in hunting and laborious idleness. The fleet was suffered to rot in harbour, and only the steady effect of such internal reforms as Peter the Great had introduced kept the country in some degree of prosperity. The old indolence returned. Since there were now no costly schemes to be realised, and the favourable turn of foreign relations brought no war, the taxes were not enforced, and the country enjoyed a fallacious happiness.

In December Natalia died of consumption. Through her Ostermann had at times got a warning word to the ear of his pupil, and the levity of the Tsar now increased. He spent his days with Elizabeth, and the Dolgorukis feared that what Ostermann had once recommended—the marriage of the aunt and nephew—would come to pass. As it was their aim, in spite of all the warnings of Russian history, to marry him to a girl of their own family, Elizabeth must go; and the frivolity of that precocious lady gave them ample opportunities.

THE ROMANCE OF THE ROMANOFFS

She was scarcely out of her teens, yet her amours were notorious, and her lovers were not of noble rank. A word was whispered to Peter, who was a sober and strict-living youth, and Aunt Elizabeth ceased to be his constant companion.

Austria, Russia's ally, looked with concern upon this reaction and indolence, and its representatives joined with Ostermann in pressing Peter to return to St. Petersburg and attend to his military resources. A tense, if more or less veiled, struggle for the guidance of the Tsar set in. For the moment the ambitious Dolgorukis won. They carried Peter a hundred miles away for a grand and prolonged hunt and series of entertainments. The entire family surrounded him and kept him for weeks in a state of febrile exhilaration. When they returned to Moscow, Alexis Dolgoruki announced that the Tsar was to wed his daughter Catherine, and the ceremony of betrothal was pompously conducted. The Dolgorukis now closed round the youthful Tsar, kept their angry rivals away, and began a premature plunder of the court and treasury as confidently as if such things had never before left their awful monuments in Russian history.

The wedding was fixed for January 30th, 1730. Peter would then be only fourteen years old, but the Dolgorukis were anxious. Already the Tsar was peevish and moody, and he gave at times

ROMANCE UPON ROMANCE

alarmingly sharp replies. One day as the favoured family gathered round him and amused him with a game of forfeits, it fell to him, as a forfeit, to kiss his betrothed. To their consternation he walked out of the room. About the middle of the month a worse cloud than ever came over their hour of sunshine. Peter fell ill and—it was whispered among the pale-faced family—the malady was the dreaded small-pox. Frantic conferences were held, and some of the family, in their sordid greed and selfishness, actually proposed to wed the semi-conscious boy and put the girl abed with him. But Ostermann guarded the chamber, and on January 30th, the day appointed for the wedding, Peter II ended his brief reign.

The succession to the throne was now so open that Moscow teemed with melodramatic conspiracies. The young bloods of the Dolgoruki party are said to have forged a will in which Peter left the crown to his betrothed, but the older men ridiculed the proposal, and the document does not seem to have been produced. On the other hand, the physician of the Tsarevna Elizabeth, a born conspirator, roused that young lady from her sleep and urged her to seize the throne. Elizabeth fluttered over the romantic proposal, then turned over in bed and deferred it to the morrow. On the morrow it was too late, for the Privy Council had held an all-night sitting and come to a singular decision.

Prince Demetrius Golitzuin, one of the older nobles who had never enjoyed what he regarded as his full share of wealth and power, felt that it was his turn to make a monarch and enjoy the reward. He decked his plan with a plausible air of reform. This recent concentration of power in the hands of an autocrat was the root of all evil, since one monarch usually meant one favourite. Let them choose a ruler who would promise in advance—promise on paper—to resign the power to the Privy Council. He drew up a scheme in which the future sovereign pledged himself or herself to take no important action—to declare war, or levy taxes, or punish a noble, or marry, and so on—without their consent. What candidate would be likely to sign and respect such a promise? Elizabeth could not be relied upon; in fact, Golitzuin, a proud and arrogant noble of the old school, detested Peter the Great and regarded his marriage as void and his daughters as illegitimate. But Peter's elder brother, the weak-minded Ivan V, had left three daughters, and the second of these, Anne, Duchess of Courland, would, it was thought, agree to almost any conditions if she were offered the crown.

Anne, who was then thirty-seven years old, had had a dull and vexatious life. Peter had made her and her mother, Prascovia, move to St. Petersburg, and he had compelled Anne, in her eighteenth year, to marry the Duke of Courland, for political reasons. The Duke, however, had found Russian hospitality so overpowering that he had died on the way home, and the young princess, childless and isolated, had been compelled to continue the journey and settle at Mitau, the capital of the Duchy. To control her purse and administer her affairs Peter had sent Count Besthuzeff, and he laughed heartily when he heard that Anne had made a lover of him. Presently there came along the familiar type of handsome and unscrupulous adventurer. The grandson of a groom of an earlier Duke, named Biren, had a sister in a modest office at court. She was, however, also a mistress of the Count, and she got a place for her brother. Biren was clever and ambitious, and it was not long before he supplanted Besthuzeff in the affection of the Duchess and got him dismissed. Biren married after a time, and it is claimed that Anne's very intimate relations to him after his marriage were purely Platonic. In any case he remained master of her court, and he would no doubt be consulted on the strange new problem that confronted her. She had costly tastes and little money, and glittering Moscow suddenly and unexpectedly rose on her horizon.

The Privy Councillors had decided that Anne was the most likely of the surviving Romanoffs—

Peter was the last male of the family—to accept the crown at a reduced price. They had sent a deputation to Mitau, and a courier presently came back with the news that she had signed the conditions. Yaguzhinsky, the drunken and turbulent general who had often given trouble, had tried a little intrigue of his own. He had sent a disguised messenger to Mitau to warn Anne, but his messenger had been caught by Golitzuin's watchful servants on the return journey. A general meeting of the great officials and nobles was called, and the Privy Councillors announced to them that Anne had accepted, and resigned all power to the Council. It is quaint to read, in letters of the time, that the once democratic Russians now trembled with anger at this surrender of the sacred autocracy. The announcement was received in ominous silence. Golitzuin turned fiercely upon Yaguzhinsky and forced him to avow his plot; and the general and his associates were arrested and disgraced. The malcontents were cowed, and Anne came to Moscow.

There can be very little doubt that Anne, who was intelligent, perfectly understood the situation and was ready, on any pretext, to disavow her oath. Although Golitzuin set a close guard of servants and soldiers about her, she soon learned that there was a powerful party in opposition to the Privy Council, and she entered into correspondence with it. Count Biren's baby was her godchild, and she insisted that it be brought to her chamber every morning to be fondled. A baby and nurse could do little harm, the sentries thought; but there were notes from the conspirators pinned underneath the baby's bib. Letters were smuggled in presents to the sovereign. Another of the older nobles, Prince Tcherkasky, was aiming at power, on the approved lines of Russian tradition (the invariable ghastly ends of which no one seemed to study), and was organising the conspiracy.

On the morning of May 8th, ten weeks after Anne's arrival, about eight hundred of the nobles and gentry assembled in the courtyard of the Kreml, and, with a select body of officers of the guard, trooped to Anne's apartments and asked a hearing. The comedy was gravely enacted. Anne, surrounded by her court, graciously received the petitioners, and heard with astonishment that there was dissatisfaction at her surrender of the autocracy. The Privy Councillors were summoned, and Tcherkasky and Dolgoruki fought for the lead. Anne hesitated, but her elder sister, the Duchess of Mecklenburg, turned the scale against the Privy Council. She would reconsider her act. In the afternoon the parties returned, and Anne turned severely upon the Councillors. "Were not those articles you submitted to me framed with the consent of my subjects?" she asked. It was boisterously affirmed by the crowd that they were not. "Then you lied," she said to the great nobles; and the autocracy was restored, and the roll of drums and roar of guns and clangour of bells announced with what joy Moscow took the yoke on its shoulders once more.

For a time it seemed as if the new ruler was too humane to exact the usual penalties. The Privy Council was abolished, but the Senate was reorganised and the Golitzuins and Dolgorukis were, to their surprise, included in the new body. Their wives were welcomed at court, their relatives promoted. But either Anne awaited the advice of Biren, who had remained at Mitau for a time, or she prudently ascertained her strength. In April a flash of the brutal Romanoff temper lit Moscow once more. Alexis Dolgoruki and his family were arrested and convicted of causing the death of the late Tsar. The aged father went to Siberia, the younger men were knouted and exiled, and the young Catherine, the betrothed of Peter II, was, with a refinement of cruelty, sent to the very spot in the frozen north where Menshikoff's daughter, the earlier aspirant to the crown, had lamented her bitter disappointment. The great proud family was shattered to atoms.

And the power that their fellow-nobles had snatched from them now passed mainly to foreigners. Biren established himself in the palace, close

ROMANCE UPON ROMANCE

to Anne's apartments, and became the real autocrat. Anne was too intelligent to part with the old and experienced ministers. Indeed an inner cabinet, consisting of Ostermann, Tcherkasky, and Golovkin, was formed, and the affairs of the State were conscientiously administered. But the bulk of the lucrative offices fell to Germans and Courlanders. Russians grumbled, and were snubbed. The fiery Yaguzhinsky was dissatisfied with his promotion and, in his cups, he spoke freely about the foreigners. One day, at table, he insulted and drew his sword upon Biren. He was appointed minister at Berlin. Other nobles were punished for criticising, and Count Biren settled down to his reign.

The external fortune of the country may be briefly sketched. In the eternal rise and fall of nations Poland had now sunk to almost its lowest depth; Sweden was sinking; France was at its zenith, and was in deadly antagonism to Austria; Prussia was watching and preparing astutely, and snatching every advantage it could from the quarrels of its neighbours. The obvious policy of Russia was to remain on good terms with the nearer of the great Powers, Austria, and it was just as obviously the policy of France to detach Russia and weaken Austria. The diplomatic battle rose to a furious pitch over the succession to the throne of Poland, which Augustus II would soon quit.

He naturally wished to leave the crown to his son, and the French king wished to secure it for his Polish father-in-law, Lesczynski. Both sides offered bribes to Biren, and he looked lovingly at the magnificent French offer of half a million ducats and the Duchy of Courland, but so violent and dangerous a change of Russian policy was not to be contemplated.

Augustus died, and the Poles were induced to accept Lesczynski. Poland was now "the sick man of Europe," as every aspirant to its throne was ready to barter away some portion of its territory to the greedy Powers. But Russia would not endure the French candidate, and in the summer of 1733 a Russian army invaded and subdued the Poles. The French retorted, in the manner of the time, by spurring the Swedes and the Turks to draw off the Russians, and a long war (1736-1739) with Turkey followed. Azoff was retaken, and the Russian generals had a hope of annexing the northern coast of the Black Sea. Anne, however, watched the progress of the long and costly operations with feminine emotion, and the withdrawal of Austria from the war gave her and her Council an opportunity to end it. It had cost the lives of a hundred thousand men and had strained the Russian treasury; and all that the grumbling country gained was the city of Azoff and a small area of the surrounding region. It should be added, however, that, cumbrous as the Russian army was, its prestige rose in the mind of Europe. Its German commanders and engineers counted for something.

To the people at large, when the last fireworks had been discharged, the burden of the war was a new grievance. Anne was not without shrewdness. She contrived to wring from the impoverished people even the arrears of taxes, which the frivolity of the late administration had allowed to accumulate, without ever confronting a serious threat to her rule. But her careful and generally intelligent government was guilty of one extravagance which further angered the people. She loved pomp and display, and she gradually impressed upon her court and aristocracy a standard of living, especially of dressing, which threatened many with ruin.

The court returned in 1732 to St. Petersburg, and Biren and she attempted to give it the elegance and splendour of the first courts of Europe. Neither had at first much refinement of taste, and foreign visitors described with amused disdain the veneer of display on the lingering barbarism of Russia. New uniforms of the most gaudy character were supplied to the guard and the servants of the court. The nobles were compelled to spend what seemed to Russians colossal sums in bringing themselves up to the new standard, and a bewigged and bepowdered crowd, in dazzling blue or green or pink silks and satins, replaced the sober-clad boyars of earlier years. Banquets and balls followed each other in rapid succession, and new dresses must adorn each occasion; while it is said that the demand for the services of the elaborate hair-dressers was such that ladies had at times to have their hair dressed two or three days in advance and carefully preserve the structure until the evening of the ball.

In her later years Anne, perhaps taught by the pungent criticisms of foreign guests, developed a sober taste. She was a very tall woman, of large and not ungraceful build, with grave dark blue eyes and black hair. In her later years she exchanged her bright blues and greens for gold brocade or brown silk, her diamonds for pearls; and her officers had black and yellow liveries, embroidered with silver braid. She did much to raise the taste of Russia. Although champagne was now introduced into Russia, she frowned upon the ancient daily habit of intoxication. Only on one day of the year —the anniversary of her coronation—did she tolerate heavy drinking. She introduced also a certain lightness and elegance into open-air feasts, which had in Peter's day been orgies of drink and roughness, and she insisted on better manners at table. It was not long since, at a Russian dinner, one plate had had to serve a guest through the long and varied series of courses—the punctilious man wiped his plate with his finger or napkin, or poured the gravy on to the floor—and a servant had torn scraps of linen or calico off a roll for the use of those who desired napkins. Into the state of such rooms when the doors were locked for many hours, as they often were, the polite modern must not inquire too closely. A good deal of this grossness lingered in Russia, and Anne set her face against it.

She—the earlier lover of Besthuzeff and Biren—was not less warmly opposed to laxity of morals. Moderate gambling she herself introduced and encouraged, but the young folk whom she liked to have about her had to be careful. When Elizabeth did not reform her free ways, after a few lovers had been sent to Siberia, she was threatened with a convent. Anne's favourite was a niece, Princess Anne of Mecklenburg, an insipid, good-natured girl whom she was preparing for the throne. The Saxon envoy, Count Lynar, was discovered in too close a relation to this young lady, and was sent back to Saxony; whence we shall find him return as soon as the Tsarina is dead and his lover is on the throne.

In other respects the character of Anne was at the lowest Romanoff level. She not only delighted in the dwarfs and buffoons, and the rough knockabout comedies, which had always been popular at the court, but she found pleasure in refinements of cruelty which Peter would have thought unchivalrous. She would rock with laughter when her dwarfs got to bloody noses in their cock-fights, and she sank to the depth of compelling noble men and women who incurred her anger to enter these vulgar troops and provide the most puerile amusement. A noble of merit was condemned to this disgraceful service because Anne hated his wife; another because he joined the Roman Church. But the most curious and brutal of all her whims was her treatment of a noble of the great Golitzuin family.

The man had travelled in Italy and married a Roman Catholic. He was forty years old and of high birth, yet he was compelled to enter the company of Anne's pages and buffoons. When his wife at length died, Anne said that she would choose a second for him, and she selected a coarse and ugly Kalmuck woman from the uncivilised fringe of her Empire. The wedding must be not merely public, but of a nature to attract the attention of the whole of Russia to his disgrace, and specimens of all the backward peoples of the Empire were summoned to it. A long procession of Finns, Lapps, Samoyedes, etc., riding in carts drawn by pigs or reindeer or other unusual animals, preceded the miserable groom and his bride, who rode on an elephant, to the church. All St. Petersburg turned out to see it. In the evening a large banquet was served to the guests, and the wedded pair then went to the house which had been made for them. It was the month of February, and a house had been cut out of solid ice. Cannons of ice exploded at the door, all the furniture was of ice, and the unfortunate noble and his hideous companion were enclosed for the night in a room, and upon a bed, of naked ice. This was in the very year of the Empress's death.

Anne was scarcely less to blame for the conduct of her favourite. While Russia groaned under her taxes, his wealth grew to a colossal fortune. His wife's diamonds alone were valued at three million rubles. His stables, his plate, his palaces, were amongst the most superb in Europe. This wealth was notoriously amassed by corruption and protected by a system of spies and bullies. In his Duchy of Courland, which he obtained in 1737 by bribing the electors, his name spelt terror to the poor folk from whom he had sprung. In Russia itself he ruled by the knout and the executioner. In 1739 he felt that the Dolgorukis were not quite beyond the power of making mischief, if the Empress died, and he dragged them from their exiles and had a fresh trial. One was broken on the wheel, two were beheaded, and others were imprisoned for life. In the following year he was insulted in the Council by a certain Voluinsky, whom he had adopted, but who had turned against him. The man must be broken or he would himself leave the country, he told the Empress. She sadly consented, and the man was taken to a scaffold which bore instruments so horrible that his robust nerve gave way. At the last moment the Empress benevolently commuted his sentence; he merely lost his right hand and his head. His companions lost their heads or their tongues, or joined the melancholy colony in Siberia.

In the summer of 1740 the Princess Anne, who had married Prince Anthony of Brunswick-Bevern, bore a son, and, as Anne's health failed, the feverish dispute about the succession reopened. It was understood that this infant was to be nominated Tsar, and the natural course would be to make his parents the Regents. Biren, however, took care to have himself nominated for the Regency, and he pressed the Empress, whose end was in sight, to endorse the arrangement. She refused for some days, but on October 26th she signed the document, and two days later she died.

Another, and still stranger romance, was now to be added to the weird chronicle of the court of the Romanoffs. Anne of Mecklenburg was the daughter of the late Empress's elder sister, who had, we saw, been a daughter of Peter the Great's elder brother. She seems to have been very unlike the other members of the family, though her mother had been a quiet and temperate princess. Anne herself was a blonde, good-natured nonentity; a

ROMANCE UPON ROMANCE

pawn in the game played by her elders. Prince Anthony, who had even less intelligence and character than she, had been brought young from Austria, and trained for his marital and royal duties under the eye of the late Empress. His wife disdained him, and Biren, seeing her dislike before they were married, suggested that she should marry instead his fifteen-year-old son. This proposal she rejected even more vehemently, and in the summer of 1739 she had coldly given her hand to Anthony.

Biren perceived the delicacy of his position, and he tried, by concessions to the troops and a reduction of the extravagance which the late Empress had imposed, to conciliate the country. But from the first day of his Regency a sullen murmur rose about him and gathered volume. Prince Anthony was the first to rebel. It was, he said, infamous to exclude him from the Regency when his son was Tsar; but when Biren brought him before an assembly of the nobles he saw the shadow of the scaffold and broke into hysterical tears. He was relieved of his appointments and ordered to confine himself to his wife's apartments. Anne herself then murmured, and Biren threatened to retain the babe, and send her and her husband to Mecklenburg.

In the group of dignitaries was a German military engineer, Münnich, who had never yet gambled in the intrigue of making a ruler of the Russian

Empire, and chance and spite now offered him an opportunity. On November 19th, a few weeks after the death of the late Empress, he had some business at the chamber of the Princess Anne, and the young mother tearfully confided to him her humiliations. She and her husband, she sobbed, would take their child and quit Russia for ever. Münnich was sympathetic: as she may have been forewarned. Biren had not given him the post of Commander in Chief, which he coveted. He told Anne to confide entirely in him, and went off to dine, jovially enough, with Biren. He was back afterwards at Anne's chamber, telling her to be ready for action at three the next morning; and, in order the better to mask his intrigue, he returned to sup and crack a bottle with the Regent.

Münnich was Lieutenant-Colonel of the Guard, and at two in the morning he told his plan to the awakened officers, and they led a picked body of troops to the Summer Palace. Bluffing the guards with a statement that he was conducting the Princess Anne to see Biren on some important business, he took his men to the room in which Biren and his wife slept. One glance at the massed uniforms behind the Colonel told the amazing adventurer that his hour had come. He fought like a madman, but was overpowered and carried off in a quilt. Before the day broke his brothers and reliable supporters were under arrest, and St.

ROMANCE UPON ROMANCE

Petersburg awoke to find that another revolution had been successfully accomplished at the palace. The hated Courlander was stripped of all his possessions, and he took that dreary route to Siberia that had been trodden by thousands of his victims.

But this last romance—of this particular series—had only begun with the pretty adventure of the German engineer. Münnich inherited Biren's vanity and corruption, as well as his power and wealth, but not his astuteness. In two months he is said to have heaped up a fortune hardly less than that of Biren, and it was at the grave cost of the State. The War of the Austrian Succession had opened, and Frederick of Prussia heavily bribed Münnich to put Russia on his side instead of that of Maria Theresa. This was too much for the sagacious Ostermann, who secured a redistribution of power and responsibility. His conceited fellow-countryman, overestimating the stupidity of the Regents, tendered his resignation, and it was accepted. Ostermann now resumed the control of foreign policy, but such matters concern us little here. It is enough to say that Sweden was spurred by France to a new attack upon Russia, and was defeated.

In the meantime the new romance was rapidly developing in the court. A young German woman named Julia Mengden secured, not merely the favours, but the passionate attachment, of the

THE ROMANCE OF THE ROMANOFFS

Regent Anne, and the court was filled afresh with disgust. Anne, an idle and insipid creature, would spend almost the whole day playing cards with Julia. She was often too lazy or too listless to dress, and courtiers found her scantily draped in Julia's room at all hours. Other Mengdens were attracted from the depths of Germany. A new brood of thick-tongued foreigners swarmed about the court.

Then Count Lynar, the Saxon envoy whom the late Empress had thought it prudent to remove, returned to St. Petersburg, and to the palace. Julia married him, but there seems no room for doubt that she was chiefly concerned to mask her royal friend's *liaison* with the Count. Anne had a second legitimate child, but within a few weeks Julia was holding her door while Lynar was within. As Anne had no redeeming charm or grace of character, the court looked on with disdain. Lynar, it was feared, would succeed to the place of Münnich, Biren, and Menshikoff, and few had a word for Anne. To her court she presented always a dull and bored look, and her husband she openly despised.

In the circumstances a fresh intrigue was almost inevitable, and the only other surviving Romanoff was the Princess Elizabeth. There was, moreover, a French envoy at St. Petersburg who had the romantic imagination in its liveliest form, and who

ROMANCE UPON ROMANCE

concluded that Elizabeth was precisely the ruler who would best suit the interests of his country. To obtain power she would, he thought, desert St. Petersburg for Moscow and surrender the Baltic provinces to the Swedes. He got into touch with Elizabeth and proposed that she should do this, if he arranged, simultaneously, a rising in St. Petersburg and an invasion by the Swedes. Elizabeth refused to yield territory, but she continued the negotiations. In December Anne detected her correspondence and warmly scolded her, but the quarrel ended in embraces. That was on December 4th; and in the early morning of December 6th, as Anne slept with her beloved Julia, a troop of grenadiers, with Princess Elizabeth at their head, entered the room and made an end of the reign of little Ivan VI and the Regency of his parents. How that was done belongs to the romance of the romantic Empress Elizabeth.

CHAPTER X

THE GAY AND PIOUS ELIZABETH

ELIZABETH has already entered so frequently, and so picturesquely, into the story that little further introduction is necessary. She was the younger of the two surviving daughters of Peter the Great and Catherine, and she inherited the independent temper of her father. Her pretty, merry figure was one of the most piquant of the court, and she had hardly attained a precocious puberty when it became necessary to watch her movements. She had, during the last three reigns, regarded both the court and its rulers with disdain. For the belated prudery of the Empress Anne she had no respect; it was the awful threat of confining her hot blood in a convent which had for a time curbed her public behaviour. For the baby-Emperor and his foolish parents she felt contempt, and she was prepared at any time to see the wheel of fortune turn toward her.

It was, as I said, the enterprising Marquis de la Chétardie who opened for her a plausible path to the throne. I would not stress her virtue in refusing to promise to yield Russian territory to Sweden.

THE GAY AND PIOUS ELIZABETH

She knew, and the Marquis ought to have known, that such a concession would have cost her the throne. But she continued to negotiate with him, and her French physician, Lestocq, assisted in the plot. Count Ostermann, the wise old German councillor who survived all revolutions at court, suspected her, and she had to use strategy. Chétardie took a villa up the Neva, and Elizabeth was fond of boating. She contrived to meet him casually and discuss the plot. She had, further, a few confidants at court, who were ready to speculate on the chances of a revolution, and she had, especially, the affection of the guards. Like her mother she was amiable with the soldiers. She held their children at the font and inquired genially about their families. Ostermann, we saw, detected the conspiracy, and Anne was directed to charge her with treasonable relations with France and Sweden, the enemies of Russia. The interview ended in sisterly tears and embraces, and the conspirators got speedily to work.

Ostermann, seeing the weakness of Anne, ordered the guard to be ready to leave for the frontier within twenty-four hours. It was probable, he mendaciously said, that Sweden was about to reopen the war. He had recently quarrelled with Elizabeth, and had no mind to see her Empress. This was on December 5th, the day after her interview with Anne. That night at ten the conspirators met to decide upon immediate action. Lestocq, the doctor, went out into the snow to see that all lights were out at Ostermann's mansion and the palace. They were as feeble a group of conspirators as ever engineered a revolution in Russia, and Elizabeth wavered between dread of a convent and eagerness for the throne. The most active and eloquent of them was the French physician. Then there were Vorontsoff, her chamberlain; Schwartz, her music-master; the brothers Shuvaloff, gentlemen of her household; and Alexis Razumovsky, her lover at the time, of whom we will see more. They raised Elizabeth's courage to the required pitch, and Lestocq stealthily introduced twenty grenadiers of the guard who professed that they were—for a consideration—ready to die for her. Elizabeth donned a cuirass under her cloak and slung a crucifix at her breast, and then, after a long and fervent prayer, committed her fortunes to Providence and the modest skill of her friends. Her lover was left to guard the house.

At two in the morning the party passed swiftly through the frozen streets to the Preobrajensky barracks. A small crowd of about two hundred soldiers gathered round Elizabeth and listened to her appeal to support her, the daughter of Peter, and exterminate the foreigners. They would cut them to pieces, they assured her; and she had to explain that she would have no bloodshed. Other

THE GAY AND PIOUS ELIZABETH

soldiers joined them, and presently a troop of four hundred marched with her and her supporters to the palace. It was the tamest revolution Russia had yet seen. Ostermann, Golovkin, and the other leading ministers were pinned into their mansions; the few loyal guards at the palace were thrust aside; and, as I said, Anne and Julia awoke to find Elizabeth in their bedroom at the head of a crowd of grenadiers.

Anne was not of the stuff of heroines. She meekly begged Elizabeth to spare her family and not take away her dear Julia, and she and her imperial baby were put upon the sledge and driven to Elizabeth's house. The blaze of fires in the courtyards and noise of soldiers soon roused the city, and courtiers and soldiers rushed out to study the situation. It is said of Lacy, the Irish commander, that, when a friend asked him which party he stood for, he promptly replied: "For the party that is in power." Few were so candid in speech, but all behaved alike. They rushed to take the new oath of allegiance, and the Empress Elizabeth inaugurated her reign.

Elizabeth insisted that there should be no bloodshed, but what happened may give the true measure of such advance as this indicated. Little Ivan and his parents must, she said, receive a pension and go back to Germany. Anne and Anthony, glad to escape so lightly, started for the frontier, but a

THE ROMANCE OF THE ROMANOFFS

courier reached them before they had left Russia, and they were imprisoned at Riga. After a time they were transferred, still prisoners, to Oranienbaum. Whether Elizabeth was struggling with her own glimmer of a conscience or with less humane counsellors it would be difficult to say. She consulted everybody. Was her life really in danger, or might she follow her impulse of humanity and let the weak-minded couple depart? Humanity was a new and rare thing in Russia.

In 1744, when Anne expected a third baby, the deposed couple were, at the instigation of Frederick of Prussia, confined in the fortress of Schlüsselburg, and four months later they were put upon sledges and driven north. They were to be imprisoned in a monastery on an island near Archangel. When, however, they reached Kholnagory, on the coast, the state of the ice would not allow the guards to take them to the island and they were left in the village. There, on the bleak shore of the Arctic, father and mother and five children— Anne added two to the family before she sickened and died three years later—lived and slept together in a common Russian hut. The children grew up feebler in mind and body even than their parents, but Russia would have it that the pale-faced Ivan was still the nucleus of a conspiracy. He was in 1756, in his thirteenth year, removed to a remote dungeon, to await his murder under the reign of

THE GAY AND PIOUS ELIZABETH

Catherine. Prince Anthony was weak-minded enough to survive the horrors for thirty years, and his children were at length released by Catherine and sent to live on a small pension in Denmark.

The "clemency" of Elizabeth—of which the decrees of the time speak—was equally exhibited toward the surviving servants of her father and her predecessor. Away with the Germans, was the cry; and a few distinguished Russians were included in the batch of prisoners who now looked forward to the customary reprisals. Old Ostermann, gouty and stoical, had fought Elizabeth, and he knew that his forty years of sound service would count for nothing. He was to be broken on the wheel. Münnich was to lose his hands and his head; Golovkin his head; and so on. A vast crowd gathered in the square on January 29th to see the "traitors" butchered. At the last moment an order of the Empress spared Ostermann the wheel and changed the sentence to decapitation. The old man moved toward the block, and a new order changed the punishment to exile. He quietly asked for his coat, and was packed off to the bleak northern region to which he had once helped to send Menshikoff. The crowd murmured when fresh orders from the Empress cheated them of the sight of blood. Münnich was sent to the spot—the very house—in Siberia to which he had sent Biren, who was summoned back to life. They met on the way, in Siberia, and bowed; and the great soldier settled down to rearing chickens and growing vegetables. The others were scattered over the bleak north. There had been no torture of witnesses—though much suborning of witnesses—and no bloodshed. Russia was improving.

While the goats were scattered, the sheep were gathered on the right hand. Vorontsoff became a leading minister, and his humble colleagues strutted also in gold lace and silks. Lestocq, first physician of the new court, was so richly rewarded with gold and favour that he imagined himself the prime spirit of the new regime, and will presently come to grief. The Marquis de la Chétardie became a saviour of Russia (which he would like to ruin in the interest of France, and indeed expected to be at least gravely weakened under the rule of Elizabeth), and soldiers kissed his hand. The guards, heavily rewarded, put on insufferable airs, and wandered insolently about the palace as if they were part owners of it. The state of the court was chaotic, and foreign envoys sent word home that Russia would sink back into barbarism.

The strange fortune of Alexis Razumovsky deserves a paragraph, since it cannot have a chapter. He was a tall, handsome Cossack, with fine black eyes and eyebrows and a rich black beard; a man in his thirty-fourth year when wealth and power were thus thrust upon him. Twenty years earlier

THE GAY AND PIOUS ELIZABETH

he had been a guardian of his father's sheep and a chorister in the church of the little Cossack village where his mother kept an inn. An imperial courier, passing through, had heard him sing, and had sent him to St. Petersburg to be trained and then got him a place in the choir of the imperial palace at Moscow. He was then twenty-two, and Elizabeth saw and appropriated him for her household. The Marquis de la Chétardie says that one of her maids first appropriated the handsome Cossack and Elizabeth got the news from her. To tell all the *legends* of the Russian court would need many volumes, and would offend the taste of our polite age, but no one seriously questions that Razumovsky took the place of Elizabeth's latest lover whom Anne had sent to Siberia.

At Elizabeth's accession he was made a Count and a Field Marshal. He was never spoiled by prosperity—"you may make me a Field Marshal," he said genially, "but you'll never make me a soldier"—and never interfered in politics. He took his great wealth pleasantly and generously, and drank royally. His brothers and relatives were—not by him, but by the Empress—similarly enriched, and even his old Cossack mother was brought from her inn, richly dressed, and presented at court. There was a story that the bewildered woman took her own reflection in the glass for the Empress and nervously curtsied to it; which would not flatter Elizabeth, as she was still one of the most handsome women of Russia.

Whether Elizabeth ever married Razumovsky cannot be exactly determined. It is generally accepted that she privately, at the instigation of her confessor, married him in the fall of 1742. Elizabeth openly doted on him and would always have him with her. He kept his even temper when, in her later years, she returned to her early license, and he was present at her death; after which, it is said, he was seen to burn a casket of papers which *may* have included a wedding-certificate.

A still greater favourite, in a different way, was Elizabeth's nephew, Karl Peter Ulrich, son of the Duke of Holstein-Gottorp and Anne of Mecklenburg, the elder daughter of Catherine and Peter. His mother had died of consumption a few months after his birth at Kiel, in 1728, and her sickly taint was on the boy. He was mean in body, intellect and character, and, as his father had died when he was eleven, his education had been rough. Elizabeth sent for him, gave him excellent tutors, and completely spoiled what bit of manliness he had. He was made a Grand Duke and heir to the throne —being the last male with any Romanoff blood— and, as he disliked the Empress's feminine circle, he surrounded himself with Germans, affected a contempt for Russia, and laughed at his aunt's amours.

PAUL THE FIRST

THE GAY AND PIOUS ELIZABETH

But Elizabeth was very far from being a fool. She adopted Peter in order to keep the crown in her father's family, making, out of dynastic feeling, a mistake which wise men like Marcus Aurelius had made. For the government of the country she chose her men well, as a rule, and she tried to put a stop to the disgraceful rivalry which had so often rent the court. At first her chief ministers were her Grand Chamberlain, Prince Tcherkasky, a corrupt old noble of the traditional school, and his son-in-law Trubetskoi. But she saw the greater merit of Michael Bestuzheff, the Grand Marshal of her household, a grave and learned man, and his able younger brother, Alexis, who was to become her chief minister.

Elizabeth herself was lazy. She let documents wait weeks for her signature and at ordinary times paid little attention to affairs. Her more resolute admirers say that she was so conscientious that she took weeks to consider a matter. She was, in point of fact, a thorough patriot, eager to maintain the work of her father; but most of her time was spent in the preservation of her health and beauty and the satisfaction of her insatiable thirst for pleasure. Her toilet took several hours every day, and it did not generally begin before midday, as she was apt to sit up with her intimate friends until the early hours of the morning. It is said that she drank heavily in her later years, but that is disputed. Her chief passion was for dress and entertainment. In a palace-fire she lost four thousand costly dresses, yet there were fifteen thousand in her wardrobe when she died. She had a large and opulent figure —a little too opulent as time went on—a face with few rivals in Russia, charming blue eyes and dark-golden hair.

One of her characteristics was a love of dressing as a soldier or sailor. She had good warrant for this in the example of her parents; and, to say the truth, she thought that no lady of her court could match her in male dress. So fancy-balls became very frequent, and Elizabeth, who was still fond of dancing and hunting until she grew too heavy, made a handsome Dutch sailor or colonel of the guard. She would change her garments three times in a ball; a dozen times in a day. Like Anne, she set her face against the old Russian debauches, and was for a French elegance, or a poor imitation of it. Luxury of every kind she encouraged, until the court shone with diamonds and gold brocade; and for her operas singers were brought from the ends of Europe. Reading was bad for the health, she said, and she avoided it.

She was, and always had been, very pious. There she differed emphatically from her father, and the orthodox clergy fell furiously upon dissenters and seceders. She observed the fasts rigorously, she knelt in prayer until she fainted, and she had a

THE GAY AND PIOUS ELIZABETH

great veneration for the relics of the saints and holy places. To the end she made pilgrimages afoot to famous shrines like the Troitsa monastery. In her youth she had made the journey in a day, and had had a lover to meet her there. Now she would walk out a few miles from Moscow—the court spent one year in four at Moscow—then ride back to the city, and begin her pilgrimage on the morrow at the point where she had left it the day before. It often took weeks to make a pilgrimage. She insisted so closely on decency that one day, as she prayed in church, it occurred to her that the angels painted on the walls were really cupids, and she had them repainted. Her own elderly gallantries we will see later.

With all this she, as I said, paid substantial attention to the interests of Russia. Sweden had collapsed in the late struggle, but Chétardie and Lestocq were instructed to induce her to be generous and give it some of the territory taken from it. It is generally difficult to disentangle the action of a sovereign from that of her advisers, and Elizabeth may have more credit for firmness than she deserves. She, at all events, refused, and the war went on until Sweden was crushed. Russia kept a large part of Finland. At last intercepted letters made it plain to the Empress that the gallant French marquis who bowed and flattered her was really trying to injure Russia in the interest of his country, and he had to go. She was, however, still infatuated with France and her French doctor, though Count Bestuzheff, who became her chief adviser, persistently warned her against France. Lestocq, who took bribes from all Powers and fancied himself a master of intrigue, now, with the aid of the French minister, made a desperate attempt to win her.

Elizabeth's chief rival in good looks was Natalia Lapukhin, a noble lady of equal freedom in manners and morals who had viciously tormented Elizabeth when she was the Cinderella of the court. To her surprise she had been, at the coronation, made a Lady in Waiting. But she remained insolent, and at a ball she appeared in a pink robe and with pink roses in her hair; and pink was understood to be an imperial monopoly at Elizabeth's court. Elizabeth's temper was much shorter than her prayers. Many a maid got the heavy imperial slipper across her mouth for talking when the Empress dozed on her couch, and her language at times resembled that of the guards. She had a buffoon cruelly tortured for playing a trick which frightened and upset her. She now fell furiously upon the audacious Lady in Waiting. She sent for scissors, made her kneel while she cut off the roses (and hair along with them), and cuffed her twice across the face. "Serves her right," she said, when they told her that the countess had fainted. To her bosom

THE GAY AND PIOUS ELIZABETH

friend, the Countess Bestuzheva, wife of the elder Bestuzheff, Natalia often told what she thought of the Empress, and in both families the talk over tea was mildly seditious. Lestocq got his agents to ply Natalia's son, young Colonel Lapukhin, with drink and learn it.

And on July 21st, 1743, the physician rushed to the palace with a report of a conspiracy. Elizabeth lived in daily dread of a conspiracy, knowing how easy such things were in Russia. She cowered behind a hedge of soldiers and let Lestocq arrest whom he would. She had humanely abolished torture and the death-sentence; but this was a different matter. Natalia and her husband and a score of others were imprisoned, and the old torture-chambers rang again with the shrieks of delicate women whose limbs were stretched until they cracked. It is said, but is difficult to believe, that Elizabeth was secretly at hand to hear their confessions. There was, in fact, no conspiracy to confess, but Lestocq was one of the three commissioners appointed to examine the prisoners, and Elizabeth was stung by the table-talk that was wrung from them. One of the women was pregnant, and the Empress was asked to spare her the torture. "She did not spare me," said the daughter of Peter the Great.

They were all condemned to death. For ten days Elizabeth lingered over the sentence, but in the end, she observed her own decree. She commuted the sentence to exile, flogging, and mutilation. Natalia Lapukhin, a beautiful woman in the prime of life, was partly stripped before an immense crowd, and brutally knouted. She sank, covered with blood, to the floor of the scaffold, and the executioner roughly finished his work, and, with a brutal laugh, offered to sell her tongue to the highest bidder. Countess Bestuzheva slipped a bribe into the man's hands. The lash fell less heavily on her white back, and less of her tongue was cut out. The mutilated wretches went the worn way to Siberia and the north. Count Michael Bestuzheff, who was innocent, was despatched on a foreign embassy. Alexis, at whom the French had chiefly aimed, was untouched. He was astute as well as able.

At the end of the year Elizabeth transferred the court to Moscow and prepared it for a new sensation. She had chosen a bride, or a girl to be trained as bride, for her wastrel of a nephew. After her weakness for France, which was then a deadly rival of Russia, came a weakness for Frederick the Great, who was far more cynical and crafty in his professions of friendship and determination to sacrifice Russia's interests to his own. He flattered Elizabeth, and laughed at her. Hearing that there was question of a future Empress, he strongly recommended the daughter of the Prince of An-

THE GAY AND PIOUS ELIZABETH

halt-Zerbst, one of his own generals. A courier sped to the little court where Sophia Augusta Frederika lived quietly with her mother, and that lady, a remarkably ambitious person for her station in life, hurried to St. Petersburg, and on to Moscow. Both Peter and Elizabeth were indecently impatient to see the bride-elect, and they professed themselves entirely satisfied with the quick-eyed, precocious maiden of fourteen who would one day be Catherine the Great.

Sophia and her mother were lodged in the Kreml, and the work of preparation began. The young princess soon realised her destiny and determined not to spoil it. But she had three near misses within a year. She worked so hard at the Russian that she would get up during the night and pace the room, repeating her lessons, in bare feet; and she caught pneumonia and nearly died a few weeks after her arrival. Incidentally she won the Empress's favour completely. In the hour of danger they asked if she would see her Lutheran pastor. No, she said, the Russian priest; and the rumour of her piety, which—she afterwards said—was really policy, spread through the court. She was received into the Russian Church in July, and solemnly betrothed to Peter. Then Peter had the smallpox and nearly died; and in fine her mother nearly spoiled her prospect. She had come with secret instructions from Frederick of Prussia, and, like a good German, she stealthily pushed his interest. The inquiry into the supposed Bestuzheff plot exposed her, and she retired to her obscure province. But Elizabeth liked her daughter, and Catherine—her name was changed on entering the Orthodox Church—remained, and married Peter in the following year.

The years that followed were filled with European struggle, which does not much concern us here. The capture of the letters of Chétardie exposed the machinations of both France and Prussia. Elizabeth found herself described as living in a state of "voluptuous lethargy," and her passion for France and Frederick suddenly chilled. Alexis Bestuzheff became her chief counsellor, and inclined her toward England and Austria. The court was honeycombed by intrigue, and even the favourite, Lestocq, was at length (1748) detected in his treachery. He was put to the torture and banished.

Elizabeth was not long drawn out of her "voluptuous lethargy." In fact, the attainment of middle age seemed to bring back the looseness of her youth, and her lovers were the jest of the courts of Europe. One of her pages, Ivan Shuvaloff, was promoted and placed in apartments near those of the Empress. Ivan took his good fortune modestly, but the customary tribe of relatives appeared and blossomed into wealthy and influential

THE GAY AND PIOUS ELIZABETH

courtiers. Count Bestuzheff and others were alarmed, and they put in the way of the Empress a very handsome young amateur actor named Beketoff. Elizabeth genially added the youth to the intimate circle which caroused in her room at night, but Peter Shuvaloff, uncle of the earlier favourite, did not like the prospect. The more credible version of his action is that he met young Beketoff one day, and, impressing upon him how much the Empress liked to see her favourites fresh and healthy, gave him a box of ointment for his face. There was in the stuff something which caused an eruption of the skin, and his condition was represented to the Empress in such a light that he fled.

It should be added that she still guarded the propriety of her subjects. The elder Count Bestuzheff held that his wife's crime had dissolved his marriage, and he wished to take a second wife. Elizabeth sternly refused to consent, holding that marriage was indissoluble. When the desperate Count did at length marry she refused to receive his "paramour" at court.

In many other respects she tried to continue the process of cleaning the face of Russia. At first she had undone her father's control of the monks, and let them gather enormous wealth. As the needs of war pressed on her, she revoked this and checked them. She endeavoured also to check the irregularities and dispel the ignorance of the secular clergy. Wandering priests would gather in the streets of Moscow and importune passers-by to give them the price of a mass. Some are said to have held a crust in their hands, and threatened to eat (which would make them unable to say mass that day), unless a man offered his purse. Elizabeth set the bishops to remove these and other irregularities. She promoted letters, since it was the proper thing for an enlightened monarch to do, and her ministers attempted to improve trade and agriculture. Agricultural banks were opened; industries were protected; mines were sunk; Siberia and the southern steppes were partly colonised. It was forbidden for men and women to mix in the public baths. These were, on the whole, slight improvements of a terribly backward country. Ignorance, violence, drunkenness, dishonesty in trade, official corruption, brigandage, listlessness, and idleness were still general.

The later years of the reign were filled with the inevitable Prussian war. After years of diplomatic struggle Elizabeth, in 1756, concluded an alliance with England. To her great disgust, and Bestuzheff's grave danger, England then formed an alliance with Frederick, and the French redoubled their efforts to oust Bestuzheff and receive the friendship of Russia. By this time the Princess Catherine openly disdained her husband and went her own way. For years the Empress, eager to

THE GAY AND PIOUS ELIZABETH

see an heir to the throne she would leave to Peter, tried to bring them together, but each hated the other, and Catherine found consolation elsewhere. In 1754, however, Catherine had a son who was presumed to be a Romanoff. Elizabeth fell ill, and Bestuzheff, believing that she would die, approached Catherine, through her latest lover, Poniatowski, and suggested that he could make her Empress if she would support his anti-French and anti-Prussian policy.

Elizabeth recovered, however, and declared that the good of the world demanded the destruction of Frederick of Prussia, who had said caustic things about her. The Seven Years' War opened, and Russia joined France and Austria against Prussia. The Russian army under General Apraksin won a great victory, and then, instead of pressing it, retired. Now this coincided with a second serious illness of the Empress, and the French envoy raised a cry of treachery. Vorontsoff, who waited impatiently for the official shoes of Count Bestuzheff, and hated Catherine, joined the French in demanding an inquiry. Bestuzheff's papers were searched, and it was found that he had been in communication with Catherine. A plot was easily constructed out of this material. Bestuzheff was to raise Catherine's baby to the throne and make her Regent; and Apraksin's troops were withdrawn toward the capital for the event of the death of Elizabeth.

Catherine in later years looked back with a shudder upon that critical time. Bestuzheff contrived to send her word that he had burned her letters, and there was no danger, but she saw a very serious danger. She wrote to Elizabeth, and for weeks she received no answer. At last she was summoned to the Empress's room. Her enemy, Alexis Shuvaloff, was with the Empress; her husband, another enemy, waited in the room; and on the table she saw letters that she had written to Apraksin. They were innocent letters, but what right had she to communicate with commanders in the field, as if she were already Empress? With tears and prayers she mollified the angry Empress, and her enemies were beaten. Apraksin died of apoplexy, and Bestuzheff was compelled to retire to his estates.

For the brief remainder of the reign of the Empress Elizabeth Catherine went warily. Elizabeth, who was little beyond her fiftieth birthday, would not control her appetites, and her health slowly departed. She became a chronic invalid and would lie for hours on a couch admiring the little babe, Paul, who would carry on the line of the Romanoffs. Some misgiving in regard to the future seemed to trouble her. Peter, though a Romanoff, was emphatically a brutal German. He lived in an entirely German atmosphere; an atmosphere of smoke and beer-fumes and Teutonic disdain of everything Russian. Catherine, on the other hand,

THE GAY AND PIOUS ELIZABETH

had developed into a thorough Russian. Her strong sense and feeling of policy told her to eradicate all Germanism from her composition and wholly transnationalise herself. Peter had an immense admiration of Prussia and Frederick, while Catherine was a Russian patriot.

And Elizabeth hated Prussia. Throughout her last years she kept alive the League against Frederick and spurred her generals in the struggle. Frederick sought peace, and she refused it. France and Austria became faint under their efforts and sacrifices, and she lashed them to the task. All through the year 1761 her strength ebbed, and she saw Frederick sinking from defeat to defeat. Would death spare her to see Prussia crushed? Would that unhappy nephew take over her power before her work was completed, and spare his idol? Her own ministers drooped, and her resources wore thin, but she cried for decisive and utter victory. In December a fit of coughing brought on hemorrhage, and she entered the last stage. She died on January 11th, 1762, in the fifty-third year of her age, not the least picturesque figure of the Romanoff gallery of monarchs.

CHAPTER XI

CATHERINE THE GREAT

WALISZEWSKI, a vivid historical writer who has covered nearly the whole period of the dynasty, calls the Empress Elizabeth "the last of the Romanoffs." If every rumour of those gossipy days were admitted, few genealogical trees of the Russian aristocracy would hold good. There have not been wanting historians who have claimed that Catherine the Great was a natural daughter of Frederick the Great; and a grave writer has said of Catherine's son, Paul, that the *only* ground for regarding him as the son of Peter III is his resemblance to that monarch. We may assume that Peter, who now peacefully ascended the throne and continued the dynasty, was the grandson of Peter the Great, the son of his daughter Anne.

It is, however, true that the moral physiognomy of the Romanoffs changes with Peter III, and it is not clear how a German father and a few years of early life in Germany could so thoroughly Teutonise his blood. We must, of course, not forget that most of what we read about him was written

CATHERINE THE GREAT

by his wife or by other enemies. Mr. Bain refuses to believe that he was brutal to Catherine, as she says. At his accession he paid her heavy debts and settled upon her the large domains of the late Empress. His unfaithfulness to her was at least balanced by her own vagaries. She, a German, took the throne from him, and she was bound to make a dark case against him in order to justify her usurpation. They were, at all events, as ill-assorted a pair as ever mounted a throne, and every informed person in Europe wondered what would be the issue, and was prepared for another revolution.

We have seen a little about their earlier years. Elizabeth drew them in their childhood from Germany, changed their religion, and appointed tutors to prepare them for the throne. Catherine prepared very diligently, but Peter went in a precisely opposite direction. While Catherine steeped herself in the Russian spirit, he remained German, looked with contempt upon Russian ways, and surrounded himself with foreigners. He had the vices, without the good qualities, of the Romanoffs. He drank heavily, was boorish to those about him, and lived loosely. Catherine tells a story which is a cameo of life at the court, if so sordid a sketch may be compared with a work of art. Empress Elizabeth's private room, in which the little suppers of the later part of her reign were held, was separated only by a door from one of Peter's rooms. The noise he heard in it at nights piqued him, and he bored holes in the door, and found Elizabeth, lightly dressed, carousing with her lover and a few intimate courtiers. He called Catherine, who (she says) refused to peep, and then he called a bunch of ladies of their court to come and enjoy the spectacle. Catherine pictures him keeping dogs in their bedroom and coming to bed, very drunk, in the early morning to kick and pummel her.

There can be little doubt that the young prince was coarse, violent, and drunken; and Catherine hated his insipid, pock-marked face and boorish ways. Long before the death of Elizabeth she took a lover, Sergius Saltykoff, a handsome young fellow of Peter's suite. Bestuzheff sent Sergius on a mission abroad, but his place was soon taken by a handsome young Pole, Count Poniatovski. In the meantime, Catherine had given birth to her son Paul, and the genuineness of the claim of the later Tsars to be considered Romanoffs hangs upon the very slender thread of Catherine's morals. Saltykoff was at the time generally regarded as the father. The boy, however, grew up to resemble Peter, morally and physically, so closely that historians now generally consider him a son of Peter. It looks as if Catherine, to save her position with Elizabeth, who pressed for an heir, reluctantly consented to provide one. Legend has it that the court deliberately instructed her to have a child by her lover if she could not be reconciled to her husband. Catherine tells us that, when the child was born, Elizabeth sent her a present of fifty thousand dollars, and that Peter got the draft cancelled.

It is sometimes said that Poniatovski, who is described as being put in Catherine's way by political schemers, was detected by Peter and fled to escape a whipping. The legend really runs that he was held up by Peter's servants, as he left the palace, and brought before Peter. He was a youth of twenty-two, of no courage, and he expected a whipping, but Peter laughed at his fright. Peter's mistress at the time, and until his death, was Elizabeth Vorontsoff, niece of a great noble of the court; a very plain and insignificant little woman whom Catherine disdained to notice. The prince felt that he could now force Catherine to be courteous to his mistress, and it is said that he arranged suppers for the quartet. The Empress, however, heard of the *liaison,* and Poniatovski had to go. Catherine had a second child, Anna, in 1758, who is believed to be the daughter of the Pole. The court was by this time, we saw, thoroughly demoralised, as all knew that the Empress herself caroused at night, and Catherine cast aside all pretence of propriety. At the time of the Empress's death her lover was Gregory Orloff, a very dashing young officer: a young man of superb and colossal frame, of features that fascinated women and of the time-honoured habits of dissipation.

If we are to understand the character of Catherine, we must endeavour to regard these irregularities with her eyes. It is sheer nonsense to seek to put her on a moral level with Elizabeth or any other aristocratic Russian dame who mingled amours with prayers, and equally venerated monks and lovers. Catherine had not the least inner respect for the Russian Church, or any branch of the Christian Church, and its ideals. For political reasons she conformed outwardly, but it is difficult to find that she had more than a vague and not very serious deism. She read and corresponded with the French "philosophers," and in her letters to them (when she became her own mistress) she ridiculed the "mummeries" of the priests. "I congratulate myself that I am one of the imbeciles who believe in God," is the extent of her profession of faith. She did not respect the authority and ideals of the Church, and so she regarded herself as free. These irregularities need not in themselves be considered inconsistent with her title of "the Great."

Liberal writers express some surprise that her lovers were never more than handsome and sensual blockheads. We shall see that Orloff, little intelligence as he had, could work for her, but that she probably never weighed. She was a woman of high

CATHERINE THE GREAT

intelligence and self-confidence. She chose ministers to do work and lovers only for enjoyment. There is no psychological mystery in such an attitude.

When Peter ascended the throne he surprised all by his policy of conciliation. He issued an amnesty, and from all the frozen recesses of the Empire came the victims—the sobered Lestocq, old Marshal Münnich, Julia Mengden and her sister, the Birens, and so on—of the earlier revolutions. Then he set himself to conciliate his subjects. Peter the Great had forced education and public service upon the reluctant nobles: Peter the Little removed the compulsion, flatteringly observing that it was no longer necessary. Peter the Great had created a secret police which had ruled the aristocracy by terror and corruption: Peter III abolished it. Peter the Great had put crushing taxes upon peasants and dissenters: Peter III relieved them, and, caring nothing about Russian orthodoxy, favoured the industrious dissenters. He abolished the corporal punishment of officers; he confiscated the wealth of the clergy and the monks, making them an annual allowance; he bade the monks educate themselves, and forbade them to take young novices.

But these reforms angered one very powerful class—the clergy and the monks—and Peter went on to alienate the army. He despised everything

Russian. Elizabeth had given him the palace (built by Menshikoff) of Oranienbaum, about twenty-seven miles from St. Petersburg, and there he had established a few companies of Holstein soldiers, the nucleus or model of his future army. He fancied himself a soldier, and spent his time there as Peter had spent his at Preobrajenshote. After his accession he announced that the army was to be Germanised. New uniforms were provided. Old regiments were threatened with extinction. What was worse, he made peace with Frederick of Prussia, who might now have been utterly crushed, and held up that monarch to Russia as a model king and soldier.

To Catherine he was at first, as I said, generous, but serious rumours got about that he intended to send her into a convent and marry his Vorontsoff. At a public and important banquet he is said to have insulted her, calling across the table that she was "a fool." In short, he put together an admirable collection of combustible material, and he was surprised when the flame of revolution burst forth.

How it was arranged is not very clear, as Catherine afterwards claimed the entire merit, yet a dozen others claimed the merit—and the reward. As far as one can judge, Catherine was nervous and did little. Gregory Orloff and his brothers had not so clear a vision of the possibilities, in case of failure, and they worked zealously. Catherine's little friend, Princess Dashkoff, a very romantic young lady who read Voltaire and Diderot and had great ideas, claims that she did more than anybody; she clearly helped to buy or convert supporters. The French agents found money, the soldiers were secretly canvassed, and the growing discontent with the Emperor was carefully nourished. A statesman, Panin, was more or less won: some say at the cost of the virtue of Princess Dashkoff. Catherine herself had, about this time (April, 1762), a third child, who was quite acknowledged to be the son of Orloff.

The last blunder of Peter was that, after making an ignominious peace with Prussia, he wanted to make war upon the Danes for his little principality of Holstein. On June 24th he went, with Elizabeth, to Oranienbaum, and ordered Catherine, whom he refused to regard as a serious danger, to the palace of Peterhof. The Emperor's nameday feast fell on July 10th, and he sent word that he would spend it with Catherine at Peterhof. He arrived there on July 9th, to find that Catherine had fled, with one of the Orloffs, in the early morning; and before many hours he learned that the capital was taking the oath of allegiance to her.

On the previous evening one of the chief conspirators, Captain Passek, had been arrested, and Gregory Orloff had been kept under observation by an agent carousing and playing cards with him all night. Princess Dashkoff says that she ran about, stirring the conspirators, and saved the situation. At all events Alexis Orloff rushed into Catherine's bedroom, at Peterhof, at five in the morning, and urged her to come to St. Petersburg and begin the revolt at once. They arrived at the barracks of the most reliable regiment at seven, and roused the soldiers. There were soon a copious supply of brandy and shouts of "Long Live the Empress." Catherine went to the Winter Palace, and courtiers stumbled over each other in their eagerness to offer allegiance. Catherine maliciously says that Princess Dashkoff was one of the last to arrive. The soldiers cast off their new German uniforms, and begged to be led against those accursed Holsteiners of Peter's; and Catherine—she and the little, snub-nosed Dashkoff dressed as officers—led twenty thousand men to Oranienbaum.

Peter had sent for his Holstein guards and loudly protested that he would fight. As the news from the capital trickled in, however, he changed his mind and took boat to Kronstadt. It is said that when the sentinel, in the dark, challenged him, and was told that he was the Emperor, the man said: "Go away; there is no Emperor." He returned, shaking with fear, to Oranienbaum, and offered to share his throne with Catherine. She contemptuously refused that dangerous half-measure. Peter, weeping like a child, and begging that they would not separate him from Elizabeth, abdicated, and was sent into the country about twenty miles away. Elizabeth Vorontsoff was sent to Moscow.

What precisely happened to Peter III is one of the many dark mysteries of the romance of the Romanoffs. Five days later Catherine coldly announced that the late Emperor had died of a colic which had sent a fatal flow of blood to his brain. There is a rumour that he was poisoned. There is another rumour, which is generally accepted, that Alexis Orloff, who conducted him to Ropcha, strangled him; and there is no evidence whether Catherine was or was not (as is generally believed) a party to the murder.

There were the usual sunny days for all who had assisted in the revolution. In three months nearly half a million dollars in money, and great gifts of land and serfs, were showered upon the new court. Many of the courtiers, however, did not long enjoy favour. In 1763, when Catherine had gone to Moscow for her coronation, a certain Feodor Hitrovo was arrested for treason. For some time there had been rumours of plots to put Ivan V, the son of Anne and Anthony whom Elizabeth had displaced, back upon the throne. Peter III had brought the poor youth, now almost an idiot, to St. Petersburg, and Catherine had confined him in the fortress of Schlüsselburg. The latest rumour in

THE ROMANCE OF THE ROMANOFFS

the capital was that Catherine was to wed Orloff, and that the jealous courtiers were determined to prevent her or to kill Orloff. Whether there was a plot or no, it is clear that the promotion of the Orloffs had caused grave murmurs. Princess Dashkoff, Panin, Captain Passek, and other conspirators of 1762, were, to their mighty indignation, arrested on suspicion of treason. They were released, but their term of favour was from that moment clouded.

Another of the blots on Catherine's reign, or one of those dark tragedies into which the historian cannot penetrate, occurred in the following year. The unfortunate Prince Ivan was killed in prison. An officer of the garrison named Mirovitch plotted to release him, and it is said that his guardians, who had orders to despatch him in case of a dangerous effort to free him, carried out that instruction. Mirovitch was executed, but it was remarked that there was no inquiry, and there was not the customary punishment of the relatives of the executed criminal. It seems, however, absurd to suppose that Mirovitch was hired to give the opportunity of killing Ivan. History, again, gives Catherine a not very cheerful verdict of "not proven."

These early threats or suspicions of revolt were attributed by Catherine to the traditional discontent and ambition of courtiers who were ever ready to create a new throne for their own profit. But

CATHERINE THE GREAT

she saw clearly enough the miserable condition of the country at large, and she opened her reign with a determination to apply the remedy prescribed by the liberal and humane principles of her French teachers. There must be education, and in 1764 she issued an instruction to the authorities who were to take up that work. Her own ideas were necessarily vague and unscientific, and she soon found herself confronted by the traditional difficulties: a massive and general ignorance so dense that it did not want education, a shortage of funds, and a corrupt and listless body of officials. A number of technical and normal schools—in all about 200 schools—were founded, and at St. Petersburg Catherine established a large and admirable school for girls, but her vague general scheme came to naught. Russia lingered on in the darkness of the Middle Ages.

The reform of law and justice was the next great need. Catherine eagerly devoured the writings of such reformers as Montesquieu and Beccaria, and in 1767 she issued an instruction which was so liberal that it was not permitted to appear in French. It abounds in humane reflections which illustrate the soundness of her attitude as a ruler in her earlier years. "The laws must see that the serfs are not left to themselves in their old age and illness," she said; and "The people are not created for us, but we for the people." She laid it down, vaguely, that "the rich must not oppress the poor," and "every man must have food and clothing according to his condition." There were even echoes of the new French words, liberty and equality. The torture of witnesses was described as a barbaric practice. Sentence of death must be imposed only in the case of political offenders.

Little came of her large scheme of reform. A Legislative Assembly, drawn from all ranks of the people, met in 1767 to give definite shape to her ideals, but its two hundred sittings ended in futile disagreement. No one wished to better the condition of the serfs at the expense of the landowners, and Catherine partly undid with one hand what she did for them with the other. The serfs of the ecclesiastical estates, which she secularised, were set on the way to freedom, and Catherine theoretically wanted to see the end of a virtual slavery which was inconsistent with her philosophy. But she herself gave enormous estates, with tens of thousands of serfs, to her favourites, and she knew that human beings who were transferred like cattle were treated like cattle. In her reign the Countess Daria Saltykoff had to be imprisoned for barbarously causing the death of a hundred and thirty-eight of her serfs. They were still bought and sold as blacks were in America, and their proprietors could for slight causes send them

CATHERINE II

CATHERINE THE GREAT

to Siberia. The great mass of the Russian people lived in this state of degradation.

Catherine's strong will nearly always failed before an internal problem of this kind. The nobles triumphed, and Russia remained in darkness and chains. In her later years, when her early benevolent despotism had given place to a fierce hatred of democracy, she persuaded herself that her people were better off than most of the peoples of Europe. She clung, however, to other parts of her programme of reform. Few were knouted, and no other torture was permitted in her reign; and she boasted that she never signed a sentence of death. Men were, nevertheless, put to death, as we shall see; and it was commonly said that the secret police were merely replaced by her mysterious official, Tchechkoffski, who suavely invited suspected folk to his house. It was believed that the chair on which his visitor sat sank below the floor, leaving only the man's face invisible to the servants in the room below who applied torture to his limbs.

While Catherine pursued these and other designs of reform, which we will consider later, her prodigality toward her favourites caused much murmuring, and to this grievance she added the costly burden of war. It is clear that in her early years she trusted to remain at peace, and had no thought of the enlargement of the country. But the greed of Frederick the Great now turned upon the decaying kingdom of Poland, and, to obtain his large share, he had to invite the participation of Russia in the plunder. Catherine, we saw, had hated Frederick, her husband's idol. It is said that amongst her husband's papers she found a letter in which Frederick spoke flatteringly of her, and she began to turn to him. She did, at all events, change her attitude, and share with him in the historic crime which is known as the partition of Poland. She joined Frederick in imposing upon the Poles her old lover, Poniatovski, and her armies went to the support of his rule against the rebellion which followed.

France and Austria were now opposed to Russia and Prussia, and France resorted to the familiar stratagem of inciting Turkey to attack Russia. Catherine, whose energy was now fully roused, spurred her generals to meet the Turks. They took the Crimea and a large part of the Slav dominions of the Turk, but Austria now threatened to oppose the southward expansion of Russia and suggested that compensation should be sought in Poland. The first partition took place in 1771, and Catherine secured "White Russia," with a population of 1,600,000 souls. Turkey, in turn, was forced to surrender the Crimea, pay a large indemnity, and open the Dardanelles to Russian ships and the Ottoman Empire to Russian trade.

But the burden of the war had fallen, as usual,

upon the impoverished people, and murmurs rumbled from one end of Russia to the other. The plague broke out at Moscow, and tens of thousands died. The country seethed with discontent, and it chanced that at that moment a figure appeared round which the discontent might crystallise. A Cossack named Pugatcheff claimed that he was the Empress's husband, Peter III, who was supposed to have been murdered at Ropcha, and his little troop quickly grew into a formidable and devastating army. Soldiers sent against him enlisted under his banner; brigands, barbarians, and Poles joined in his campaign of loot and slaughter; an immense area of the country was captured or laid waste by him. The revolt went on for four years, when Pugatcheff was captured and beheaded. From that date Catherine's zeal for "the people" abated; and it was with some recollection of this that she in a later year put an end for ever to the power and remaining independence of the Cossacks.

The Empress, nevertheless, continued her work of reform. Official and judicial corruption was as rife as ever, and she retraced more practically the spheres of jurisdiction, and separated the administrative from the judiciary officers. Like Peter (though unlike him in her extravagant liberality to favourites, which increased the evil) she hated and sternly prosecuted official corruption. Her scheme, both of administration and of the dispensing of justice, was a great reform, embracing every class of her people, if we take a liberal view of the little she did for the serfs. She encouraged agriculture and industry, made wise efforts to ensure the colonisation of the fertile steppes of the south which she had acquired, founded about two hundred new towns, and secularised (with just compensation) the enormous property of the clergy and the monks. She pressed the introduction of medical service, in order to combat the appalling death-rate of the prolific people, and boldly submitted to vaccination and imposed it upon her people. Her philanthropic institutions included a school for nearly 500 girls and a large Foundling Hospital which, during her reign, received forty thousand children. In reforming the terribly loose fiscal system she made notable improvements and raised the national revenue from ten to eighty million roubles; but the increasing extravagance of her court made a mockery of her financial reforms.

In fine, as is well known, she corresponded with Voltaire and the other leading French thinkers, and made strenuous efforts, in her earlier years, to arouse a corresponding culture in Russia. Her letters to Voltaire are now believed to have been written, at least in part, by Alexis Shuvaloff, and one cannot say, nor would one expect, that her genuine letters and other writings indicate any

CATHERINE THE GREAT

great literary skill; though her constant humour and vivacious personality make them good reading. She purchased the libraries of Voltaire and Diderot, and made famous collections of works of art, rather because it was the part of a great monarch to patronise art than from any personal taste. To Russian art and science, apart from (to some extent) letters and history, she gave no impulse; and her own "discoveries" in the field of science were amiable nonsense. However, the great literary output which she stimulated, the foundation of an Academy (on the Parisian model) at St. Petersburg, and the encouragement of the theatre must be counted amongst her untiring efforts to educate Russia. How the French Revolution checked her ardour, and turned her love of France into hatred, we shall see later.

This programme of work, which I am compelled to compress into a few paragraphs, fairly entitles Catherine, when we take its results in conjunction with her extension of her Empire, to the epithet of "the Great." That she chose men of ability to carry out her will, even to assist her in making plans, goes without saying; but she paid close and industrious attention to all that was done, and she fierily resented the obstacles to the complete realisation of her scheme. I have doubted if the modern spirit can grant Peter the title of "the Great" for two reasons: first, because of features of his character which we must describe as brutal; secondly, because of the vagueness and casualness of many of his plans and the lack of obstinacy in realising them. Catherine was far from brutal. Her character had defects, which we will consider, but they are not such as to make us refuse her the homage her work deserves. That, on the other hand, her plans were imperfect, inadequate to the vast need, often sketchy and not enforced with masculine stubbornness, we must admit; but she was a great ruler. Let us complete her work before we regard the personal features that lower her prestige.

The Crimea, now part of Russia, remained in a state of constant disorder, and this became at length an open revolt. Catherine suppressed the rebellion, and a few years later Turkey was induced to relinquish all claim to the old Tatar principality. Catherine was now supremely eager for a further extension toward the blue waters of the Mediterranean, the immovable goal of all Russian policy. She suggested to the Austrian Emperor, with whom she was now on excellent terms, that Turkey should be dismembered. Austria should take the nearer provinces; a new kingdom of Dacia should be founded, recognising the Orthodox Church; and the Greek Empire should be revived and extended so as to embrace Constantinople. Her grandson Constantine was to be the first Greek Emperor.

Austria accepted the scheme, and Russian agents

CATHERINE THE GREAT

were sent to agitate in the Slav provinces of Turkey. In 1787 Catherine herself made an imposing journey in the south. Turkey clearly saw the threat to its Empire, and in 1787 it declared war. Potiamkin, Catherine's favourite at the time, was entrusted with the supreme command, and marched south. Then the ever-ready Swede fell upon the flank of Russia, and Catherine, who could from St. Petersburg hear the roar of the Swedish guns on the Baltic, had a momentary fright. She called up all her energy and stirred her commanders, and in the following year she had peace with Sweden and was free to attack Turkey, in conjunction with the Austrians. The details do not concern us. The war lasted five years, and a little more of the coast of the Black Sea was brought within the Russian Empire. It may be added, briefly, that continued internal trouble in Poland, of which Catherine took as mean an advantage as any, led to the second and third partitions of that country. Poland ceased to exist; the once great kingdom, ruined by the quarrels and obstinate conservatism of its nobles, was divided between Russia, Prussia, and Austria.

The vast addition to her territory which Catherine obtained from the spoils of Poland will not be regarded by the modern mind as a title to glory. More creditable was the wresting of territory from the Turks, but her chief merit lies in the reform-

THE ROMANCE OF THE ROMANOFFS

edicts (she counted 211 of her ukases under that head) with which she sought to uplift Russia. Against this we have her personal repute as it is given in many historians. There were those at the time who called her "the Messalina of the north," and writers on her still differ in their estimate of her moral personality.

That she was, in the narrow sense of the word, flagrantly immoral no one questions. We may recall that Europe at large was still very far from the standard of these matters which adorns our generation. Paris under Louis XV, or the Directorate, or even Napoleon; London under the Georges; even Rome under the Popes of the period would not pass modern scrutiny. Russia was a little more mediæval than the others, and Catherine inherited a court in which an Empress of advanced years and conspicuous piety had given an example of wild debauch. To a woman of Catherine's views and strong personality there would seem to be no reason for restraint; and she observed none.

We have seen her early lovers, and I do not intend to examine the lengthy gallery with any minuteness. Gregory Orloff, an indolent and very sensuous Adonis, enjoyed her extravagant favour until 1772. His three brothers and he cost her, in those few years, about nine million dollars. In 1772 she sent Orloff on a mission to the Turks, and during his absence another mere sensualist, Vassiltchikoff, earned her favour. Gregory heard it, and covered the two thousand miles which separated him from St. Petersburg with a speed that beat all records. He was directed to retire to his provincial estate, and from there he bombarded the palace with entreaties. Catherine hardly attended to imperial business for several months. At length she definitely discharged Orloff with an annual income of 75,000 dollars, a present of 10,000 peasants, and the right to use the imperial palaces and horses when he willed.

Vassiltchikoff made way in 1774 to the famous Patiomkin, a different type of man from any of the others. He was in his thirty-fifth year and, as we saw, he had ability. Her letters to him show the nearest approach to tender feeling that we ever find in Catherine, except in her relations with her grandchildren and her dogs. Patiomkin was of an age to take his position philosophically when his two years of intimate relationship were over, and he remained her favourite minister. From first to last it is calculated that he cost her about twenty-five million dollars.

After Patiomkin there was a period of what one is almost tempted to call promiscuity. Man after man was lodged for a brief period in the luxurious chambers near Catherine's room, and any handsome young officer felt that promotion lay within his power. Stories are told of ambitious young men persistently mistaking their rooms and of Catherine maternally sending them home for correction. No young soldier of athletic build and fair face knew when he would be drafted to the well-known suite, and find a preliminary present of 50,000 dollars in gold in his cabinet. For the closer details of his initiation I must refer the reader to Waliszewski's "Roman d'une Impératrice." In 1780 Lanskoi seemed to have taken firmer root, but he died in Catherine's arms in the same year. Jermoloff succeeded him, and in 1792, when Catherine was sixty-three years old, she adopted her last and strangest lover, Plato Zuboff, a handsome youth of twenty-two. On this series of mere ministers to her pleasure Catherine spent a sum which is estimated at more than forty million dollars. That was a national scandal and entirely unworthy of her character.

It is curious that in other respects Catherine had a great regard for propriety. None dared repeat in her presence the kind of story or verse that would have pleased Peter the Great, and she discharged several officials for loose conduct. She also forbade mixed bathing; though she allowed artists to enter the women's baths. She was sober in eating and drinking. The chief luxury of her plain table was boiled beef with salted cucumbers, and until her later years, when she took a little wine, she generally drank water coloured with a little gooseberry-juice. She knew well, however, that in other parts of her palace her favourites were enjoying the most luxurious banquets, and she never checked their criminal waste. Her own son, Bobrinski, whom she seems to have regarded with indifference, continually outran his generous income and contracted heavy debts. She virtually exiled him to the provinces. It was reserved for her lovers to riot as they pleased; that is to say, as far as money was concerned, for she had the strictest guard kept upon their conduct.

With all her strength of will and tireless energy she loved social intercourse of the liveliest description. She would play with children, especially her grandchildren, for hours, and she had not the least affectation of haughtiness. Although she never visited her nobles, she was just as reluctant to receive the ceremonious and tedious visits of foreign sovereigns. To her smiling favourites she responded, as we saw, with an almost criminal generosity. When Potiamkin's niece married, she gave her half a million dollars, though her uncle had already been enriched beyond any man in Russia; and she gave the same sum to the bridegroom to pay his debts. When, on the other hand, she wanted some difficult work done, especially by her commanders, she had a persuasiveness that none could resist. Scores of times her mingled pleading

THE ROMANCE OF THE ROMANOFFS

and driving induced her armies to do what seemed to her generals impossible.

She had occasional flashes of temper, but her quick humour seized upon this defect and helped her to control it. This other, occasional self she called "my cousin," and she watched it carefully. Normally her good nature was remarkable, and one could give three anecdotes in illustration of it for every anecdote that refers to her irregularities. She rose at five or six every morning, and would often light the fire herself. One morning, when she had done this, she heard shrieks and curses up the chimney, and realised that a sweep was at work in it. She hastily put out her fire and asked the man's pardon. On another occasion it occurred to her to ask, during a long drive, if the coachman and servants had dined. She learned that they had not, and she held up the carriage while they did so. When she heard that a lady she liked was undergoing a dangerous delivery, she had herself driven to the house, and she put on an apron and assisted the midwife. If her pen became bad, she would (or did in one case) scribble on and tell her correspondent that she had not courage to trouble a valet to bring a new one. On one occasion she went out of her room to find a valet for that purpose. She found him playing cards, and she took his hand while he ran for a pen. But perhaps the best anecdote is that which tells of one of her secretaries whom she overheard saying, after she had angrily scolded an ambassador: "What a pity she loses her temper." He was summoned to her room, and in an agony of apprehension he fell upon his knees. Catherine handed him a diamond snuff-box and quietly advised him in future to take a pinch when he was tempted to give useful advice to his sovereign.

This geniality was in her later years somewhat soured. The first cause of the change was the French Revolution; the second was the unfortunate development of her son Paul. A short consideration of these two points will form a useful introduction to the change which, with the nineteenth century, comes over the rule of the Romanoffs.

That humanitarian zeal with which Catherine sought to reform her country, and which she was careful to communicate to the grandson Alexander whom she reared for the throne, was plainly due to the influence of the French philosophers. If, like modern Europe, she learned irreligion from them, she also, like the modern world, learned the elementary lesson of the rights of man. She introduced tolerance into Russia. That she sheltered the Jesuits, when even the Pope sought to extinguish them, was not wholly a matter of toleration. "Scoundrels" as they were (to use her own genial description), they helped her to keep Poland quiet. But she believed in toleration, and she believed that the state of the mass of the people was a reproach to

THE ROMANCE OF THE ROMANOFFS

any right-minded monarch. Peter's reforms had had a utilitarian basis: Catherine's were humanitarian, learned from the French humanitarians.

But the dark development of the Revolution turned her zeal for France and democracy into hatred. In 1791 she wrote that if the Revolution succeeded it would be as bad for Europe as if Dchingis Khan had come to life again. In 1793, when she heard of the execution of the king, she wrote: "The very name of the French must be exterminated." She proposed that all the Protestant nations should embrace the Greek religion "in order to preserve themselves from the irreligious, immoral, anarchic, scoundrelly, and diabolical pest, the enemy of God and of thrones; it alone is apostolic and truly Christian." We see the new Russia already foreshadowed: a Russia fighting western ideas in the name of sound ideals. But Catherine took no action beyond controlling the importation of French literature. Even in that she showed her old personality. She read the Parisian journal, the *Moniteur,* herself before she allowed it to circulate. One day she found herself described in it as "the Messalina of the North." "That's my business," she said; and she allowed the issue to pass.

The second source of annoyance was her son Paul. It seems—though the point is disputed—that from the first she was cold to him (a fair indication that he was Peter's son), and to her grief he grew up into a counterpart, in some respects, of Peter. It is said that she one day learned that he asked why his mother had killed his father and occupied the throne. He visited Frederick at Berlin against her wish, and he married a German princess, the Princess of Hesse, whom she disliked. This lady died in 1776, and he then married another German princess, the Princess of Württemberg. He was thoroughly German, flattered and duped by Frederick. "Russia will become a province of Prussia when I am dead," Catherine sighed.

In 1781 she sent the pair on a tour of Europe. "The Count and Countess du Nord," as they styled themselves, had a magnificent reception at Paris, which made little impression on Paul, and a fresh grievance awaited them on their return. Their sons, the little grand Dukes Alexander and Constantine, had been removed by the Tsarina for education, and she declined to give them up. The Prince and his wife had to live apart, and Paul brooded darkly over every feature of his mother's conduct. He had the Romanoff taint in a form not unlike that we find in Peter III, except as regards drink and coarseness. He was moody, irritable, sensitive, suspicious, and obstinate. He quarrelled with every good man, and as a result had about him a circle of dissembling adventurers. Some said that he was epileptic; others that he took drugs. It is said that when he was at Vienna an actor refused

THE ROMANCE OF THE ROMANOFFS

to play Hamlet, observing that one Hamlet was enough.

Such a man readily accepted the rumour that Catherine intended to disinherit him and pass on the crown to his elder son. She kept him out of affairs, and, although he fancied himself a soldier and, like Peter, brooded over dreams of military reform, she kept him out of the war. He retorted with pungent criticisms of her young lovers; and they insolently repaid him. "Have I said something silly?" Zuboff asked one day when Paul expressed approval of what he had said.

It is believed that if Catherine had lived six months longer, Paul would have been excluded from the succession. The Grand Duke Alexander, his eldest son, was now a fine and promising youth of twenty. Catherine had taken minute pains with his education, and even with the choice of a bride for him. Eleven German princesses were invited to St. Petersburg, and sent away disappointed, before the young Princess of Baden-Durlach was selected. The parents were not consulted. Everybody expected that Alexander would succeed his grandmother; indeed it was rumoured that the decree was already composed and would be published on January 1st, 1797.

And on November 17th, 1796, Catherine died suddenly of apoplexy. There seems little doubt that the cynical sensuality of her seventh decade of life destroyed her strong constitution. I say cynical, not that she was ordinarily cynical, but because there seems to be in her later conduct a somewhat cynical defiance of moral and religious traditions. This was weakness rather than strength; the same weakness which squandered forty million dollars upon lovers when the national treasury had to be replenished by extortion. Her mind was greater than her character; her achievements were greater than both. Russia—the mighty Russian people—was still chained in the dungeon of mediævalism. But Catherine, the German who divested herself of Germanism—"Take out the last drop of German blood from my veins," she said to her physician —the pupil of the French humanitarians, impressed the fact upon the Romanoffs that they ruled a semi-civilised world.

CHAPTER XII

IN THE DAYS OF NAPOLEON

THE story of the Romanoffs has three phases. The first is the preparation, when the primitive democracy of the Slavs is slowly destroyed and the people are enslaved to an autocracy. The second, and longest, phase is the enjoyment of power by the Romanoffs: the succession of brutal or genial, strong or weak, merry or pious sovereigns whom the accident of birth or the red hand of revolution raises to the throne. A certain nervous instability runs through nearly the whole series, but it is almost invariably expressed in a determination to enjoy—to kill, to drink, to love, to spend, to seize territory, to use power for self-gratification. In Peter the Great we find a glimmer, amidst the old disorder, of a new day. In Catherine the Great it revives and grows. Now the middle phase is over. We enter upon a period of grave and sober-living monarchs, at first bent upon the reform of their people, according to their ideals, then struggling in fear against the people they have awakened from a long slumber.

IN THE DAYS OF NAPOLEON

The reign of Paul I is merely a dark episode between the second and the third phase. He was now forty-two years old: a short, ugly, bald, sour-tempered man, of diseased nerves. He hardly concealed his joy as he hastened to the throne and strove to obliterate the memory of his great mother. If she must have an imperial funeral, his martyred father shall have one also. He digs up the corpse, or what is left of it after thirty-four years, puts it in a magnificent coffin, and makes the survivors of the conspiracy of 1762 walk humbly behind it, before they are exiled. St. Petersburg is still a land of rumours, and we do not know precisely what form his mad idea took. Some say that there was body enough left to seat in the throne; some say that the skull was put upon the altar and crowned with a superb diadem; some say that only the boots and a few fragments of Peter III were found. Whatever there was received an imperial funeral; and the bones of Potiamkin were dug up and cast into a ditch. The usual golden shower descended upon the new brood of favourites.

Then Paul began to enforce his grand schemes of military reform—and alienate the army. They must abandon those new and serviceable uniforms which Potiamkin had given them. They must return to powdered hair and pigtails. Paul went along the line, on parade, and used his cane freely. Old General Suvoroff grumbled, and was banished;

though he had to be recalled when war broke out. A regiment one day threw Paul into one of his hurricanes of rage. "March—to Siberia," he thundered; and they marched, but were stopped on the way. Everything must be done on the German model. Anything that reminded him of France was anathema. More than 12,000 people were exiled or imprisoned in four years, generally for trivial offences. He made some useful changes, but so many that were petty and irritating that men thought him insane. He was, in fact, on the road to insanity. He suffered from insomnia, and took opium. People fled at his approach.

Paul sincerely wanted peace, but the French were overrunning Europe, and he joined forces with Austria against them. Austria co-operated so badly that his army, ably led by Suvoroff, had to retreat disastrously. Bonaparte watched him astutely, and bribed his chief ministers. Next England irritated him. Like Catherine, he challenged England's right to search neutral vessels, and, whereas England kept its Russian prisoners, Bonaparte sent home, neatly dressed and armed, those that had been taken by France. When England went on to take Malta, Bonaparte had an easy victim. Paul had become grand master of the Order of St. John of Jerusalem, and he considered that this gave him a special interest in Malta.

At the beginning of 1801 Paul was pledged to

IN THE DAYS OF NAPOLEON

France and set about the formation of a league against England. And on March 24th, after a gloomy reign of four and a half years, Paul met the end he had expected. He had heavily fortified the Mikhailovski Palace, in which he lived, but about midnight (March 23-24) Count Zuboff, Count Pahlen, General Bennigsen, and a few others entered his chamber, roused him, and invited him to abdicate. He refused, and it is presumed that a scuffle followed. It is at least certain that Paul was strangled. It was officially announced that Paul died of "apoplexy." "Isn't it time they invented a new disease in Russia?" said Talleyrand when he heard. Napoleon was furious.

Alexander I lay upon his bed, dressed, when Count Zuboff rushed in to say that "all was over." He started, but he was at once addressed as Emperor and could not misunderstand. He had agreed to the enforcement of his father's abdication, but had assuredly done no more. Whether he had looked beyond or no we cannot say, but Alexander was a high-minded man, a new type of Romanoff. While they talked, Paul's widow came and heard the news. She shrieked that she was Empress, and begged the soldiers to support her rights. There was a second horrible scene in the darkness of that winter night. They drew her away, and, when the day broke, St. Petersburg burst into open and enthusiastic rejoicing, such as Romans had shown at the death of Domitian, that the gloomy and misguided Paul had gone the way of so many Tsars and princes. Strangers embraced in the streets. There was no trial, but those who had been in the plot were leniently removed.

Alexander I, the monarch who opens the new phase, came to the throne with large and vague and lofty ideals. Not only should Russia become happy and prosperous under his benevolent despotism, but all Europe should be illumined. He averted the threatened war with England, which had sent a fleet to the Baltic, and reaffirmed the friendship with Napoleon. His new minister of foreign affairs, Kotchubey, agreed with him. Russia must be kept clear of the entanglement of war and concentrate upon internal reform. Kotchubey had soon to give place to the Pole Czartoryski, who more sincerely shared Alexander's romantic idealism. The Tsar of Russia was to inaugurate "a new era of justice and right" for the whole of Europe. An envoy was sent to London to propose —there is nothing new under the sun—a sort of League to Enforce Peace. England and Russia, the two powers which desired no further territory, were to form its nucleus. Other Powers might join.

One hears plainly the echo of the French humanitarians and the English whom they inspired. But how was the league to enforce peace upon France?

IN THE DAYS OF NAPOLEON

Russia moved slowly toward war. In 1804 the Duc d'Enghien was murdered, and Alexander was outraged. He came to an agreement with England to chastise Napoleon: only—as far as Alexander was concerned—for his monstrous breaches of international law. Napoleon became Emperor and King of Italy, and Alexander was further outraged. Kings were born, not made. In 1805 he joined the Austrians on the battle-fields of Italy.

The story of Alexander I, the monarch who was going to impose peace upon a foolish and distracted world, is one long story of wars, and it does not enter into the scheme of this book to describe wars. How far Alexander was to blame for the entry of his country into the struggle against Napoleon, or into Napoleon's struggle against England, is a point on which opinions differ. His entire change of attitude—from neutrality to war against France, then to friendship with Napoleon, then back to the English alliance—annoyed his ministers and people, and lays him open to a charge of nervous instability. Such a charge he would have rebutted with warmth and astonishment. His portrait is familiar: a smooth-faced, dignified man, reflecting righteousness in every feature. He would have given a hundred reasons for each change in his policy. We will notice these and the issues of his wars briefly, before we consider his personality and his domestic work.

THE ROMANCE OF THE ROMANOFFS

His first war ended in the historic rout of Austerlitz (1805), and his optimism was sadly clouded. But when his mind was fixed upon what he regarded as a righteous cause, he could be obstinate. Prussia and Austria came to terms with France, and Alexander's advisers were for doing the same, but he refused. He entered the new coalition (Russia, Prussia, Sweden, and England). Napoleon smote the Prussians at Jena, frightened the Swedes into peace, and inflicted appalling losses upon the Russians at Eylau. Alexander would not desist. He saw the King of Prussia and swore eternal alliance, and Napoleon overran Poland (1806-7). But Napoleon understood the naïve mind of the Tsar, and knew that he was angry at the remissness of England in supporting him. Before long he met Alexander on a raft in the middle of the Niemen, and the charm of his manner and righteousness of his proposals won the large heart of the Tsar; besides that Napoleon cleverly conveyed to his mind the impression that he thought seriously of choosing Alexander's sister Anna as his second wife. At the entreaty of his new friend Napoleon spared the sovereignty of Frederick William of Prussia, though he relieved him of his Polish gains and turned Poland into a Duchy of Warsaw.

Kornilov, the ablest of recent Russian historians, maintains that Alexander was not duped. He wanted time, and played his cards skilfully. It is not easy to credit Alexander with such subtlety; and there are those who think that Alexander sacrificed his honour and the interest of his country. He was to break with England, when all St. Petersburg had been educated to admire England, and he was *not* to receive Constantinople as his reward. St. Petersburg was thoroughly angry at the change of policy, and Alexander had to change his ministers. The Russian ambassador at Paris secured a confidential document in which Napoleon declared that Russia was the natural ally of Austria and inevitable enemy of France. Still Alexander persisted, though he was not a very useful ally. He did, it is true, make war upon Sweden because it would not place an embargo on British ships; but out of that war he got the remainder of Finland, with 900,000 souls, for Russia.

The two Emperors met again at Erfurt in 1810. Napoleon had there a mighty gathering of his royal vassals, partly to impress Alexander, and he seemed to succeed. In later years, however, Napoleon himself considered that Alexander was fooling him. He said that the Tsar had "the duplicity of a Byzantine Greek." Napoleon was a judge of duplicity, but I prefer to believe in the simple-mindedness of Alexander, and do not even see ground to seek psychological explanations of his vacillations. He respected to the end the genius of Napoleon, but the alliance was hollow, and in the next year the causes of quarrel multiplied. Napoleon said no more about the Tsarevna Anna: he married an Austrian. He seemed anxious to turn Poland into a French province. On the other hand, Napoleon complained that his ally spoiled his continental blockade against England, and put heavy duties on French wine. Alexander, pushed by intriguers, got rid of his ablest minister, Speranski, who was pro-French, made peace with Turkey and Sweden, and at length entered into an alliance with England and Sweden. Both Emperors now massed their troops at the frontier and joined them.

Napoleon's famous Russian campaign of 1812 need not be described here. The Poles hailed him as a deliverer, and he ran on until the continuous retreat of the Russians and the appalling desolation they created as they retreated made him uneasy. It was Alexander's generals who were responsible for that strategy. The Tsar himself expressed impatience. At length, on September 15th, Napoleon gazed upon the golden roofs of Moscow and felt that the end was in sight. How could Russia yield its ancient capital and not acknowledge defeat? The next day began the historic fire of Moscow, already evacuated by its population. Whether or no General Rostopchin ordered the fire, the Tsar was not privy to it. He wept when he heard of the tragedy. But it was a

The Red Square, Church of St. Basil and Redeemer Gate, Moscow

IN THE DAYS OF NAPOLEON

tragedy for Napoleon also. The grip of winter soon began to close upon the desolated land. The Tsar was whipping up his weary people with manifests after manifests, imploring them to break the tyrant and help to take "the blessings of liberty" to other nations. We shall see presently that at this period he became almost fanatically religious.

At the head of his inspirited troops—he would, he said, not again leave his armies to unenterprising generals, who could only retreat—Alexander followed the pale and emaciated remnant of Napoleon's "grand army" across the corpse-strewn wastes. Then came Leipsic, the first nail in Napoleon's coffin. The Austrian statesman Metternich saw the Tsar at Frankfort, and was for moderation in victory. On to Paris, said the Tsar; and the encircling movement pushed the French gradually in toward their capital. He was at Paris for the end, and he spent a few weeks in London before he returned to receive a magnificent, and not unmerited, ovation at St. Petersburg.

Alexander went himself to Vienna for the Congress which was to settle the map of Europe. Again one must glance at his portrait to imagine him at Vienna. He was the modest arbiter of the destinies of Europe, the conqueror of Napoleon. Behind the scenes, however, was a limping diplomatist named Talleyrand, who had returned to office with Louis XVIII, and he and Metternich and

THE ROMANCE OF THE ROMANOFFS

Castlereagh ruled. Against Alexander's wish Poland was again divided, only Cracow and its district receiving a republican independence. Napoleon suspended their intrigues for a season by his dramatic return, but after Waterloo the monarchs and statesmen met again at Paris to complete their work.

Here the personality of Alexander attracted considerable, and not very flattering, attention, and we may linger over one of the last bits of personal romance—of very chaste romance—in the story of the Romanoffs. In the house adjoining his hotel, and connected with it, Alexander established a lady who was soon known to all Paris. This was the Baroness Barbara Juliana von Krüdener. In her youth Juliana had been a fascinating and gay lady, of Prussian birth, who had virtually deserted her elderly and prosy German baron for a French officer. Her nerves deteriorated with her charms, and in 1804, her fortieth year, she had been very seriously converted. A gentleman who was paying court to her had fallen dead at her feet. Wandering to and fro in a state of extreme nervousness, she came into touch with the Moravian Brethren and "got religion." The long war and comprehensive disturbance of Europe had led to remarkable eruptions of mysticism. Napoleon was anti-Christ: the end of the world was at hand. Prophets arose in every German village; and Juliana eagerly sought them. She became convinced that it was her mission to preach the millennium which was to precede the end.

In 1814 she met the Tsarina Elizabeth at Baden, and through her she attempted to reach the Tsar. Alexander refused for some time to see her, but he in turn went to Baden in 1815 and he allowed her to call. She found him in a receptive mood. Since the burning of Moscow he had spent much time over the Scriptures, and he was at this moment brooding over the open page, seeking in vain the remedy of his mysterious restlessness. Juliana harangued him, stormily, for three hours, and captured him. He brought her to Paris, put her in the house next his own, and attended her prayer-meetings. Nobles and famous writers of Paris attended. Over all the horrors of the past men saw dawning the glory of a new religious epoch.

All this has more historical and practical import than may be imagined. Alexander invented a "Holy Alliance" of monarchs to put into force the lofty moral tenets of the new mysticism. He showed the Baroness one day—she annoyed him afterwards by claiming that she had written it—the draft of a manifest of the Alliance. In three short articles the royal signatories would bind themselves thenceforward to be guided, in domestic and foreign policy, by "the precepts of that holy religion [Christianity], namely, the precepts of Justice, Charity, and Peace." The whole document breathed the spiritual exaltation in which the Tsar was at the time. The King of Prussia signed it without wincing—to oblige his friend. Francis of Austria, very pious, but taught by the Jesuits to suspect heresy everywhere, consulted Metternich, who said it was a harmless piece of folly. He signed it. Castlereagh advised the English Prince Regent that it was a piece of sublime mysticism and nonsense; and the gay Regent accepted it in principle, without signing it, and assured the Tsar that he would follow its "sacred maxims." The Pope refused to sign.

The practical importance of the matter is that the Holy Alliance became, in effect, an alliance for the bloody suppression of democracy and enlightenment, and the charter drawn up by Alexander became the code of his persecuting successors and their nationalist supporters. Western Christianity became faithless; it compromised with democracy, with science, with liberalism. So the "holy religion" must be the uncompromising Church of Russia, with its profound reverence for autocracy and its hostility to enlightenment.

Alexander became sensitive that his association with the Baroness made him seem rather ridiculous. He got rid of her, and from that time maintained only a coldly polite correspondence. The astute Metternich gained increasing influence over him,

IN THE DAYS OF NAPOLEON

and there was no vagueness about Metternich. Kings must guard their crowns, and ministers their portfolios, against anybody—adventurers or democracies—who wanted them. When the Greeks rose against Turkey in 1821 the Baroness rushed to St. Petersburg and urged her pupil to take up "the holy war." Metternich told him that the situation was that the Greeks had rebelled against their lawful sovereign, the Sultan. So Alexander would not send a gun to aid either the Slav or Greek victims of the terrible Turk. The whole Russian nation opposed him. When a great flood brought tragedy upon St. Petersburg in 1824, men said that God was punishing the Tsar. He was troubled, but did nothing. Justice, Charity, and Peace he still loved; but he would lend no aid to insurrection. For the remainder of his life he defended the absolute divine right of kings and assisted in attempting to retard the birth of modernism.

The Poles felt his gradual deterioration. Russian Poland was at first, with a show of generosity, converted into an autonomous kingdom under the Russian crown. Alexander was the king; though the Poles had their old flag with the white eagle. The Grand Duke Constantine was commander of the army; though it was a Polish army. An officer of Napoleon's army was made Viceroy, and a general amnesty was granted. But Warsaw was far away, and the harsh Constantine and the Tsar's more reactionary ministers ruled it. The Diet was soon left in abeyance, and the promises of reform unfulfilled. The Poles angrily muttered that they had been duped, and secret societies spread, with a result which we shall see later.

But we are passing to Alexander's last phase, the phase of reaction, without having considered the reforms which came of his early humanitarian zeal. He had, we saw, been educated (in part) by humanitarians like La Harpe, imbued with the French spirit. Catherine herself had, as I said, leaned to reaction, and let her reforms droop, in her later years; and the interlude of Paul's reign had been thoroughly bad. Yet Alexander came to the throne with a magnificent resolution to reform Russia. He was dreamy by temperament, and he had neither the positive knowledge nor the quality of painstaking perseverance which were necessary to construct a detailed scheme of reform for so comprehensively backward a country. However, he appointed a Committee of Reform, and he followed its deliberations with keen interest.

During many years, especially from 1807-1812, Alexander had for this work the splendid ability and devotion of a remarkably enlightened and democratic statesman named Speranski. Professor Kornilov regards him as "one of the most remarkable statesmen in all Russian history." He was the son of an obscure priest, a child of the people; and his large mind and great capacity for detail enabled him to give definite shape to the Tsar's vague dreams of justice. He not only studied the new democratic constitution of the United States, of which the Tsar obtained a copy from Washington, but he followed Napoleon's constructive work with much sympathy and admiration. To Speranski the Tsar owed the great scheme of reform which at first he made some effort to impose upon Russia. It, unhappily, remained for the most part a paper-scheme. Years afterwards, in 1830, the rebellious Poles found a copy of Speranski's liberal constitution and printed it, but Nicholas I emphatically suppressed it.

The first task was to reform the central part of the administration, which was chaotic. Eight ministries were created, and, although the Tsar made the inevitable blunder of appointing favourites rather than competent men in some cases, the change helped to create a more effective machine. The heads of the departments were to form a cabinet, or Council of Ministers, responsible to the Emperor, and below them the administrative structure went down gradually as far as the Mir, or village-council. The legislative machinery also began with the Mir, and ended with the Duma, or national council, from which there could be an appeal to the Imperial Council. The administration of justice was to begin in the village and end in a reconstituted Senate; and Speranski sketched a new code of laws on the model of the Code Napoleon.

Of this great scheme very little was carried out. The reformed Senate found most of its proposals opposed by the Imperial Council, and the Tsar himself, who was to be guided by it, chafed when it did not fall in with his wishes, and often issued ukases in defiance of the opinion of the majority. The new code of laws was put upon the shelf, and remained there until the reign of Nicholas I. The hierarchy of popular councils was not created. Alexander seemed to shrink from the logical consequences of his "sacred maxims" when they were drawn out on paper by a practical statesman, and he lent too ready an ear to the reactionaries. As his piety increased, the conservatives found it convenient to represent to him that these progressive ideas were associated with atheism and revolt. The familiar type of political adventurer, a man named Arakcheeff, appeared at court and secured wealth and power. This man and his associates suggested to Alexander, in 1812, that Speranski was promoting Freemasonry and subversive ideas, and the great statesman—a man so far from Voltaireanism that he had translated "The Imitation of Christ" into Russian—had to go. The Tsar wept maudlin tears while he dismissed him.

The ministry of education, or of National Enlightenment, whose task was vital to the reform of the country, seemed to make greater progress. Alexander entrusted it to his mother's educational adviser, Count Tzadovski, and his own tutor Muravieff. Afterwards it was controlled by Prince Golitzin, a follower of the new mysticism, but a serious and liberal statesman. He was a patron of the Protestant Bible Society, which Alexander permitted to open premises in St. Petersburg in 1812. Alexander found from two to three million rubles a year for the education department, and paid out of his own purse for the translation of western works. Students were sent abroad for pedagogical training, and after a time training-colleges were established in Russia. Three new universities (Dorpat, Kazan, and Kharkoff) were founded, and these and the older universities were to become central points in a scheme of enlightenment for the various districts of Russia.

It is, however, usual to exaggerate the work done. We have already heard much about the reforms of various rulers—of Philaret, of Peter I, of Elizabeth, and of Catherine—but the fact remains that far more than ninety per cent of the Russian people were still illiterate and densely ignorant at the death of Alexander, and, although we shall hear of further reforms, at least eighty-five per cent of the Russian people were illiterate at the beginning of the twentieth century. The sum provided for education was ludicrously insufficient for the task, and the opposition was considerable. Merchants grumbled that they must pay for the teaching of something more than reading, writing, and arithmetic; the bulk of the nobles wanted only a military education for their sons. In all about 200 higher schools (with classes of Latin and Greek) and 2,000 elementary schools were founded: barely enough to educate the five per cent of the population which was attracted to new ideas. The work, like all the other reforms, languished in Alexander's later years, and was deliberately checked, in the interest of the dynasty, by his successor.

The next great problem was the emancipation of the serfs, and here the Tsar's vacillation between his sentiments of benevolence and his vague perception that they threatened the aristocratic system is more apparent than ever. Catherine had had the same experience. She had spoken of liberty and equality; and she had bestowed upon her favourites hundreds of thousands of serfs who would, she must have known, be regarded and treated as cattle. The restriction of the freedom of the peasant, by which Godunoff had converted him into a serf, really handed over his freedom to the higher authorities or put it into the hand of the landowner. When a peasant wished to move, he might secure permission from his lord by a payment of money.

IN THE DAYS OF NAPOLEON

When a noble obtained a grant of new lands he had to buy, or obtain by favour, a great batch of serfs to work it. In practice the wealthy landowners bought and sold the population just as cotton-planters then did in America, and the serfs were generally treated with brutality.

Nearly every other country in Europe had long since abolished serfdom, and Alexander saw clearly enough how inconsistent the institution was with his "sacred maxims." He discussed with his friends this "barbarous" traffic in human beings, and we can understand how they assisted him to salve his conscience. Reform must be gradual; an evil which was centuries old, and rooted in the very structure of Russian society, could not be cured in a day. In other words, the great sacrifice, which justice demanded, must be thrown upon a later generation. Alexander expended his zeal upon small alleviations of the sufferings of the serfs. He forbade the masters to break up families, or to enforce marriage upon reluctant serfs. He restricted the right of punishment, opened the courts to the serf, and set aside large sums for the emancipation of batches of serfs. He had a pamphlet published in which owners were urged to treat the serfs humanely and promote emancipation. So much was done under pressure of the humanitarians, but it was only a trifling mitigation of the worst evil of mediæval Russia, and the new regulations were not properly enforced. Russia was the land of the wealthy. The millions of descendants of the original free Slavs must toil on in squalor and ignorance. The day of reckoning was still to come.

Arakcheeff tried an experiment in this connection which was bitterly resented. He induced the Tsar to settle regiments of soldiers, with their families, on the crown-lands, in military colonies. They were to be special breeding grounds for recruits, and were to spread amongst the peasants the spirit of military discipline. They were so carefully organised—for Arakcheeff had ability—that even the mother was provided with a set of rules which she must hang beside the holy ikons. The peasants hated the innovation, and on Arakcheeff's own estate they rebelled and killed his mistress, who ruled them with the brutality that he encouraged. The institution was afterward suffered to decay.

In the fiscal world, which was but another section of the Augean stable of the Russian system, Alexander set out to make enlightened reforms, and ended in the usual listlessness. The treasury had long been artificially filled by the excessive creation of paper-money. Alexander recalled a large proportion of it, but the strain of the war put an end to this reform. An Imperial Bank was founded, a sinking fund was started, and it was decided to publish an annual budget. It was proposed, and partly attempted, to relieve the duty on the importation of raw materials and impose heavy duties on luxuries. At the same time the abandonment of Catherine's extravagance at court relieved the exchequer. These reforms were, like the others, a comparatively slight mitigation of a great evil, and were in Alexander's later years suffered to droop.

In fine one must mention prison-reform, though the state of Russian jails decades later does not dispose us to attach much importance to it. During Alexander's earlier years, we saw, there was at St. Petersburg a great regard for English ideas, and at that time England was producing many humanitarians. Robert Owen was then elaborating his comprehensive and advanced schemes of reform, from the betterment of schools and prisons to the substitution of arbitration for war. It is the enfeebled echo of these liberal English ideas, and of American and French ideas, that we find in the Russian schemes. One of the English prison-reformers, Mr. Venning, asked permission to visit the Russian jails. The Tsar, who was still in his early humanitarian fervour, gladly assented, and asked Venning to make a report to him on what he saw. As a result a Society for the Welfare of Prisoners was founded at St. Petersburg, and afterwards at Moscow.

These liberal ideas represent, it must be understood, the early attitude of the Emperor. After the fall of Speranski in 1812, and especially after the Tsar's close association with Metternich in 1814, Alexander passed slowly from a state of nebulous zeal for Charity and Justice to an attitude of positive reaction, tempered by a faint lingering glow of his early dreams. Metternich persuaded him that the real struggle of light and darkness was the struggle of the enlightened monarchies against these democratic and "atheistic" emanations from the smothered volcano of the French Revolution. In private he cynically observed to his friends: "I have the Tsar safely at anchor." The humanitarian ideas on which the United States had been set up, and the early and sane part of the French Revolution had been based, remained in the mind of Europe. They threatened the restored monarchies, which reverted to mediæval ideas of their power, and the terrible conflict which fills the first half of the nineteenth century in Europe began long before the death of Alexander. It is to his credit that he recognised the blunders and crimes of his fellow-monarchs and never entirely sacrificed his early ideals.

But the sinister Arakcheeff and the dreamy Golitzin spoiled the efforts of Speranski. Golitzin introduced to the Tsar a "converted atheist" named Magnitski, an abominable adventurer, and the man was put in control of the universities. The higher teaching was reduced to a comedy. Golitzin himself was too liberal and cultivated for the plotters, and Admiral Shishkoff replaced him in charge of the ministry of National Enlightenment. Shishkoff hated liberalism, and would suffer no education that did not strengthen in the pupils' mind a spirit of blind subservience to the Church and the autocracy. A third power among the reactionary forces was the Novgorod abbot, Photi, a zealot of the old type who gathered about him a crowd of aristocratic women and worked through them. Professors who had any tincture of liberalism were now expelled from the schools. Some of the new schools were suffered to disappear, and in all, lower and higher, the teaching was rendered ridiculous by the fierce determination to protect the pupils' respect for his pastors and masters. Political economy and the new discoveries of science were rigorously banned. The Russophile school was established; the fight against enlightenment was inaugurated.

But enlightenment could no more be suppressed in Russia than in Italy, Spain, Portugal, and France, where the Papacy and the restored monarchs used the old bludgeons against it. A large part of the nobles was, as in France before the Revolution, imbued with the new ideas; and the economic and other reforms were creating a middle class which, as in England, gave many recruits to the humanitarian cause. Students, teachers, writers, medical and other professional men joined the emancipated nobles. The army of light began slowly to gather round its various banners and face the army of darkness. As repression increased, the many societies and liberal journals were merely driven underground and their rhetoric became more fiery. There were "unions" for everything of an advanced nature. In obscure clubs young men began to talk even of a Russian Republic. The Tsar's refusal to help the Slav and Greek rebels against the Turk increased the anger of the liberals and gave them a basis in the popular mind.

By the year 1824 Alexander had fallen into so morbid a state that he spoke of resigning. He wept over his Bible and wondered if his sins were not the curse of Russia. Even his domestic life was a burden. He had married a Princess of Baden, and her lack of good looks was not redeemed by any other charm except the cold adornments of virtue and piety. She dressed dowdily, and she generally presented at his board a face as melancholy as her creed. For many years Alexander had lived apart from her, and he had no children. The genial dignity and self-esteem of his earlier years broke down altogether. His next brother, Constantine, had made a morganatic marriage, and forfeited the throne, and Alexander distrusted the third brother, Nicholas. Alexander

IN THE DAYS OF NAPOLEON

slowly and sadly drifted toward the grave. His courtiers discovered a plot against the autocracy, but he would do nothing. He died on December 1st, 1825: a high-minded, well-meaning man, too little endowed in intellect and strength of will to solve the mighty problems which were raised by his own ideals.

CHAPTER XIII

THE FIGHT AGAINST LIBERALISM

ON an earlier page I remarked that the element of romance passed out of the story of the Romanoffs with the last lovers of Catherine and the murder of Paul. This is true of what we may call personal romance, but it will have been apparent that a larger, impersonal romance now opens. Not individual Romanoffs, but the Romanoff dynasty, must fight for existence. Life at court is now too earnest for bibulous companions of monarchs, and handsome lovers of queens, and plots of the anteroom. The comedy is over; if one may call a comedy the enthronement of a selfish and profligate monarchy upon the poverty and ignorance of millions of human beings. The play now assumes the sombre note of tragedy. The people, represented by a few of the educated few, begin to awaken and claim their rights. The rest of the story is a ghastly record of the efforts of the Romanoffs to prevent the spread of that awakening.

Nicholas I, who succeeded Alexander, represents the struggle of the dynasty in a form which

THE FIGHT AGAINST LIBERALISM

might be reconciled with conscience. He differed materially from Alexander in two respects. First, although he was, like Alexander, moderately endowed in intellect, he had great strength of character and would stubbornly pursue any policy which he adopted. In the second place, that policy was inevitably shaped by the accident that he was born many years after Alexander. The eldest son of Paul I had received his education at a time when Catherine was under the influence of the French humanitarians. Nicholas came to the years of discretion during her second phase, when the Revolution had soured her taste of all things French and liberal. His chief tutor had been a French emigrant, an incompetent teacher and a bitter enemy of liberal ideas. Nicholas had grown up a rough and conceited boy. Later he had had abler teachers, but he had yawned over their lessons. He had in 1817 married a daughter of the King of Prussia, and, like almost all the Romanoffs, he thought a minute acquaintance with military drill the first equipment for life. In spite of hints from Alexander he refused to prepare for the serious task of governing a great nation. By an unfortunate accident his vague despotic mood was at the very opening of his reign hardened into an attitude of fierce hostility to the new culture.

His elder brother Constantine had, as I said, forfeited his right to the throne. He had fallen in love with a charming Polish lady, the Countess Jeannette Grudzinsky, after divorcing his first wife. As no amount of personal charm, not associated with royal blood, fitted a woman to occupy the throne of Elizabeth and Catherine, the Tsar had, in 1822, given him the alternative of losing either the lady or his right to the throne. Constantine had not a regal disposition. He married Jeannette and abdicated the right he had to the throne on the restored principle of inheritance.

Nicholas knew of this abdication, though it was otherwise known only to a few intimate councillors. But he knew that there was much feeling against him in St. Petersburg, and he proceeded diplomatically. He proclaimed Constantine Tsar. Prince Golitzin and others who knew of the abdication begged him to refrain until the Council had opened a certain sealed letter which Alexander had left, but Nicholas persisted and sent word to his brother at Warsaw. Constantine refused the throne, and for several weeks letters went backward and forward. Nicholas was very much attached to his brother, but it is probable that he wanted time to study the threatening situation in St. Petersburg and secure the stability of his throne. He yielded on December 13th, and fixed the following day for the taking of the oath of allegiance.

On the 14th a large body of troops and the customary crowd of citizens assembled in the square,

THE FIGHT AGAINST LIBERALISM

and suddenly the cry "Long Live Constantine" rang from the lips of various companies of the soldiers. "Long Live the Constitution" was also shouted; and it is said that the ignorant troops, who had been told to add this, thought that it was the name of Constantine's Polish wife. Nicholas, who did not lack courage, came out of the palace and endeavoured quietly to convince the soldiers that his brother had abdicated. They repeated their cries, and the nucleus of mutineers began to grow and form a compact body. It is thought that if those who had arranged the plot had had more courage it might have succeeded. But Prince Trubetzkoi, the leader, kept out of sight, and there was no vigorous direction. General Miloradovitch approached the soldiers to reason with them, and was shot. The Metropolitan of St. Petersburg, his golden cross lifted high in the air, next addressed them, and he was contemptuously told to go home and mind his own business. The night was falling, and it was feared that under its cover a serious riot would occur. Nicholas ordered blank firing and, when the rebels jeered, ordered grapeshot; and the rebellion was over.

After the burial of the victims came the inquiry, and it was thorough and protracted. Two hundred and forty were arrested, and they included men of the highest rank in St. Petersburg and many officers of the army. Princes, counts, barons, and generals were on the list of the condemned. The five ringleaders, including two colonels of military distinction, were sentenced to be quartered, but the Tsar commuted the sentence to hanging. The death-sentence had become so unusual in Russia that a bungling amateur made a horrible tragedy of the business; but those five first martyrs of the Russian people met their death with impressive dignity and courage. Thirty-one were sentenced to be beheaded, and were sent to the mines for life. Seventeen were condemned to the mines, and had their sentences changed to twenty years' imprisonment. Others went, with their wives and families, to Siberia or to remote provinces. And Tsar Nicholas I went to Moscow to be crowned.

Nicholas was sufficiently intelligent to realise that this conspiracy of soldiers and nobles and intellectuals was a new thing in the annals of Russia. He had a very candid memorandum drawn up from the subversive literature which was taken with the conspirators, and he carefully studied the condition of Russia as they had seen it. The new Tsar had a type of mind entirely different from that of his brother. He had a clear, robust, and narrow intelligence, unclouded either by mysticism or moral hypocrisy. He seriously considered the evils of the Empire: the corruption of officials, the arrears of payment which led to extortion, the heavy taxes, the parody of justice, the general squalor and igno-

THE FIGHT AGAINST LIBERALISM

rance, the State-monopoly of drink, the shocking condition of the serfs, and so on. These things must be remedied; and they must be remedied by the god-appointed person—the Tsar. That was his attitude. In his Coronation-Manifesto he said:

"The statutes of the land are gradually perfected, the faults corrected, the abuses remedied, not by insolent dreams of destruction, but from above."

The new Tsar was for "true enlightenment." Any other enlightenment, any unauthorised enlightener, must look out.

That was the note of the early part of the reign of Nicholas I. Speranski was brought from his retirement and told to carry out the reforms he had projected. His older code of laws was not passed, but he was directed to codify the existing laws of Russia; which was something. There were not competent lawyers in Russia to ensure the proper administration of justice, and young men were sent abroad to study law. But no youth must go and acquire education abroad for any other purpose. No foreign teachers or tutors must be tolerated any more in Russia. No foreign ideas must be permitted to taint the purity of the docile Russian soul. No noble could remain abroad more than five years, and no commoner more than three years.

A very rigorous and complete censorship was set up. All manuscripts, even the manuscripts of journalistic copy, must be revised before they reached the printer. Any that ventured to recommend the ideas which were in France leading up to the Revolution of 1830, and in England to the Reform Bill of 1832, were suppressed. Intellectual life must concern itself with the native contents of the Russian tradition. It was stifled. Russia was just at the stage of a literary renaissance, but it was directed into this channel, and, as it was mainly artistic, it contrived to thrive on nationalist soil. Pushkin and Gogol wrote their famous stories and poems. Karamsin founded Russian history—of the dynastic type. Young men like Turgenieff, Dostoievski, and Tolstoi began, at the end of the reign, to take up the artistic tradition. The national drama was advanced. But it was all genuinely Russian. The new theologies and philosophies and sciences of the west were banned.

The censorship was moderated a little in 1830, when Prince Lieven, a religious but cultivated man, became minister of education. For a time the anathema was confined to matters which had a plain political import. But after a few years a reactionary succeeded Prince Lieven, and the task of preventing enlightenment was rigorously resumed. The second revolutionary wave was slowly spreading over Europe. The stupid and harsh dynasty of the French kings went forever. The reform of the parliamentary franchise was now won in Eng-

WINTER PALACE, PETROGRAD

THE FIGHT AGAINST LIBERALISM

land. An historic fight for freedom and knowledge was raging in Austria, Italy, Spain, and Portugal.

Everywhere it was this detestable new middle class which was assailing the old traditions. Young men of the working class to-day have little conception in how overwhelming a proportion the champions and martyrs of "the people" in those sanguinary days belonged to the middle class. The task of rulers plainly was to check literature and the university-life, which were manufacturing this intellectual middle class. Literature of a modern kind was entirely suppressed. The universities were watched by the police—the new secret police which Nicholas created as an instrument of the threatened autocracy—and controlled after a time by the clergy. The Slavophile creed was elevated to the rank of a philosophy. Against this bold scheme of human development which the liberals were basing upon the philosophy of Hegel, the "sound" teachers pitted a very plausible static creed. It was, they said, the peculiar gift of the Russian soul to reconcile the jarring elements of life, which in the west created only discord. These new notions of democracy and evolution (which was just emerging from the pit in England) and rationalism only increased the misery of life. Look at the contrast of the restless proletariate of England or France and the Russian peasant! Self-absorption in love, as taught by Russian Christianity, not self-assertion, as taught by religious and political rationalism, was the creed to make people happy.

The influence of the Church was ardently enlisted. Nicholas was sincere—he read a page of the Bible every night to his wife—and liked to have sincere people about him. He got rid of Arakcheeff and the converted atheist Magnitski, and he upheld the abbot Photi. The Bible Society was directed to return to England, and its property was confiscated. The Roman Catholic Church had made progress under the liberal Alexander. It was checked, and its property confiscated. The secret police penetrated study and boudoir in search of traces of heresy. In Poland four and a half million Roman Catholics were "converted" to the Orthodox Church. In Protestant Livonia the Russian priests and officials did almost as they willed. School-children were damped with holy water and oil, and counted members of the Orthodox Church. Presents of money or land settled the hesitating consciences of their parents. The Russian Church supported the autocracy and anathematised culture: all Russians must therefore belong to the Russian Church.

It must not be supposed that this drastic campaign extinguished the light in Russia. It merely compelled men to hide their light underground, or to speak and write with discretion. A sullen and stern fight went on all the time. Once the Catho-

THE FIGHT AGAINST LIBERALISM

lies of Poland and Hungary had tried to shut off Russia from the culture of the west and they had eventually failed. Now the Tsars, who had torn down the barrier, would set up a barrier of their own. It had no greater chance of lasting success, though it did postpone the awakening of Russia. In the end, when a third revolutionary wave spread over Europe, Nicholas doubled his precautions. Not more than three hundred students were allowed at each university. This was "true enlightenment." But a nobler race was rising amidst the densely ignorant mass, and Nicholas I could not crush it.

It may be asked what he did for the honest improvement of the country which he had sincerely regarded as the task of the autocracy. Very little. To educate the mass of the people was, of course, a mischievous delusion in the creed of Nicholas I. The spread of elementary education was either arrested or carefully controlled. Under Speranski's early influence he appointed an official, Count Kisseleff, to look after the eighteen million serfs on the Crown Estates, and the official was a good man. Schools of a kind were established. The filthy and unhealthy habits of the people were partly corrected. In 1842 a serf was enabled by statute to purchase his freedom. In 1848 it was enacted that the serfs of an insolvent landowner might collectively purchase the estate. Nicholas encouraged nobles to free their serfs. Then came the French Revolution of 1848, with its echoes all over Europe, and Nicholas abandoned reform. Even within the limits of his own plan he had rendered insignificant service, in comparison with the task which the papers of the conspirators had impressed on him. The thirty years of his reign were occupied in fighting the light which from all sides now sought to penetrate the darkness of Russia.

The wars which interrupted or accompanied the Emperor's efforts do not properly concern us, but in some features they illustrate his personality and work. On this side also the new morality of the Romanoffs was degenerating rapidly into casuistry. Alexander had sought neither war nor territory. The dynasty was converted from the brutal attitude which had put the quintessence of glory in conquest by the sword. Alexander interfered in European affairs only in the lofty interests of justice and civilisation. Nicholas also was a lover of peace and justice, and on this plea he started, or resumed, the Russian policy of expansion southward which has since cost Europe so much blood.

As is well-known, Nicholas had provocation; indeed, until some other force can secure protection for the weak, it remains an act of chivalry for the strong to do battle for them. That at least was the almost universal sentiment in the earlier half of the nineteenth century, and we saw that the people of

THE FIGHT AGAINST LIBERALISM

St. Petersburg bitterly blamed Alexander for not interfering on behalf of the Greeks. Nicholas at once took up the task that his brother had declined. Greeks and Serbs were trying to throw off the brutal tyranny of the Turk, and the Sultan had sent the most fanatical and least civilised of his soldiers to chastise the insolent Christians. Europe rang with the horror of the massacres, the mutilations, the rapes and burnings. It was assuredly the place of a monarch who was of like creed to the Greeks and of the same blood as the Serbs to demand justice for them, and Nicholas promptly demanded it. He bade the Sultan evacuate the Balkans and grant autonomy to his Christian provinces. England and France were equally moved by the outrages, and not a little jealous of any action of Russia, and the three Powers gave the Sultan an ultimatum. His refusal to comply led to the destruction of his fleet at Navarino in 1828, and Greece won its independence.

It was the beginning of the abominable international jealousy which has so long suffered the Turk to play the savage in Europe. The Sultan knew that Austria was sufficiently jealous of Russia to support him, and he believed that England was in the same frame of mind. He therefore sent a pompous complaint to Russia, and demanded an indemnity. Nicholas, knowing well the jealousy of the other Powers, baffled them by a straightforward inquiry whether he would not be justified in chastising the Turks. He would, he said, seize no territory in Europe, and would be content to reduce the Sultan merely to a decent sense of his duty to his Christian subjects. Austria trimmed in its reply, but England, France, and Prussia consented, and Nicholas led his legions southward. Again I refer to histories of Russia for the details of the eighteen months' war. It ended with the victory of Russia and the Treaty of Adrianople (September 14th, 1829). Moldavia and Wallachia (now Rumania) and Serbia were declared autonomous. The Dardanelles was opened to Russian commerce. Russia secured an indemnity and the right to protect Orthodox Christians in the Ottoman Empire.

In the meantime a new page had opened in the relations of Russia and Poland. The Grand Duke Constantine ruled the kingdom with more force than wisdom, and he begged his brother, who had not been crowned King of Poland, to come and impress the people of Warsaw by that ceremony. Nicholas went, and swore to maintain the constitution which Alexander had granted the Poles in 1818. He made matters worse, however, by his arbitrariness. It was with difficulty that he could be induced to tolerate a service of thanksgiving in the Roman Catholic cathedral; he opened the Diet with a speech in French; and he usurped a func-

THE FIGHT AGAINST LIBERALISM

tion of the Diet in nominating Senators. The discontent of the Poles, who had absorbed western ideas, was greatly increased. It is said that there was a plot to kidnap the Tsar. At all events, the complaints in the Diet became so bitter that he closed it, in violation of the constitution, and the discontent ran to underground conspiracy.

This plot was another element in the autocratic education of Nicholas I and his successors. In July (1830) occurred the second French Revolution, followed by an insurrection at Berlin. Nicholas was so indignant that he thought of declaring war upon France, and he did offer troops to the King of Prussia. But at the end of September he was infuriated to learn that the spirit of revolt had spread to his own kingdom of Poland. Pro-Russians had been massacred, and an attempt had been made to capture the person of the Grand Duke, who had fled to Russia with his few troops. General Chlopicki and the Polish regiments had joined the revolutionaries. A Provisional Government, including Princes Czartoriski and Radziwill, had been established.

In his sternest mood Nicholas sent 120,000 men against the Poles, who hastily closed their intestine differences and gathered an army of 90,000 men. They fought with magnificent bravery, but the superior Russian forces wore them down and entered Warsaw (September 7th, 1831). It suited the humour of Nicholas to suppress a rebellion; and the suppression, like the earlier partition, is one of the grim memories which lie between Poland and Russia to-day. After punishing the captured rebels, Nicholas went on to remove the very soil in which another rebellion might grow. He destroyed almost the last remnant of Polish nationality. The flag of the white eagle was abolished, the constitution torn up, the higher schools and universities closed. On February 26th Poland was declared to be henceforth a province of Russia.

At the other end of the Empire trouble in Georgia and Circassia gave occasion to strengthen in that direction the rule of the Tsar. He now reigned over the largest Empire in Europe, and almost every other Power, but especially England and France, regarded the growth of Russia with apprehension. Nicholas got the Dardanelles closed against foreign warships, and so secured his Black Sea coast against attack. He had assisted the Sultan to chastise one of *his* rebels—Mehemed Ali, of Egypt—and was rewarded with this concession. Europe moved toward the Crimean War.

First, however, Nicholas had an opportunity of crushing another revolt and chastising the supporters of the new ideas. The third revolutionary wave, which was definitely to destroy the old political order in Europe, began in 1848; and it be-

THE FIGHT AGAINST LIBERALISM

gan, as usual, in France. Louis Napoleon, who was destined to give that country its last and not most fortunate experiment in kingship, made an appeal to Nicholas for friendship, if not alliance. But Nicholas liked neither an authority which was set up by the will of the people nor a programme that pandered to the will of the people. He rejected Napoleon's appeal, and turned rather to Austria, where insurrection seemed to be well on the way to shake even the Hapsburgs from the throne. The Hungarians were on the point of securing their independence, and the mediæval system which Metternich had so long maintained was about to be destroyed. Nicholas gladly supported his brother-autocrat. It was the Russian army of 190,000 men which propped up once more the tottering throne of the Hapsburgs and prolonged the struggle of darkness against light. Nicholas would learn presently the utter selfishness and ungratefulness of Austrian policy, as his last successor would learn at a later date.

The eyes of Nicholas were still upon the south, and the eyes of Europe were upon Nicholas. There can be very little doubt that the whole of the moralising Romanoffs of the nineteenth century had, behind their professions of disinterested regard for the victims of the Turk, a more or less clearly conceived design of gaining Constantinople and passing over the Balkans to the Mediterranean. Whatever sincerity there was in their zeal for the protection of the Christian subjects of the Sultan, they were far from insensible to the fact that these helpless Greek Christians occupied territory which would, if it were annexed, bring Russia at last to a free and warm sea. In Alexander this motive was so far checked by an effort at sincerity, that he would not interfere between the Greek and the Turk; he would be true to his later resolution to help no insurgents. Nicholas held an even sterner attitude toward insurgents, but the moment Christian subjects of the Sultan rose against *their* ruler he entirely forgot that they were rebels against an hereditary autocracy. We shall find his successors equally lenient to rebellion in the Balkans; and it is scarcely a diplomatic secret that the Serbs, when they received the brotherly support of the last of the Romanoffs in 1914, looked silently and anxiously for a less disinterested purpose in the act of that monarch.

Nicholas now had the Sultan almost in a state of vassalage, and it seemed to him that he had so far raised the prestige of Russia, and won the gratitude of Austria, that he need hardly consider the western Powers. Hence in 1853 he made a pompous objection when the Sultan granted the French certain privileges in regard to the Christians of Palestine. He sent Prince Menshikoff to Constantinople to establish a definite Russian

THE FIGHT AGAINST LIBERALISM

protectorate over all the Greek Christians in the Ottoman Empire. Secretly, however, Menshikoff was to arrange an alliance with Turkey against France, in case that Power gave trouble, and the secret mission became known to the other Powers. It has been the diplomatic pastime of the Sultans for several generations to take advantage of the mutual jealousy of the Christian Powers which read them such admirable lessons in virtue. Supported, behind the scenes, by the English ambassador, the Sultan refused the Russian proposals, and Nicholas decided upon war. He so little knew the secret action of England that he discussed with the English ambassador at St. Petersburg a plan for the division of the Ottoman Empire: England should, in the teeth of France, occupy Egypt, and Russia should take Constantinople. He at least expected England to be neutral.

It may at least be said for England, which naturally did not care to see the Russian giant cast his shadow over Egypt and the route to India, that it tried earnestly to avert war. France was less pacific. It would like to see Russia in difficulties with England, and it secured an alliance with England to the extent of pressing upon the Tsar a round-table conference on the matters in dispute. The conference was held at Vienna and a scheme of settlement was drawn up. This scheme the Sultan, supported by a growing feeling in his own country and an astute perception of the international jealousy, declined to accept without modification; and Russia refused to admit the modifications he suggested. Austria had played the Tsar false. In January (1854) the English and French fleets had entered the Black Sea. The Sultan had at the last moment signed the Vienna Note, and the Tsar had agreed to sign it with certain modifications. It was Austria that procured the rejection of these reserves. What came to be known as the Crimean War opened.

Nicholas has been severely judged by some historians for his policy. This censure is easy for the historian who has before his eyes the issue as well as the commencement of the war. Russia was beaten and humiliated. After appalling sacrifices she was compelled to sign a very disadvantageous peace, and her new prestige in Europe fell considerably. It is, perhaps, unfair to judge the man by the issue. But we may very well surmise that Nicholas did little more than cloak an aggressive design in the new mantle of righteousness which the Tsars affected. It was, as usual, the people who paid.

The course of the war need not be described here. By a rapid assault—which was represented in France and England as a premature outrage, and did much to influence popular passion—the Russian fleet destroyed the Turkish, and the Russian

THE FIGHT AGAINST LIBERALISM

armies descended south once more. Before the end of March England and France declared war on Russia in alliance with the monarch who had for years reddened the soil of Greece and the Balkans with Christian blood. The language of the time reads curiously to-day. Nicholas issued a manifesto in which he warmly disclaimed any idea of conquest; he drew the sword, he said, only in defence of Christianity, and he was outraged to find France and England supporting the Mohammedan murderer. They must, he said, be jealous of Russia's prosperity and eager to destroy it. England frankly sang in its streets that it would never let the Russians get Constantinople. France openly used the same language; though there were those who said that Napoleon was personally irritated at the Tsar's haughty disdain of his credentials.

The war soon centred upon the Crimea, and its historic milestones—Alma, Balaclava, Inkermann, Sevastopol—are well known. It entered upon a second year, 1855, and the Russian people murmured bitterly. Nicholas himself must have felt the sting of many of the criticisms. During the long reign of his censors, when public opinion could not be brought to bear upon the administration, official corruption had increased, and both army and navy were far below the required standard of efficiency. Nicholas had isolated Russia from the west; yet from the west had come every stimulus to the improvement of the Russian forces. He had reversed the policy of Peter and Catherine, and he seemed to be in danger of losing the lands they had taken. A terrible fire of criticism and invective was maintained at St. Petersburg. The censors controlled the press—men circulated their views in manuscript. Nicholas was honest, and it is said that he at times doubted if the policy to which he had devoted his life was sound. But he was stubborn, and he thrust aside all suggestions of peace. In the midst of the struggle he caught a chill which led to pneumonia. He died on March 3rd, 1855.

Such was the opening of the last phase of the romance of the Romanoffs. The dynasty is sobered, not merely by the spirit of the age into which it has passed, but by the very impossibility of sustaining its gaieties. No monarch who showered the precious national revenues upon lovers or drinking comrades could long hold the throne in such an age. Insurrection has taken a new form. It is no longer the work of a coterie who would place a new monarch on the throne in order that they, the conspirators, may take the place of the late favourites in the golden rain. A new phrase, the rights of the people, is born, or re-born, in the world. A monarchy by the grace of God must do the work of God, not the work of the devil. Nicholas tries to reconcile the new and the old: the new idea of service and the old idea of autocracy. He will better the lot of the people, not because it is their will, but because it is his divine mission. And in order to protect his scheme he constructs a new machinery of despotism: secret police, and Cossacks, and priests, and censors, and sophists. Against this machinery we have now to see the Russian people bruise and crush their limbs until it and its autocratic makers are destroyed. First, however, one more effort will be made to pose as autocratic dispenser of Justice and Charity.

CHAPTER XIV

THE TRAGEDY OF ALEXANDER II

It is said that in his last year Nicholas I observed that he would leave a terrible burden to his son. He left a very costly war which turned monthly against Russia. He left an empty treasury, and a privy purse that was a million rubles in debt. He left a city and country that bitterly murmured against the rule which he had intended to make so benevolent. He left forty millions of his people in the condition of serfdom which the whole of the remaining civilised world had outgrown. He left a nation outpaced industrially and commercially by every other Power because he could not admit into it the science which made the others superior. As he brooded over his Bible at night he saw no solution. He died in distress; and, as in the case of the death of nearly every Romanoff, few mourned.

His son, Alexander II, who confidently took over the legacy, was much closer to Alexander I than to his father. He had the mediocre intellect of the dynasty (after Peter I), but the sunny tempera-

THE TRAGEDY OF ALEXANDER II

ment of Catherine, sobered. Unlike his father, who had listened only to the wrong teachers, Alexander II had been an exemplary pupil, and he had had good teachers. The new domestic atmosphere of the court is less interesting than the old, and we need not linger over it. The picture of Nicholas reading the Bible every night to his wife will suffice. The Tsarina was a model German *Hausfrau* on an imperial scale. Alexander breathed this atmosphere easily. He was an exemplary youth. On the night after the death of his father he took the Bible to his mother's room and read to her. His chief tutor had learned teaching from Pestalozzi, and his lessons, which we have in part, were worthy of Marcus Aurelius. They were exalted in principle, if vague in application. Alexander was to make duty his star: his duty to his people and to civilisation. He had travelled all over the Empire, even in Siberia; and the sight of the exiles had so touched his warm heart that he had persuaded his stern father to modify the treatment even of some of the conspirators at his accession.

What would a young monarch—Alexander was thirty-seven years old—of this type make of the formidable problem which his father had created? We are quite prepared to hear that he is going to disarm rebellion and win his subjects by kindness. He will make the autocracy so beneficent that men will love it. A comparatively simple thing, the young man thought. But the tragedy of the life of Alexander II is that it was during his reign that Nihilism arose, dagger in hand, and he himself fell by the bomb of an assassin who represented "the people."

Russian funds rose in the European market when Alexander II mounted the throne. He was well known: an amiable, kindly man, gently punctilious about etiquette, very sober in meat and drink, very cold to flatterers. Europe looked to him for peace; his people, who sank under their burdens, looked to him for relief; liberals looked, not too confidently, to him for justice. But Alexander felt that his first duty was to bring the war, not merely to an end, but a successful end. He would not be crowned until that was attained. A few weeks after the death of his father he sent a representative to Vienna to take part in a peace-conference. When France demanded that the Black Sea should be neutralised and the naval strength of Russia limited by agreement, he refused and he bade the war go on.

It went on, as is known, until Sevastopol fell, and Russia soothed her feelings a little by taking Kars. Then the diplomats gathered round a table to see what difference to the world the death of hundreds of thousands of men and the squandering of three nations' resources must make. There was in Russia no chance of disguising the defeat. The Black

THE TRAGEDY OF ALEXANDER II

Sea *was* neutralised. All the ships and forts on which so much had been spent must go. Kars must be surrendered. The mouth of the Danube must be yielded. The protectorate of the Christian subjects of the Sultan must be abandoned. One war had put Turkey at the feet of Russia; another war had put Turkey upon its own feet once more, and had set back Russia.

It was, however, peace, and the country looked eagerly for the domestic programme of the young Tsar. He was crowned in August, 1856, and he at once disclosed his policy. He would, of course, maintain the work of his revered father; but it soon fell to pieces. An amnesty was granted, and the rebels came back to the sunlight. The military colonies of Arakcheeff were finally abandoned. Arrears of taxes to the extent of twenty-four million rubles were remitted to the impoverished people. The censorship was suspended, and St. Petersburg poured into liberalism like a stream when the dam is broken. The manuscripts that had passed stealthily from hand to hand, and been read behind locked doors, were now sent to the press. Periodicals and pamphlets snowed upon the metropolis. Unions and leagues for everything new and beneficent and western sprang up like mushrooms. All the talk of English radicalism filled the salons: self-government and emancipation of women, biblical criticism and Darwinism, banks and railways and manufactures, education and co-operation and political reform.

Presently the discussion would strike a deeper note. A certain Robert Owen of England had advocated a scheme which he called Socialism. Certain Germans were beginning to take the germ of Owen's patriarchal theory and make a "scientific system" of it. Russia was now free to travel, and to import books. The mind which has been artificially repressed will, if the process be not continued too long, expand more rapidly than the mind which is suffered to grow normally.

In all this babel of humanitarian tongues, each reformer stridently denouncing his brother as a charlatan, as is the way of reformers, there was one steady and persistent note. Serfdom must be abolished. Here the mass of the people agreed with the intellectuals. We are tempted to picture the great body of the Russian people as too stunted in mind, too dazed by labour and the stupefying conditions of their life, to understand anything of this reform-language. But there is plenty of evidence that they were quite alive to the idea of emancipation. They had looked to each new Tsar, as he eloquently unfolded his lofty aims on coronation-day, to abolish serfdom. They looked with particular eagerness to Alexander. "Constitution" was too large a word for them. But they knew what it meant to be free and to have their *Mir* and their bit of land.

THE TRAGEDY OF ALEXANDER II

Forty-two and a half million people in Russia were still serfs in the year 1856: nine centuries after the establishment of the Russian Church, two hundred years after the beginning of the rule of the Romanoffs. I have, incidentally, given sufficient evidence in earlier chapters that this serfdom differed little from slavery. The peasant was, in polite phraseology, attached to the glebe. When a rich man ruined himself in the dissipations of St. Petersburg and sold his estates, he sold the peasants with the land. When a man opened new estates, he bought peasants to work it. They had no liberty of movement, which is the fundamental condition of liberty. They owned no land (except a small number who secured the advantages offered by the last two Tsars) and were therefore not masters of their own labour. Half their labour must be given gratuitously to their lord—this was the new, decent sort of serfdom—who would then allow them to wring a miserable living for themselves and family out of a fraction of his land with the other half of their time. Not much earlier, we saw, great land-owners, even women, could inflict on them such torture and death as few Romans are said to have inflicted on their slaves in the worst days of the Empire. They were still slaves, though humanely treated on the Crown Lands, much as a wise farmer gives good conditions to his cattle. The lot of the peasant of Russia to-day is hard enough. Imagine it sixty years ago with the added yoke of serfdom.

Assuredly serfdom was the first and most monstrous evil to be removed, and we saw that for fifty years or more the rulers of Russia had been ashamed of this great stigma on their civilisation. At the very beginning of the reign the rumour went out that Alexander would free the serfs, and their wealthy owners were anxious. Alexander reassured them to some extent. He would like to see an end of serfdom, but it was an evil to be remedied gradually. He would like to see individuals reduce it by freeing their serfs. Soon after the close of the war the Tsar again addressed the nobles, and begged them to give serious attention to the emancipation of the serfs. It was plain that little would be done in this fashion, and a few months later he appointed Provincial Committees of land-owners to give practical consideration to the problem.

Historians seem to differ in discussing whether Alexander was moved by his own idealism or by the pressure of the growing liberalism of St. Petersburg and the clamours of the peasants. The point is of some interest in forming a general estimate of the Tsar-Emancipator. Professor Kornilov, while ascribing great reforms to Alexander II, maintains that he was impelled from without rather than within: that his moralising tutor had not been a liberal or a man of definite social views,

CATHEDRAL ERECTED IN PETROGRAD IN MEMORY OF ALEXANDER II

THE TRAGEDY OF ALEXANDER II

and had implanted in his mind only such general regard for humanity and justice as a conservative may profess. Others would represent the Tsar as a practical reformer of a liberal type, a little soured in the end by the excesses and violence of "advanced" people. Perhaps we are nearest to the truth if we picture Alexander II as a man who united a real detestation of serfdom with a sincere regard for justice in the abstract, yet would never have overcome the conservatism of many of his advisers and the immense practical difficulties but for the very effective pressure put upon him by the rising impatience of educated Russians.

The Provincial Committees wasted many months in futile discussion and wrangling. Around them there now waged a great battle of amateur sociologists, and half a dozen different theories of emancipation had their schools of defenders. There was, to begin with, a vital difference of views between the serfs and their owners. The peasant wanted land even more than liberty; the owner felt that it was emancipation to give liberty, and he was, as a rule, unwilling to part with land. There was the question of compensation, which inspired endless discussion. A serf was worth a hundred dollars. In short, the committees of local owners did not want the work to proceed, and Alexander formed, at the beginning of 1857, a Central Committee of twelve members under his own presidency. The work was to be done "from on high." Emancipation was to be a voluntary gift from the Tsar.

The work still dragged. In 1855 Alexander had appointed the liberal Lanskoi Minister of the Interior, and he zealously promoted the scheme and secured the liberal Milyutin as colleague. But other ministers were of the old school and unsympathetic. They pointed out that behind the demand for emancipation other and more disturbing demands were becoming articulate. Liberal nobles who were ready to emancipate their serfs already claimed that this ought to be followed by their own political emancipation. They demanded a Duma. However, even members of the imperial family, like the Grand Duke Constantine, pressed for the reform, and the Tsar at length formed an Imperial Commission, on which the conservative opposition was checked. A law was drafted, and on February 19th, 1861, Alexander announced to Russia and the world, with a very natural exaltation, that the serfs were to be freed.

The serfs fell into three classes. Those on the Crown Lands were, as we saw, already in an improved condition. The law of 1861 did not affect them, but they were later (1866) put in the same position as the emancipated serfs. Then there were a million and a half serfs who were not on the land, but in personal service. These were ordered to continue their service for two further years, and

THE TRAGEDY OF ALEXANDER II

they would then be free. The main body were the twenty-one million serfs on the estates of private owners. Each was now to own his house, and the small strip of land encircling it, and the entire community of peasants in a village were to have, in common, a part of the arable land of the owner. The Slavophiles had secured this reversion to the primitive custom of owning in common, and one may justly suspect that they felt that the arrangement would make the peasants more or less impervious to the new ideas about property which were being imported from Germany. The *Mir* was re-established. But the land-owners were to sell, not give, their land; and they were to be compensated for the loss of serf-labour. The entire value was estimated, the State paid it, and the peasants were to refund the sum within a space of forty-nine years. The *Mir* was responsible for the payments.

Alexander looked out upon his Empire for the signs of jubilation, and at first he saw many. Even so drastic a rebel as Hertzen rejoiced. The journals and pamphlets of the metropolis turned from acidity to a temporary sweetness. Deputations of peasants, carefully chosen, were brought to thank the Tsar, and in the tearful accents of the aged serfs he thought that he heard the voice of twenty millions. But it was not long before the reaction began, and a chill affected the liberalism of the Tsar.

THE ROMANCE OF THE ROMANOFFS

It was a very general belief of the peasants that the land belonged, by ancient right, to them, and it had been in some way stolen from them by the wealthy and noble. When, therefore, they heard of the scheme of compensation, the payments which must be made annually until the death of the youngest of them, they began to murmur. The officials, they said in many places, must have falsified the words of the Tsar. There were other grievances. The allowance of land to each had, in the heat of discussion, been cut down to very small proportions. The owners were not *bound* to sell even this, and in many places they refused; and, where they sold, they generally attempted to sell inferior land. Officials, charged with the administration of the law, took bribes, and there was a vast amount of foul play. In fine, the emancipated serfs now found that a free man had to shoulder a burden of taxes heavier than they had imagined.

In short, hopes had been improperly inflated, and the disillusion was exasperating; nor was there now any lack of men imbued with the new ideas who fostered the discontent. Lanskoi and Milyutin were dismissed from office, through the intrigue of the conservatives, and the new minister, Valuyeff, had not the same scrupulous regard for the success of the law. In various places there were risings of the peasants, and the troops had to use their muskets. In the government of Kazan ten thousand

THE TRAGEDY OF ALEXANDER II

peasants revolted, under the lead of Anton Petroff, and the new era was stained heavily with blood. Petroff was executed; eighty of the emancipated serfs were shot with arms in their hands. At the university of Kazan the students boldly held a requiem service in honour of the dead, and Alexander had to punish even the monks who celebrated it. The "Tsar-Emancipator" did not long enjoy his popularity. The clouds closed slowly, after the short burst of sunshine, and would cover the skies of Russia henceforward until the last Romanoff quitted the throne.

An even graver cause of distrust now arose. Alexander had visited Poland soon after his accession and had paternally promised to make the Poles happy, if they were good. "No more dreams," he said genially to them. His father's work was to be maintained, he told them. Poland was to be a province of Russia. He appointed a moderate governor, Prince Gorchakoff, and declared an amnesty. Since the terrible repression of the rebellion by Nicholas I a large number of Poles had lived in the various capitals of Europe, and there they had been thoroughly educated in modern ideas. In London, particularly, they had been steeped in the sober radicalism that had followed the failure of the Chartist movement, the fervour for the deliverance of Hungarians and Italians, the popular indignation against Russia.

Most of them would not return to a Poland which was not free, but some did, and they assisted in the education of the Poles. There arose a very general cry among the educated Poles for a constitution; and Alexander believed no more than his fathers, or than Pius IX, in giving a constitution that was asked as a right.

In November, 1860, a great demonstration was held in memory of the revolution of 1830, and the authorities were annoyed. Demonstrations increased for all kinds of undesirable objects, and the troops at Warsaw fired and killed five Poles. A vast crowd of one hundred thousand attended the funeral. The Tsar tried to conciliate them by small gifts. He appointed a Polish Director of Public Instruction and Cults. He created municipal councils for the large towns, and electoral councils for each government and district. But he would not grant a constitution, and the agitation increased. A great crowd went to the Viceroy's palace to formulate their demands, and soon two hundred of them lay dead upon the pavement. The whole city went into mourning.

A new Viceroy, General Lambert, was appointed, and the Tsar instructed him to carry out conscientiously the reforms he had promised. But the officials who were to carry them out were Russians, and the greater reforms were withheld. There were further demonstrations, and further shootings. A reactionary soldier, Count Luders, was then made Viceroy. His life was attempted. The Poles now openly demanded independence and a restoration of Lithuania. Arrests and banishment were useless. The whole educated nation seemed to be aflame. So on January 15th the authorities decided to decimate the enthusiasts by an enforced recruiting for the army, and Poland entered upon another futile rebellion. Those who escaped the police fled to the country, secured arms, and formed guerilla bands.

It was one of the most pathetic of rebellions. The insurgents had no artillery, no transport or medical service. They moved about, often led by priests, as they were hunted, living on the sympathetic gentry and peasants, occasionally hanging or shooting a pro-Russian landowner. It was not war, and the Russian troops hanged or shot all they captured. The most curious feature of it was that a secret committee or council guided the insurrection, levied taxes, and issued decrees from the University of Warsaw itself without being detected by the police. Poles abroad fierily preached the wrongs of their countrymen, and the English, French, and Austrian governments formally requested the Tsar (1863) to put an end to the anarchy. Two months later they formulated for the Tsar what seemed to them the reasonable demands of the Poles: a general amnesty, parliamentary representation, reform of the law of recruiting, complete liberty of religion, admission of Poles to office, and so on. Alexander indignantly refused. He did not add—one wonders if he reflected—that it was precisely because the Sultan would not grant such rights to his Christian subjects that Russia had made war upon the Turk. Prussia supported, and promised assistance to, the Tsar.

The last sparks of the rebellion were stamped out in May (1864), and the punishment began. The few traces that Nicholas had left of a Polish nationality were now destroyed. The Polish language was banned from schools and universities, and the chief rebels were executed. It was the nobles, the educated class, that Alexander chiefly blamed; and it was on that account that he granted the peasants of Poland the right to share the land.

Alexander was less to blame in connection with another event, two years later, which moved Europe to express its indignation. The settlement of the Caucasic region was completed, and some hundreds of thousands of Mohammedan Circassians and Georgians migrated from the occupied territory and sought shelter in Turkey. The English Government again made a protest at St. Petersburg, which was neatly countered by a reminder that the state of Ireland hardly justified England in posing as a moralist. The Circassians were, in fact, handsome ruffians with whose ways the English were

THE TRAGEDY OF ALEXANDER II

imperfectly acquainted. They freely sold their daughters, the famous Circassian maids, to the harems of Constantinople, and they were the most expert cattle-thieves and least industrious workers of Europe or Asia. They were largely settled by the Turks on the farms of the reluctant Bulgarians, and they willingly joined the bashi-bazouks in cutting off Christian ears.

The brutality that was used in the suppression of the Polish insurrection reacted upon the intellectuals of St. Petersburg, just as the insurrection itself reacted upon the more or less benevolent designs of the Tsar. But before we consider how the reign of Alexander II came to inaugurate the terror which would for the next sixty years brood over Russia, it is proper that we should briefly examine the remainder of his reforms.

The emancipation of the serfs, though a measure of elementary justice that had been too long denied, must nevertheless command our admiration when we consider the stubborn opposition which the Tsar had to overcome. It was not followed by the political emancipation of the nation at large, but the Tsar created a popular institution which would, at a later date, prove a valuable instrument of reform. The *Mir* was re-established by the communal ownership of the land. The district council, the *Zemstvo,* was now established (1864). Each government (or province) of Russia was already divided into districts, and there was to be in each of these a Zemstvo, or popular council, formed of deputies who were elected for a term of three years. They included representatives of the landowners, the artisans, and the peasants, and were to meet at least once a year, with a permanent executive committee. A general Zemstvo for each province was also created.

At the time the Zemstvo had, in so far as it was obliged to act, few and simple functions—the care of roads, bridges, sanitation, etc.—and the imperial taxes were so heavy that it could not raise sufficient money for other work. The Imperial Government, moreover, jealously watched, and often interfered with, the work of the popular council. Yet it was an important instalment of reform, and at a later date we shall find the Zemstvo playing a greater part than the Tsar intended, in the enlightenment and emancipation of Russia. Already it had the option of building schools, and in many places it did so.

There was a corresponding improvement in the administration of justice. The slovenly and corrupt traditional system was condemned, and an entire series of new tribunals, framed on western models, was created. There was a court for each district and a court of appeal, from which a final appeal for revision might be made to the Senate. On the French model the magistrates were to conduct the preliminary inquiry which had hitherto been left, with disastrous results, to the police, and public trial by jury was introduced. In the rural districts justices of the peace, who were generally large landed proprietors, heard the petty cases which had earlier been made a matter of rough justice, or injustice, between the serf and his master. In such cases an appeal might be made to a bench of justices if there was question of a fine of more than thirty rubles (fifteen dollars) or more than three days' imprisonment. Such appeals were rare, as it was found that the hardy peasant preferred a few strokes of the lash, as in the old days, to a loss of his money or his time. In the higher courts, as well as in the army, flogging was abolished.

Here again the demands of the liberals were, in theory, generously met; and in practice they were largely evaded. Incompetence was inevitable at the beginning of so large a reform, and some degree of ill-will and abuse of power had to be expected. These defects do not detract from the merit of the Tsar and his liberal ministers. But there was from the first a tendency on the part of the imperial government to regard cases as political and reserve them for the kind of treatment they had always received. As the radical agitation grew, and the Tsar was driven into the arms of the reactionaries at the court, this interference naturally increased. Long before the end of Alexander's reign the civil courts were habitually ignored in precisely those cases which needed the most impartial consideration, and men were detained and punished in thousands at the whim of brutal and irresponsible servants of the autocracy.

These were the principal measures of reform granted by Alexander II in his period of benevolence. With the fiscal improvements we are not much concerned, but it may be noted that for a time a Budget was published. Much was done in those early years (1861-1866) for education. The restriction upon the number of students attending the universities was removed, and there was a remarkable eagerness to obtain higher education. Youths earned their living while they attended the classes, and some scholarships were founded. Girls were excluded from the universities, but we shall see presently how they broke through the barriers and joined the youths of Russia in the demand for enlightenment. A large number of secondary and elementary schools were established. In 1877 it was claimed that there were 25,000 schools. The press was offered the alternative of submitting its copy to a censorship or risking the attentions of the police. The very name of Censor was hated, after the experience under Nicholas I, and for a time periodicals and books poured out upon an eager public. The restriction upon travel also was re-

THE TRAGEDY OF ALEXANDER II

moved, and men passed freely to the outer world which terrified the Slavophiles, and came back with the language of Mazzini and other apostles upon their lips. Foreigners in Russia received civil rights for the first time. The restrictions upon the movements of the Jews were modified, though "the Pale" was not abolished.

The history of that stirring period has been so frequently written in the last thirty years that we no longer profess to find a mystery in the fact that this reforming Romanoff fell by the hand of an assassin. Here it is necessary only to give a short summary of the development after 1860 which entirely changed the character of his reign. We must remember that from the first Alexander II did not recognise the rights of man. In his best and most benevolent mood he was concerned only with the duties of monarchs. The authority divinely entrusted to him was accompanied by a divine mandate to make his people virtuous and happy. Within the limits of a strict maintenance of the authority of the autocracy and of the clergy he would do so. The more enlightened of his subjects might respectfully offer suggestions, though that was properly the function of the ministers he chose to guide him, but the correct attitude of the people was to await, in patience and respect, the measures of reform which the wisdom of his council sanctioned him in granting.

THE ROMANCE OF THE ROMANOFFS

This was a fundamental anachronism, and, however generous the intentions of the Tsar may have been and however misguided and exaggerated some of the radicals, a conflict was as inevitable as the sunrise. Seeing that the policy of his early liberal ministers did not pacify the country, which became louder and bolder in its demands the more he gave it, Alexander fell back upon the worn maxims of autocracy and surrounded himself more and more with reactionaries. The wealth of the great landowners and the power of the clergy and monks were as much threatened by the new spirit as was the autocracy of the Tsars. In the recesses of the court there was, therefore, a complacent agreement upon the kind of theory which has at all times reconciled the consciences of good men with persecution. The "extremists," it was said, were few in number and morbid or perverse in sentiment. They must not be suffered to abuse liberty to the detriment of the nation. Coercion was justified. To coercion—which meant, in practice, the most wanton brutality and violence on the part of baffled police—some replied with violence. In effect, war was declared.

The crowd of young men who flocked to the University of St. Petersburg when the restrictions were removed were the nucleus of the radical movement which was gradually raised to a revolutionary heat. The teaching of liberal professors, who were reconciled to gradual and moderate reforms, only prepared them for a more highly seasoned political diet, and there were powerful writers to purvey it. Hertzen, who was in exile, sent his propaganda into the country much as Mazzini taught the youth of Italy. His very radical organ, "The Bell," was the delight of the young folk who, in all ages, scorn the timidity of age and are convinced that the immaturity of the youthful mind is amply compensated by its superior candour. Bakunin, who for a time joined Hertzen in London, and then settled in Switzerland, taught a gospel which gradually approached, and finally reached, anarchy. Tschaikovsky, who also was compelled to leave Russia, was the inspiration of a "circle," or discussion-society, at St. Petersburg which had branches or affiliated societies in every town of Russia. Bielinski and other radicals assisted the ferment of emotions and philosophies. Krapotkin and Stepiak were coming upon the scene.

We have seen how the mind of Russian youth was prepared for these advanced gospels. The monotonous misery and poverty of the country in spite of every change of ruler, the corruption and brutality of officials, the harsh measures of Nicholas I, the disastrous issue of the Crimean War, the severity of the repression of the Poles, the disappointing results of the emancipation of the serfs, and the increasing perception that Russia lagged behind every other country in Europe put a mass of inflammable material into the minds of the educated. As early as 1862 a student was caught spreading a pamphlet in which he advocated a bloody revolution against the dynasty, and was exiled to Siberia. In the same year a series of mysterious fires in St. Petersburg increased the agitation. Conservatives ascribed them to the violent radicals: the radicals retorted that they were due to agents of the reactionaries who wanted to provide a ground for stringent action. The left wing of the reformers moved rapidly further west, and its language increased in violence. The authorities raised the fees at the universities and endeavoured to suppress the numerous students' societies, but the agitation continued. Many of the nobles themselves were in sympathy with the intellectual revolt. In 1862 several gatherings of nobles and gentry passed a demand for parliamentary institutions.

At the other end of the movement the conviction increased that no form of centralised government would remain honest and disinterested, and the philosophy of anarchy was framed. At first it was moral rather than political, as it is in the minds of many Anarchists to-day. The individual was to be relieved of the swathing bonds of all religious and moral and other traditions, and the theory was that he would then develop healthily. To this theory was first applied the name "Nihilism," which was afterwards, as Anarchy became more and more po-

THE TRAGEDY OF ALEXANDER II

litical in complexion, extended to the whole revolutionary movement; though Socialism gained considerably on Anarchy as time went on. It was the period of Karl Marx and the early German Socialists, and the imposing structure of Marx's argument won large numbers of adherents.

One of the most disturbing features in the mind of conservatives was the way in which young women adopted the advanced creed. The attempts of Peter the Great to break down the barriers which confined the life of women had almost ceased at his death. In the world of wealth, as Tolstoi's novels show, women kept the liberty of the reigns of Elizabeth and Catherine. The new austerity of the court was not accompanied by any general asceticism amongst the aristocracy. The philosophy of anarchy provided a principle for what had hitherto been an inconsistent defiance of religious traditions which were nominally respected. But the mass of Russian women and girls, above the level of the peasantry, had hitherto been unaffected by these liberties of the aristocracy. Now the cry of the emancipation of woman penetrated remote country houses, and many a girl broke loose from the control of a tearful mother or an infuriated father, and sought the centre of enlightenment in the city. The authorities refused to allow unmarried women to attend the higher schools. They retorted, as Roman women had done nearly two thousand years before, by entering into fictitious marriages. Gradually they won the right to attend certain lectures at the university, and many of them were found in the students' circles where the reconstruction of the universe was heatedly discussed.

The next development was that the intellectuals decided to educate the workers. An officer of the army resigned his commission and turned weaver. Sophia Perovskaia and other daughters of wealthy parents got into touch with the working and domestic women. The police of the "Third Section" (the secret police created by Nicholas) grew in numbers and dogged the steps of these fiery young apostles. In 1866 a man named Karakosoff, who had formed a society to promote the welfare of the people, attempted to shoot the Tsar. An isolated fanatic, the Tsar was told; and at that time there was certainly no real organisation of assassination. But the pressure of the police and the daily risk of arrest drove the agitation underground, and to their new quarters the spies and informers and police followed them. There was now, plainly, no question of persuading Alexander II to complete his scheme of reform. There was increasing question of making war upon him and the autocracy. It was the Russian tradition. When a Tsar was obnoxious you removed him; but to do so in the name of justice, not in the name of a covetous group of courtiers, was revolution of the worst order.

THE TRAGEDY OF ALEXANDER II

By this time, the early seventies, the Tsar saw that he had not merely to deal with a few unbalanced individuals. The jails were full of political prisoners. All the well-known leaders were in jail or exile, yet the work proceeded amazingly. In 1874 there were 1,500 arrests. The new courts were not called upon to decide the guilt of the prisoners. They were knouted, or thrust into prison, or sent to Siberia. Large numbers died in the overcrowded jails. Some went insane or committed suicide. When the experiment of a public trial was at last made, in 1877, people were amazed at the calm courage and high idealism of the young "criminals." In 1878 nearly two hundred of them were tried. Many received terms of imprisonment, or penal servitude, of from ten to twenty years.

The rebels were now at war with the brutal ministers of the autocracy, and they began to use the same weapons. A young girl from the country came to St. Petersburg and shot the head of the police; and, amidst great enthusiasm, she was acquitted by a jury. Another head of the police was in the same year (1878) stabbed at Odessa. Spies were shot. Groups of young men who were surprised in secret council by the police produced revolvers and fought. The governor of Kharkoff, who treated political prisoners with great brutality, was assassinated. Another attempt was made to shoot the Tsar (1879).

In the meantime, it will be remembered, the Russo-Turkish war had occurred, and it had the customary effect of increasing the people's burden and the discontent. The Slavophile party naturally gave birth to a Pan-Slav party, and the traditional Russian ambition to spread over the Balkans was revived. The Turks continued to treat their Balkan subjects with great brutality, and in 1874 Bosnia and Herzegovina broke into revolt, while Serbia and Montenegro, which were semi-independent, joined with their compatriots in the war. The Pan-Slavs now pressed for war, and there were those in the Tsar's circle, such as his brother, the Grand Duke Nicholas, who warmly supported the agitation. The financial minister, on the other hand, who had carefully nursed the treasury into something like prosperity, strongly opposed the adventure. The Tsar wavered between his hope of getting the ignominious treaty of 1856 set aside and his love of peace and dread of the costly chances of war.

There is now no doubt that Bismarck helped to urge him to war. Alexander was pro-German, and had in 1870 secured the neutrality of Austria while Prussia attacked France. It is true that, when the Germans meditated a fresh attack upon the French in 1875, the Tsar interfered on behalf of France

THE TRAGEDY OF ALEXANDER II

and greatly angered Bismarck. That statesman, however, retained influence at St. Petersburg, and, on the Frederician tradition of encouraging rivals to wear out each other, he urged Russia to attack Turkey. In 1877 (April) Russia entered the war, and its progress was so rapid that in the following March it compelled Turkey to sign the humiliating Treaty of San Stefano. Russia took from it very little territory directly, but, besides securing the recognition of the complete independence of Serbia and Rumania, it created a large principality of Bulgaria in which it hoped to have a predominant interest.

England was, unfortunately, still in its mood of favouring the Turk, through jealousy of Russia, and Austria was less openly hostile. A desultory war continued, and Bismarck astutely offered the services of Germany as mediator, with the intention of curtailing its gains. By the Treaty of Berlin (July 13th, 1878) the San Stefano Treaty was torn up, and Bulgaria was cut down by half. Once more a costly war had, in the eyes of the people, done little for Russia; and there was the customary, and not unjust, cry that the course of the war had revealed a great deal of official corruption. The tragedy of the reign of Alexander ran on to its ghastly finale.

In 1878 it was decreed that in future political prisoners should be tried by courts martial, and in the following year the Tsar appointed Governors General of St. Petersburg, Kharkoff, and Odessa, and gave additional and formidable powers to the Governors of Moscow, Warsaw, and Kieff. The system of repression was to be drastically pursued. The revolutionaries retorted by attempting to blow up the train in which Alexander returned from a visit to the Crimea. Three mines were laid. Near Moscow Sophia Perovskaia and a few associates had worked for two months digging a tunnel to the line from a house they had taken. The preparations were in this case perfect, but the Tsar escaped. The police had arranged three trains, and, as the Tsar changed train on approaching Moscow, leaving the middle for the first train, he was allowed to pass unharmed, and it was the second train that was blown to pieces. Sophia Perovskaia and her associates escaped and returned to their plotting. The heads of the revolutionary movement had decreed the death of Alexander II.

For the next fifteen months there was a thrilling war between the revolutionaries and the "Third Section." Time and again the Tsar's advisers declared that only a few dozen rebels were left, and the country was substantially loyal. But, although hundreds were arrested annually, though bribes and spies and all the ignominious machinery of the police were brought into play, the "red terror" held the field against the "white terror." In February,

THE TRAGEDY OF ALEXANDER II

1880, not only the Tsar, but all the imperial family, had a narrow escape. A revolutionary named Halturin entered the service of the Winter Palace as waiter. He discovered that the waiters' quarters were, with an intervening floor occupied by troops, directly underneath the dining-room, and he proposed to fire a mine there. Day by day he smuggled into the palace small quantities of dynamite and stored them with his belongings. The police discovered a plan, on which the imperial dining-room was marked with a cross, and they searched the floors beneath it. They did not find the explosive, but from that day a stricter watch was kept, and no more dynamite could be introduced. Halturin believed that he had enough, and on February 17th he fired the mine at a time when the imperial family ought to be assembled for a festive dinner. But the Tsar was late for dinner, and again he escaped unhurt.

The closing scene is one of dramatic interest. It was decided to lay a mine under a street through which the Tsar had frequently to pass, near the palace, and at the same time station men with special bombs to throw at the carriage, in case the mine failed. The conspirators hired a shop, and, while some of them conducted a brisk and honest trade in eggs and butter, others tunnelled beneath the street. The soil was removed in the empty boxes, and, though the police several times visited the shop, they detected nothing beyond a popular grocery business. The tunnel was complete, and the mine ready, about the middle of March (1881).

The dramatic feature is that meantime Alexander II was being induced to consider proposals of reform. He had, after the outrage at the palace, removed the Governor General of St. Petersburg and entrusted the repression of anarchy to a Supreme Commanding Commission. The leading spirit of this was General Loris Melikoff, who had had some success as Governor General of Kharkoff. Melikoff's method was to isolate the terrorists by granting reforms which would conciliate the general body of malcontents. He pressed this method upon the Tsar, as Alexander, distracted and weary, perhaps a little anxious about his life, decided to try it. The prisons and the settlements of Siberia were explored, and large numbers were restored to their homes. About two thousand students were permitted to return to the universities, and the scholarships were restored. Melikoff then proposed a scheme of popular representation which, though it did not exactly give Russia a constitution, might have conciliated many. The reactionary ministers and courtiers now doubled their efforts to restrain the Tsar, but he accepted Melikoff's draft, and kept it several days for revision. He probably wavered and postponed the fatal decision. And it

THE TRAGEDY OF ALEXANDER II

was during that week of delay that the conspirators completed their preparations.

On March 16th Alexander read the draft to his ministers and approved it. His relief at having reached a definite policy was great, and in happier mood he drove out to review his troops. As he returned to the palace a young woman in the street waved her handkerchief. She was the redoubtable Sophia Perovskaia, and was giving the signal. A bomb was thrown, and the carriage was wrapped in a cloud of smoke, while Cossacks writhed on the ground. But out of the smoke and litter the Tsar again emerged unhurt. Against the advice of his officers he lingered to say a word to the wounded, and it is said that he congratulated himself on his escape. "It is too early to congratulate yourself," said a young man who, through some oversight, had been permitted to approach. He flung his bomb, and the Tsar fell, fearfully and mortally wounded. He died at the palace two hours later. "They who draw the sword shall perish by the sword," the rebels grimly commented. The doctrine of the assassination of tyrants—of men who stifled constitutional demands by the shedding of blood—was then held by even moderate radicals in many lands. There were others who pointed out that Alexander II, who had inherited an empty purse, left many millions of rubles to be divided amongst his family.

CHAPTER XV

ENTER POBIEDONOSTSEFF

THE romance of the Romanoffs has now passed the phase of comparative dulness which set in with the conversion of the dynasty from its license of personal conduct, and has entered upon its final stage of mingled melodrama and tragedy. The Russian people is awakening to a consciousness that what some call an autocracy by divine right is a foreign intrusion into the life of the Slavs, an infringement of the rights of man. Three ways of meeting the crisis were open to the new Emperor, Alexander III. He might grant the full constitutional liberty that had now been won in every civilisation of the world except China; he might follow the course traced by Melikoff and prolong the life of the dynasty; he might prefer to extinguish every demand and insist upon an unadulterated autocracy. Alexander III chose, with such modifications as his vacillations allowed, the third course.

He was the second son of Alexander II. The eldest son had died in 1865 of consumption, but Alexander was a man of exceptionally strong con-

ENTER POBIEDONOSTSEFF

stitution. There is a tradition that he could take a horse-shoe in his mighty hand and bend it until the points touched. Such a youth would make a fine soldier, and as a soldier he was trained. He was cool, courageous (as he showed on various occasions), regular in life, sincerely religious, and very little cultivated. When his brother died, he had to be prepared for the business of ruling a very unruly Empire. But he was now twenty years old, dull in intellect, and altogether indisposed to acquire the varied culture which his future required. One of his tutors was the famous Pobiedonostseff: who was not at that time a pronounced reactionary, but his office prepared the way for power in his reactionary days. It is said that his wife, the Princess Dagmar of Denmark, induced him to prepare more carefully for the throne; but that seems to be a legend of the court. All that men knew about him was that he liked soldiering and music and patronised historical research, and thought that there were far too many Germans in Russia.

On this last feature some built a faint hope. Germany was now an Empire, and the "League of the Three Emperors" (Germany, Austria and Russia) boded no good for democracy. Bismarck encouraged both the policy of repression in Russia and the policy of aggression abroad because he did *not* wish to see Russia develop her mighty resources. On the other hand, Alexander was a soldier, a man steeped in the Romanoff tradition of a divine autocracy and entirely out of sympathy with humanitarian or progressive ideas. The only question was whether from policy he would follow the lead of Melikoff. When the oath of allegiance was taken he announced, ambiguously, that he would walk in the steps of his father. Which set of steps? Melikoff showed him the draft of a pseudo-constitution initialled by the late Tsar. "There will be no change," he said. But men were uncertain. The fearful end of his father must have embittered him. The rebels were, of course, drastically punished. Eight hundred more arrests were made. Sophia Perovskaia, the wonderful woman of those bloody days, and four others were executed. There is a grounded suspicion that they were first tortured. Another woman was condemned, but she was pregnant, and her sentence was changed to exile.

It is thought by many that an injudicious step taken by the revolutionaries helped to fix the Tsar's plan. They somehow got into his hands a long letter or manifesto, in which, while pleading for reform, they very plainly held a sword over his head; and their demands were not at all moderate. I doubt if Alexander III ever hesitated. His strong and narrow mind and soldierly attitude disposed him to "enforce discipline." Pobiedonostseff was soon at his side. He was Procurator of the Holy Synod (since the preceding year). When

ENTER POBIEDONOSTSEFF

Melikoff's scheme was brought forward for discussion he bitterly opposed it, and predicted that it would ruin Russia. He was now a Russophile of the narrowest and most fanatical description. Alexander leaned to that side. The German Emperor had, he said, warned his father against making any concessions to constitutionalism. The "Holy League"—a fanatical Russophile society led by the Grand Duke Vladimir—pressed for coercion.

Out of the struggle there emerged at last (on April 29th) the new Tsar's message to his people. It was probably written by Pobiedonostseff. In it Alexander firmly contended that the autocracy was of divine origin, and he would protect it against all encroachments. But the reforms granted by his father would not be withdrawn. Education, popular councils, municipal institutions, and so on, were to be maintained. The people were to be admitted to some share in the management of the Empire's affairs. That was to be the note of the new reign: something more moderate than Pobiedonostseff and less "advanced" than Melikoff.

Melikoff resigned, and his place as Minister of the Interior was taken by General Ignatieff, a man of moderate conservative views, or a man who at least felt the need of concessions. On the one hand he looked with criminal toleration upon the massacres of the Jews which now broke out all over

Russia. On the other he advised the Tsar that large reforms were needed. The peasants were assisted in paying off the crippling annual interest on their "emancipation." Popular councils were set up in Poland, Siberia, and the Baltic provinces, which had not hitherto had them. Above all he devised, and imposed upon the Tsar, a feeble pretence of a national parliament. Members of the provincial councils—"informed men," as they were diplomatically called—were gathered into a deliberating assembly at St. Petersburg, and it was through them that the reforms were gradually drafted. There was an improvement in the harsh manner of collecting the taxes, and the burden was shifted a little more on to the shoulders of the wealthy. Banks were opened for the peasants.

The conservatives stormed the Tsar with protests against these dangerous concessions, and in the spring of 1882 General Ignatieff was forced to retire. His place was taken by Count Dmitri Tolstoi, one of the men of the last reign whom liberals hated above all others. He had been the Minister of Education during the late Tsar's drastic restriction of the schools and universities. He and Pobiedonostseff and a few other rabid Slavophiles now closed round Alexander III and dictated the policy of his reign. That policy was one of, at home, unswerving, unscrupulous, unmerciful Russification; that is to say, complete obliteration of all

ENTER POBIEDONOSTSEFF

criticism of the autocracy in native Russia and all religious or racial characters in the subject-provinces of alien race or religion. Abroad, the policy was naturally Pan-Slav, aggressive, imperialistic; but here the Emperor and his limited resources curbed the fanatics, so that the reign passed without a war. Russia was orientated for the final struggle in the next reign. For the reign of Alexander we need only glance at the various branches of the machinery of despotism which was created for the defence of the Romanoffs.

Education was the great source of evil, but in a world where education was now adopted as an elementary principle of civilisation it was no longer possible to return to the absolute illiteracy of the Middle Ages. A compromise was found in the easy distinction between sound and unsound education. The figures of educational progress during the reign of Alexander III are at first sight impressive. In 1877 the eight universities had had 5629 students: in 1886 the number had arisen to 14,000. In the same period the number of high schools rose from 200 to about a thousand: the number of elementary schools from 25,077 to 35,517. There were now, in all, more than two million pupils in the elementary schools of the Empire. It should be added that the population of the Empire was now 113,000,000; that most of the schools were founded, independently of St. Petersburg, by the zealous

Zemstvos; and that very many of them were mere huts or sheds with ludicrously incompetent teachers.

Count Tolstoi, having been for sixteen years Minister of Education, controlled this department in the interest of the Slavophiles and imperialists. Pobiedonostseff, indeed, wanted to have all the elementary schools put under the control of the Holy Synod, or under the clergy. I have said little about the Russian Church during this period for a reason which will be understood. It was a mere docile instrument of the dynasty. Its ordinary priests were rough, ignorant men, little superior to the peasants themselves. Its higher clergy murmured not one single syllable at the cruelty, just as they had murmured none at the earlier vices, of the Romanoffs.

The Zemstvos, however, in most cases refused to hand over their schools, and the secular part of the government had neither the funds to devote to the work nor the wish to have serious trouble with the Zemstvos. We shall see that they found it easier to capture the Zemstvos themselves and control their action. The Holy Synod also began the policy of creating religious schools in opposition to those of the Zemstvos, and securing imperial favour for these nurseries of docility. The high schools were re-modelled, and were now forbidden by law to admit the children of the poorer types of workers. Some technical improvements were made in them,

ENTER POBIEDONOSTSEFF

but the general effect was to reduce the stimulating influence of the education. The universities were more drastically controlled. No students' societies were permitted, and the curriculum was carefully purged. Inspectors were attached to them, and the grant of scholarships was made to depend upon the reports of these spies of orthodoxy. There were serious riots of the students in 1882 and 1887, but the energy of the reactionary officials gradually drove professors into silence or exile and pupils into subjection.

The press was in 1882 controlled by "temporary rules," which proved to have a long duration. If a journal had, after three warnings, incurred suspension, it must, at the expiration of the term, henceforward submit a copy of the next day's issue to the censors before eleven at night. This effectively silenced the majority of the liberal periodicals, and eviscerated the others. When some tried to evade the gag by using language of a veiled or ambiguous character, a junta of four Ministers was empowered to suppress any periodical which seemed to them to have a mischievous tendency. By these and other means progressive literature was extinguished. The few revolutionaries continued, of course, to establish private presses, which were constantly detected and the workers sent to Siberia or the mines, but the work of political education was generally suspended.

THE ROMANCE OF THE ROMANOFFS

The political scheme which had been set up was similarly "revised." The Zemstvos were, as I said, stubborn. Even the nobles were jealous of their local powers, and at first antagonistic to the new regime. Large numbers of them were won by stories of dangerous tendencies amongst the peasantry. It is said that in their attacks upon the Jews the people had said: "We will make our breakfast of the Jews, our dinner of the landowners, and our supper of the priests." Priests and nobles fell into line with the ministers. In 1889 and 1890 the nobles were given a preponderating influence over the other representatives in the Zemstvos. They became little more than assemblies of loyal landowners, open to the direct influence of the government. The Mir was similarly enfeebled, and lost its popular representative value.

The judicial system was correspondingly modified. Public executions were abandoned, in the spirit of the age, and some other improvements were introduced. But the general scheme set up by Alexander II had been too grossly ignored in the later years of that monarch, and it was now modified by decree. The jury-system was reduced; the justices of the peace abolished. Petty cases fell back to the reorganised Zemstvos.

The financial system, on the other hand, remained for many years under the control of an enlightened minister, Bunge, and was greatly improved.

ENTER POBIEDONOSTSEFF

Finance was in any case a department into which it was profitable to admit modern science. The coinage was improved, and more banks were established. Home-industry was fostered, and the great extension of the Empire in Asia opened new markets. Railways were multiplied, and in 1891 the Grand Duke Nicholas opened the terminal station of the proposed Trans-Siberian railway at Vladivostock. Russia had already made commercial treaties with Korea and Japan. We will return presently to this dangerous extension of Russian ambition.

Most important and characteristic of all was the process of Russification in which all these engines of reaction were combined. One can understand the fascination of the Slavophile dream as it was formed in the mind of honest conservatives. Every concession made in the western democracies and limited monarchies had led to further demands. Napoleon III had lost his throne. The Papacy had lost its temporal power. William I and Bismarck were struggling against a portentous growth of Socialism. France was rapidly shedding its religion. Even in England the republican movement was at that time (the eighties) strong, and lower depths of radicalism were disclosed every decade. Liberalism, either in religion or politics, was evidently a slope; you could not remain long elsewhere than at the top or the bottom. So Russia must be made thoroughly, homogeneously autocratic and religious. In spite of the well-known facts of Russian history the Church agreed warmly with the Romanoffs that the autocracy was divinely appointed. If all could be made docile to the Church, the autocracy would have an easier task.

So began the process of Russification which passed with the brutality of a steam-roller over every sect or fragment of the nation that was not Russian in creed and dynastic in politics. The Jews formed the gravest problem. Long experience had shown that no power on earth could erase the religious and racial peculiarities of the Jew, yet there were nearly five million Jews in the Russian Empire. Their intelligence and skill in trade were but additional grievances. There were, even then, parts of Russia in which the Jews showed that, under proper treatment, they were as capable as any of settling upon the soil, but as a rule they avoided agriculture. The slightest relaxation of pressure allowed them to pour into a city or even a district, and as traders and money-lenders they soon had the poor and thriftless Russians in their power. Hence, in great measure, the readiness of the people to rise against them, which was gradually exploited rather than checked from St. Petersburg.

The first procedure of the reactionary ministers was to overlook the massacres which took place from the beginning of the rule of Alexander III.

Tauride Palace, Petrograd, Meeting Place of the Duma

Session Chamber of the Duma, Tauride Palace, Petrograd

ENTER POBIEDONOSTSEFF

Presently, a series of "temporary rules" were issued against them. Even in the Pale of Settlement they were compelled to live in the towns and were forbidden to purchase real estate in the country. In 1888 they were ordered to go back to the place in which they had lived before the year 1882. About a million and a half of the Jews were affected by this rule, and the chaotic abandonment of their several businesses and properties cast large numbers of them into deep and undeserved poverty. Vast aggregations of them, growing at a prodigious rate on account of their high fertility, huddled together in the towns of the Pale, and lived in great privation. In 1891 a new application of the rules exiled and ruined seventeen thousand Jewish artisans of Moscow.

Still more stupid, and hardly less cruel, was the restriction upon the development of their ability. The civil service and the professions were closed against them. They might not, without special license, have a Christian servant, and notaries were forbidden to have Jewish clerks. Their zeal for education was similarly repressed. In the universities which were situated in the Pale Jewish students must not number more than a tenth of the whole. At other provincial universities they must not number more than five per cent.; at the metropolitan universities not more than two per cent. By these contemptuous repressive measures the ignorant people were prepared for the pogroms which would disgrace the reign of the last of the Romanoffs.

The Poles were the next most conspicuous victims of the Slavophile policy. We saw that Alexander II had ordered the extinction of their nationality, but a people with an acute memory of having been a great civilisation at a time when the Russians were a disorderly mass of semi-barbarians could not easily resign itself to obliteration. The religious tradition here coincided with the national, as in Ireland (the Poland of the west), and the priests generally fostered insurgence. Alexander's ruthless ministers had but to apply more stringently the laws already in force against the Poles. From the University of Warsaw to the smallest elementary school the teaching was entirely Russianised. Even the Bank of Warsaw was suppressed, and Polish trade forced into a branch of the Russian bank. There was a futile rising in 1885, but four executions and two hundred arrests completed the work of "pacifying" the country, or eliminating from it every man of spirit and courage. Even Finland, which was still autonomous, had to complain to the Tsar of encroachments upon the liberties which his father had sworn to respect. In the other Baltic provinces the Russian roller was used as in Poland.

The dissenters and heretics of every kind in Rus-

ENTER POBIEDONOSTSEFF

sia itself were similarly treated. To the tenacious dissenters of the last century or two were now added sects like the Doukhobors and the followers of Tolstoi, and upon these the Tsar's ministers fell with particular malevolence. Alexander was ignorant enough to believe quite sincerely in the doctrines of the Orthodox Church, but he knew that these new sects had more than a religious significance. Prayer-meetings were prohibited. Even children were separated in some cases from their parents and forced into the rigid Slavophile mould.

It will be understood, after this description of the machinery that was set up by Tolstoi and Pobiedonostseff, that the chronicle of revolt in the reign of Alexander II is comparatively slender. It is computed that by the end of the reign there were about a hundred thousand rebels in the jails, the mines, and the Siberian colonies, and to these one must add the graves of the bolder spirits and the large numbers of Russians who sought abroad the liberty that had died in Russia. Men still risked their lives in printing and disseminating the new ideas, but as the long reign wore on, and tyranny was still enthroned, the open spurts of defiance grew less in number. The revolutionaries and liberals felt that, if their race was not to be extinguished, as the reactionaries desired, the work must proceed in different form. We shall see in the next and final chapter how it proceeded until, after further bloody revolts against the intolerable tyranny, it succeeded in awakening the people and shaking the Romanoffs from their throne.

It remains to see how the Pan-Slav movement, the twin-brother of the Slavophile philosophy, also prepared the way for the next reign. We have seen how every expansion of Russia, every enlargement of its stupendous population and therefore ultimate resources, alarmed some other European Power. Russia now made new advances and opened the way for fresh conflicts. It had reached the eastern coast of Asia. Now it began its interference in Korea and attracted the attention of Japan. It spread south toward India and still further alarmed England. Journals of the imperialist school at St. Petersburg openly boasted that their armies were beating a path to the Indian Ocean, and it may be said in justification of England's long distrust of Russia that the Romanoffs wholly encouraged this dream until an Asiatic Power proved to them that Asia was not the helpless world they had imagined. When the southern limit of Asiatic Russia was extended until it came, at certain points, within a hundred and forty miles of India, when Russian agents swarmed in Afghanistan, it was not unnatural that London should be nervous. Alexander III, however, took a keen personal interest in foreign affairs, and he succeeded in averting serious trouble with England.

ENTER POBIEDONOSTSEFF

Still more dangerous to the peace of the world was the ambition of the Pan-Slavs to overrun the Balkans. Our generation is familiar enough with the philosophy in the form of Pan-Germanism, and from this the mood of Russia in the days of Alexander III will be understood. The creed of the Pan-Slavs was a mixture of commercial greed, imperialistic ambition, the impulses of soldiers to use their weapons, and the desire of priests to enlarge their Church. As the little peoples of the Balkans were largely Slav—though the Bulgars are as much Asiatic as Slav, and the Rumans take more pride in their remote descent from the Romans—it was inevitable that, in spite of the jealous watchfulness of all the Great Powers of Europe, the new imperialists of St. Petersburg should push their work in the Balkans.

There is this almost single advantage in the reign of Alexander III that he distrusted Germany and did not allow his ambitious ministers to embroil the country in war. Bismarck would like to see Russia weakened, as it periodically was, by war, and there seemed to be every prospect of war over the Balkan peoples. Behind the specious plea of liberating Christians from the brutality of the Turk and conveying civilisation to the backward peoples of the Balkans there was at that time, as in our own days, a dual rivalry. Austria and the Papacy had an ambition which was directly opposed to the ambition of the statesmen and priests of St. Petersburg. The path to the Mediterranean and the commercial advantage of exploiting the Balkan peoples were not more eagerly sought by politicians and merchants than the religious allegiance of the independent Balkan Churches was sought by the Vatican and the Holy Synod.

Russia pushed its ambition in Bulgaria—Austria in Bosnia and Herzegovina, which had been entrusted to its "protection." But the little Balkan peoples were now almost entirely awake to the designs of the ministers of Alexander III. The Tsar said on one occasion that the King of Montenegro was the only friend he had in Europe. The Serbs and Rumans drew nearer to Austria, the Bulgars began to resent the presence amongst them of so many officers of the Russian army and agents of the Russian Government. After the Bulgar revolution of 1885 there seemed to be grave prospect of a war between Austria and Russia. But Alexander was made sensible of the disgusting duplicity with which Bismarck tried to draw Russia into dangerous waters in the south, and he withdrew his officers from Bulgaria. He complained to the German Emperor of the procedure of the Chancellor, but he maintained the commercial alliance with Germany and the ostensibly friendly relations.

Out of this rivalry of interests and clash of intrigue, in which Alexander III acted with caution

ENTER POBIEDONOSTSEFF

and shrewdness, there gradually emerged the set of alliances which would one day deluge Europe with blood. Germany and Austria made a common lot of their interests and drew together. Italy, jealous of the French support of the Papacy and won by the deceitful promises of Germany, joined them and formed the Triple Alliance. Russia could no longer remain isolated and Alexander III slowly and reluctantly overcame his imperial dislike of the French Republic. Little acts of mutual courtesy led up to the floating of a large loan in France in 1887. The financial link with Germany was almost severed. In the following year a Russian representative was appointed to the Vatican. In 1890 a large French fleet appeared at Cronstadt, and was boisterously welcomed. In 1893, the year before the death of Alexander, a commercial treaty with France was signed.

Thus in both domestic and foreign policy the reign of Alexander III was one of preparation for the final chapter of the romance of the Romanoffs. It created at home a machinery of despotism which would prove so heavy that it roused the very people whom it was designed to suppress. Abroad it entered upon imperialistic ventures which would lead to wars that would expose the disgusting growth of corruption under the shelter of the universal censorship. Alexander III died in 1894 (November 1st), and left to the last of his line a country which he had apparently pacified. He was honest in his creed of orthodoxy and autocracy, though we will not suppose that he was insensible of its profit to himself and his family; but he had not the intelligence to see that such an anachronism as his mediæval suppression of a people's sentiments could not live in the atmosphere of the end of the nineteenth century.

CHAPTER XVI

THE LAST OF THE ROMANOFFS

THE crowning act of the drama of the Romanoffs has a peculiar irony. One could well imagine a Romanoff of the seventeenth or eighteenth century making a ferocious struggle against the democratic forces which now threatened the autocracy. For those older monarchs power had been a means of obtaining wealth, of enlarging their individual pleasures to royal or imperial proportions, and they would use all the machinery of despotism to maintain their splendid privileges. But in proportion as the democratic menace grew in the nineteenth century the voluptuous selfishness of the Russian monarchs diminished. The serious, almost ascetic, standard set up by Alexander I lingered in the imperial palaces, and it seemed that the less personal gratification the monarch received from his autocratic power the more resolutely he fought to retain it. The last of the Romanoffs was one of the most sober and industrious of his line; and his reign was disgraced by a more bloody and cruel coercion than had reddened the reign of any of his predecessors.

Nicholas II, son of Alexander III and Princess Dagmar of Denmark, is one of those tantalising personalities whom one knows to be in themselves far removed from subtlety, yet whom one cannot honestly pretend to understand. He came to the throne an unknown man, eagerly scrutinised by every moderate reformer in Russia. He departs from it with his personality and actions still largely enveloped in mystery. This obscurity is, as I said, not due to any depth or subtlety in the mind of the Tsar; it is due rather to the weakness of his character. Two sets of influences surrounded him, bending to their will his frail personality and substituting their cupidity or prejudice for his native impulses. The inner circle was that of his family, in which his mother and uncles were the leading and most mischievous figures. The outer circle was the ring of adventurers or reactionaries whom the strength of his older relatives or the febrility of his own character invested successively with ministerial power. Beyond these, again, were the religious charlatans who at times preyed upon the superstition of the Tsar and Tsarina, the great body of ecclesiastical and other officers whose interest it was to maintain the existing system, and the doctrinaire conservatives who, with purblind eyes, insisted upon the isolation of Russia from the

THE LAST OF THE ROMANOFFS

progress of the world. Through this maze of intrigue and influence it is difficult to reach the personality of Nicholas II with confidence, and the fierce partisanship of writers on both sides in the great struggle increases our task of disentangling the precise parts in the final catastrophe.

It seems, however, to be an error to regard the last of the Romanoffs as a mere puppet, a tearful and hysterical implement, of the reactionary influences which surrounded him. Nicholas had not the robustness of his father, whose dwarf intellect had been lodged in the frame of a Russian giant, but he was stronger than many literary portraits of him suggest to us. His education had been severely controlled. Distinguished experts had taught him those branches of culture—law, history, and political economy—which were deemed necessary in a successor of Alexander III, and a rigorous physical training had braced the comparative feebleness of his person. He swam and rowed with skill, he played tennis and hunted, and throughout his reign he loved a long walk, often of ten or fifteen miles, and would at times burden himself with all the equipment of a common infantryman. It is said that the sabre-cut on the head which he received from a Japanese fanatic in 1891, when he made a tour of the Empire and further Asia, injured his brain and led to nervous instability; but this is one of the many statements of revolutionary writers which have not been checked by sober criticism. He came to the throne in 1894, a cool, self-possessed, carefully-educated young man of twenty-six, and some hope was excited in the breast of moderate Russian liberalism.

To this it may be added that throughout his reign Nicholas II adhered to a sober and industrious standard of life. Here, indeed, the writers of the opposing schools begin to differ. That he was a man of comparatively simple and sober tastes none disputes. His table was temperate and conspicuous for old Russian dishes. He spent his leisure in the domestic circle, playing dominoes or billiards in the metropolitan palaces, sharing walks or rides or sails with his family in the provinces. He opened every day with religious observances, had the family ikons brought on voyages, and rigorously kept the fasts of the Church.

But his industry and attention to affairs are differently represented. Conservatives picture him a model of severe self-sacrifice. He worked, they say, without secretaries, ten or twelve hours every day. He minutely studied and annotated every document. He wore his pencil to the stump—the conservative pen records this with awed amazement—and then gave the stump gravely to his son. One imagines him relaxing from the cares of Empire but for an hour in the evening. The revolutionary writers, however, depict him differently.

THE LAST OF THE ROMANOFFS

They represent that he attended impatiently to serious affairs and spent an abnormal proportion of the day in the petty amusements of the domestic circle. The truth lies between the extremes. Nicholas II was industrious, and he attempted to discharge his functions very seriously within the limits of his narrow and mediocre conceptions.

His people were not long in doubt as to the nature of his ideal. It was the ideal which each Romanoff of the century had naïvely conceived afresh; a complete retention of the autocracy coupled with a benevolent intention to help his people. On the day of his father's death Nicholas issued a manifesto in which he promised to promote "the progress and peaceful glory of his dear Russia and the happiness of his faithful subjects." To the deputies who came to congratulate him he said that—as his foreign minister, M. de Giers, also assured foreign Powers—he would maintain his father's policy. Plainly the young Emperor approached his task with the customary confidence of youth. He would avoid the error of his predecessors and, by wise moderation, disarm the malcontents and sustain a benevolent despotism.

But Nicholas soon discovered that the last reign still survived in such power as to admit no new experiments. His mother, the Dowager-Empress, was a harsh and arrogant woman, uniting to her political ignorance and incompetence a fierce resolution to have her husband's policy sustained. Nicholas's uncles, the Grand Dukes Sergius and Alexander, were of the same harshly despotic temper, and Pobiedonostseff, the head of the Holy Synod, was the enthusiastic supporter of their wishes. These four, with the reactionary ministers Plehve, Muravieff, and Brezobrazoff (later Admiral Alexieff and others), whom they gradually discovered and promoted, formed what came to be known as the "Immortal Seven," the caucus which led the dynasty to its destruction.

Nicholas was not married at the time of his accession. It was not until November that he married Princess Alix of Hesse-Darmstadt, who entered the Orthodox Church and adopted the name of Alexandra Feodorovna. It is said that at the last moment the Dowager-Empress took a violent dislike to her and enlivened the palace with lamentable exhibitions of her violent temper. It is at least clear that in the earlier years the Tsarina had no influence. Only in the last phase did she, by her pro-German leanings and her ignorant susceptibility to the intrigues of religious adventurers, contribute to the downfall of the monarchy.

Nicholas was crowned at Moscow on May 26th, 1895, and a terrible catastrophe clouded the very opening of his reign. Hundreds of thousands of peasants flocked to Moscow for the festivity, and for the presents which were promised them, and they spent the night packed into the field of Khodynski. A panic arose amongst them, and about a thousand of them—some say several thousand—were trodden under foot or cast into the ditch and perished. It was a bad beginning, and the Tsar soon made matters worse. In July nearly two hundred delegations brought to his palace the congratulations of every class of his people, and faint and respectful suggestions of reform were inserted in the bouquets of traditional compliment. From the province of Tver, especially, came a demand for liberal institutions, and the Emperor received it with a smiling disdain which showed how little he understood his country. These were "foolish dreams," he said; he would devote all his strength to the welfare of his country, but he would, "with equal firmness, maintain the autocracy."

A few reforms were introduced. Count de Witte fought his way to the head of the Treasury and improved the finances. The immense flow of paper money was checked, and gold was accumulated at the banks or put into circulation. Ukases were passed which directed the building of model houses for the workers, and regulated to some extent their condition in the growing industries of Russia. New railways were built and canals projected. The army was partly reorganised; the administrative and judiciary institutions of the Empire extended to Siberia, the development of which was energetically pushed; a measure to give separated married women the control of their property was passed; education was further enforced, though in this respect the reform was weakened or undone by the desperate efforts of the clergy to wrest the elementary schools from the Zemstvos.

These reforms, however, like those of the preceding reigns, were trivial in comparison with the mighty needs of Russia, and it was now felt by all but the incurable conservatives and the parasites of the autocracy that self-government, through popular institutions, was the first and essential condition of reform. On this issue the dynasty, or the misguided group who undertook to guide its fortunes, staked its existence. How far any of the reactionaries really believed that the autocracy was for the welfare of the Russian people it is not our place to consider here. The antagonistic forces moved slowly toward the field of battle.

With the general policy and personal adventures of Nicholas II I am not concerned. The whole interest of the story is now concentrated in the growth of the conflict which will presently put an end to the Romanoffs. It suffices to say that Russophilism and Pan-Slavism continued to act together, and were equally responsible for the fall of the dynasty. Nicholas II professed a humane dislike of the coercive policy of his father, and in some respects, in the early years, the zeal of officials in

THE LAST OF THE ROMANOFFS

persecuting dissenters was moderated. But the facts of the entire reign are within the memory of my readers and their ghastly inconsistence with this humane profession need scarcely be emphasised. Never since the Middle Ages had the Jews suffered so brutally at the hands of their Christian masters. Unscrupulous officials and bodies of ignorant men like the "Black Hundreds" soon learned that massacre and pillage of the Jews were looked upon with favour at the palace, and the repeated "pogroms" are in themselves an indelible disgrace upon the name of Nicholas II. The Russianisation of the Poles—for which Russia pays heavily to-day—and the Lithuanians was maintained with all the earlier brutality, and in regard to the Finns Nicholas II incurred a peculiar stigma. He had at his accession sworn to respect the rights and the constitution of the Finns, but before long his officials tore up his oath and began to strip the vigorous little people of its nationality. Hardly a year of the Tsar's reign passed without some callous violation of his solemn promise, done with his express authority. The whole Empire must, in spite of every obligation, be squeezed into the Russian mould. The only extenuating feature of this section of the Tsar's work that one can suggest is that the Russian people generally were in accord with this harsh and unjust procedure.

The imperialistic tendency which led to this injustice equally shaped the disastrous foreign policy of Nicholas II. There can be little doubt that the Tsar desired a continuance of the peace which Russia had enjoyed during his father's reign, and for my part I am ready to recognise his sincerity in issuing a summons to a Peace Congress (August 24th, 1898), the aims of which Nicholas defined in a personal letter (January 11th, 1899). It was, as we now know, Germany which chiefly frustrated that well-meant effort. The Tsar remained friendly with Germany, which then wavered between a Russian and an English *entente,* while further strengthening his alliance with France.

But the Tsar's desire of peace was, from the general practical point of view, rendered nugatory by his imperialistic policy. In the Balkans he maintained that policy of secret and subtle infiltration which prepared the way for a conflict with Austria. Alexander III had in effect retired from the Balkans, disgusted at the ingratitude of the principalities Russia had helped to set up. Nicholas II resumed the policy of disguised penetration, and it is not too much to say that the southern Slavs felt almost as much apprehension at the shadow of Russia as at the encroachments of Austria. It was, however, the imperialist adventures in the Far East which contained the gravest danger and were least respectable in principle.

It was entirely natural that Russia should spread

The Tsarina Alexandra

THE LAST OF THE ROMANOFFS

along its Trans-Siberian line, develop its vast domains in Asia, and seek ice-free ports on the eastern coast. This national ambition was, however, complicated by sordid speculations on the part of men and women who, directly or indirectly, had influence over the Tsar. Revolutionary writers say that the Dowager-Empress herself speculated heavily in Asiatic properties, and at least it may be regarded as certain that the Grand Dukes and adherents of the court sought fortune in that direction. From Siberia these cupidities reached out toward Manchuria and Korea, and had large and vague designs upon helpless China. Russia—so the formula ran—was the heir of Dchingis Khan and Timur. It had a "divine mission" to impose its Kultur upon Asia. The very thin strain of Tatar blood in the veins of Russia was at length discovered to have some value.

The Chino-Japanese War occurred in the first year of the reign of Nicholas II, and the rise of an Asiatic power in the path of Russian ambition caused a momentary concern. Japan must be promptly checked, and at the close of the war Russia bluntly refused to allow Japan to occupy any of the territory it had seized. Germany astutely watched and fostered the dangerous adventure which diverted Russia from Europe to the Far East. Under cover of its supposed protection of China, Russia then established itself in Manchuria, secured (with money borrowed from France and England) a financial hold on China, and in 1898 obtained a long lease of Port Arthur and Talienwan. The cold anger of the Japanese at this piece of perfidy was little disguised, and presently Russia was requested to carry out its promise to evacuate Manchuria. From its new ports, it was plain to all, Russia would spread to Korea. The other European Powers now joined in the protest of Japan, and Russia sought to gain time by long negotiations, while it pressed the development of Port Arthur and Dalny. These devices Japan, in 1904, sternly cut short by making war.

The documentary evidence in regard to those aspects of the Russo-Japanese War which concern us here is in the same unsatisfactory condition as so much of the evidence on which we must rely in this chapter. It awaits the impartial sifting of history. The suppression of truth in Russia throughout the reign of Nicholas II had the inevitable effect of provoking abroad a stream of something more than the truth. Writers and orators of revolutionary parties do not usually make calm and conscientious reflection on the statements they repeat, and in every country of the world the Russian writers found a large public eager to hear sensational stories about the court and the bureaucracy. It is at present entirely impossible to select with any confidence the reliable statements from the mass of legends which

THE LAST OF THE ROMANOFFS

were published in Europe and America by the critics of the dynasty. Their fellows in Russia were, we shall see, being butchered in thousands, and were in tens of thousands suffering an agony which they often terminated by suicide; and, on the other hand, many of the chief agents of this bloody system were undoubtedly corrupt adventurers or cynical egoists. In the vast anti-Romanoff literature, therefore, we cannot look for judicious impartiality, and if the reader misses from this chapter many a picturesque legend which he has read in the scorching pages of revolutionary writers he must not be surprised. The history of that appalling reign is still to be written.

As far as the Russo-Japanese War is concerned we need not hesitate to admit three points. The first is that the Tsar, if not some of his ministers, sincerely believed that the little nation of the Far East would never have the audacity to fight mighty Russia; and that Germany encouraged the Russian court in this view. Japan was bluffing, the Tsar was assured, and he might pursue his eastern extension under cover of a hollow and dilatory diplomatic negotiation. The second clear point is that this eastern extension of Russia was very largely due to the corrupt and selfish ambitions of influential individuals. Stories about the investments of the Dowager-Empress or the Grand Dukes or other persons of the Tsar's circle may or may not be true. There is fair evidence that the speculative fever penetrated the court. In any case the "divine mission" of Russia in the Far East was as hollow a pretence as the divine mission of Germany in the west in 1914. The third established point, and the one of most importance for our purpose, is that members of the imperial family and servants of the reactionary regime made vast sums of money by a corrupt diversion of goods and funds from the purposes of war to their private purses.

The knowledge of these facts came to thoughtful people in Russia as the ignominious campaign dragged on from month to month. Public opinion, startled by the success of what they had been taught to regard as a tribe of "monkeys" against their great army, looked for hidden reasons of Russia's failure, and they were brought to light. It was known that aristocratic officers gambled and rioted in the Asiatic towns; it was known that trained regiments of the regular army were kept at home to coerce Russia while crowds of reservists were hurried out to meet the deadly Japanese fire; it was known that the large sums extorted from the people for the prosecution of the war were to a great extent diverted; it was known that Count de Witte and Count Lamsdorff had tried to avert war, and that Manchurian affairs had then been entrusted to a favourite of the palace-clique, Admiral Alexieff.

THE LAST OF THE ROMANOFFS

Before the war was half over the revolution was again aflame in Russia, and it grew daily.

We are told by writers who seem to have had the confidence of the revolutionaries that the complete suppression of overt criticism by Alexander III and his son had led to the formation of a new and very powerful secret movement. It had branches in all parts of Russia, and it is said to have had as many as three million members in the year 1904. Twelve men of distinguished ability directed its propaganda, and many wealthy Russians, disgusted at or injured by the atrocious system which Nicholas II maintained, devoted their whole fortunes to its work. Many of the stories told of its secret action are melodramatic and improbable, but it cannot be doubted that a vast and well-organised movement existed, not unlike the secret republican organisation which was then being formed in Portugal. The Russian movement, however, was not definitely republican. It aimed at converting the Tsar, under pressure of his people, to constitutional views. It resented and despised the turbulent movements of the students and Socialists, and it countenanced assassination only in very grave and carefully-selected cases. We are told that its agents repeatedly placed on the Tsar's desk letters in which the situation was fully described and Nicholas was urged to make peace with his people

THE ROMANCE OF THE ROMANOFFS

by granting a constitution and casting off the influence of the Dowager-Empress.

The early agitation was crushed with the customary brutality. One of the most repulsive adventurers of the time, Plehve, had become Minister of the Interior, and under his genial lead the police and magistrates fell upon every suspicion of revolt. Over the greater part of Russia the protection of civil law had been virtually suspended since 1881. Under what was called "The Regulation for Reinforced Protection" suspects might be at any time arrested and imprisoned, journals suppressed, the civil courts entirely ignored. In the year 1903 nearly 400 men and women had been arrested under this barbarous system, and it was estimated that there were already more than 100,000 in the jails of Russia and in Siberia. The work had continued, however, and the revolutionaries boast that in the very year before the war, the year when they seemed to be feeblest, they circulated two million pamphlets among the Russian people. As the agitation grew with the war, Plehve retorted with increased savagery; and on July 28th (1904), he was, in spite of his extraordinary precautions, assassinated. The murderer, Sazonoff, was sentenced only to twenty years' imprisonment, and Nicholas reduced this to fourteen years. The revolutionaries claim that they warned the Tsar that he answered with his life for the life of Sazonoff. It

THE LAST OF THE ROMANOFFS

was, at all events, made plain to the Tsar by the press of Europe that his system of ruling was regarded as barbarous.

A more moderate man, or one who claimed at least to have some sympathy with liberalism, Prince Sviatopolk-Mirski, was put in charge of the ministry of the interior, and the struggle passed to a new phase. On November 19th the police of St. Petersburg permitted a large meeting of members of the provincial Zemstvos, and a deputation of these was allowed to see Prince Mirski. They demanded free parliamentary institutions and manhood suffrage, and the Prince undertook to lay their demands before the Tsar. It is reported that the Dowager-Empress, the Grand Dukes, and the reactionary ministers violently opposed any concession, and we must assume both that they would be consulted and that they would give this advice. The Tsar was nervous and timorous, physically and mentally unequal to the great burden which now lay upon him. On December 12th he issued a ukase in which he promised reforms, but he described the demands of the representatives of the Zemstvos as "inadmissible" and inconsistent with "the fundamental laws of the Empire." The bulk of his people were, he said, "true to the old foundations of the State-organisation," and he would protect them from the intrigues of agitators.

The battle continued. A great meeting at St.

THE ROMANCE OF THE ROMANOFFS

Petersburg was addressed openly by writers and scholars of distinction, and amongst the crowd the cry "Down with the Autocracy" was heard. Petitions and demands for representative institutions rained upon the Tsar from all classes of his subjects. Strikes and riots filled the daily press. On January 9th the notorious Father Gapon led 300,000 workers to the Winter Palace, to lay their grievances before the "Little Father," and before evening the snows of St. Petersburg were stained with the blood of thousands. There were spurts of revolt at Kichineff, Odessa, Moscow, and even Kronstadt.

On February 4th the Grand Duke Sergius, the most corrupt of the reactionaries, was assassinated. Prince Mirski resigned and was succeeded by Bulygin. Before the new minister was established, the Tsar issued a new ukase affirming the autocratic principle, but Bulygin insisted that he should modify this act of mad defiance, dictated by the palace-clique, by issuing on the same day a promise to convoke a consultative assembly of representatives of the people. He appointed a commission of inquiry, and in reply to a deputation from a second conference of the Zemstvos he announced that a National Assembly would soon be granted. The long-expected ukase appeared on May 10th. It opened on a note of repentance:

"A State cannot be solid unless it holds as sacred

the traditions of the past. We have failed in this, and God has punished us. The sovereignty of ancient Russia was indissolubly bound up with 'the voice of the land,' with the representatives of the people assembled in council."

For the first time the Romanoffs perceived that, centuries before their dynasty was cradled, Russia had had a past, and a democratic past.

But the project of the new assembly, the first Duma, turned this avowal into derision. The business of the representatives of the people was merely to examine proposals which would be laid before the Imperial Council: the Tsar alone could initiate and pass legislation. By further regulations, in fact, the members of the Duma were put at the mercy of the conservative Senate. The autocracy was maintained in all its mediævalism. Liberals and radicals now united in a fierce demand of reform. Russia was paralysed by a general strike and the suspension of traffic. More than a million workers were on strike. In a momentary panic the Tsar directed Count de Witte to draw up a list of reforms, and on October 30th (1905) he issued the famous ukase which has since given a name to the vast body of moderate Russian reformers (the "Octobrists"). He would grant manhood suffrage, real national representation, freedom of speech and religion, and so on. As usual, the first breath of liberty let loose a passion of discussion.

THE ROMANCE OF THE ROMANOFFS

The radicals and independents united to form the powerful body of the Constitutional Democrats (the "Cadets," or K. D.s). A council of labour deputies was formed with the express purpose of holding the supreme power when the Tsar had been deposed.

In brief, Russia was seen aflame with revolution. There were mutinies in the fleet at Kronstadt and at Sevastopol, and the audacity of the more radical elements led, at Moscow, to the futile and pathetic rebellion in which large numbers of students lost their lives. The revolution was premature. The troops were unprepared for revolt on such an issue as the constitution, and the "Black Bands" everywhere aided the police and dipped their hands in the blood of Jews and radicals. The active rebellion was truculently suppressed, and the jails were packed to suffocation. His reactionary advisers urged the triumphant Tsar to refuse all concessions, but the rumble of the more moderate malcontents was still heard on every side, and the promise of some sort of national assembly had to be carried out.

It was in these circumstances that, on May 10th, 1906, Nicholas opened the first Duma. The name had been invented by the reforming minister of Alexander I, Speranski, and it represented the measure of popular representation which might have been regarded as satisfactory in those semi-

THE LAST OF THE ROMANOFFS

feudal days. For a civilisation of the twentieth century it was ridiculously inadequate, and it soon proved only a channel for the comparatively safe release of the boiling sentiment which filled the country. Before the Romanoff dynasty fell it was customary for polite journalists and essayists to explain that the excesses of the radicals frustrated the work of the new institution. It is unhappily true that the left wing of every reform-movement uses a rhetoric which is little in accord with its loud insistence on justice, but in this case even the work of moderate members of the Duma was obnoxious to the authorities. Day by day the state of the Russian jails, the gross conduct of police and military authorities, and the barbarous practices of their subordinates were brought to light. Week by week men waited, and waited in vain, for the further instalments of reform which had been promised.

The Duma grew more and more vehement in its attacks upon the Government. The Cadets formed the majority of its members, and they formulated their demands for adult suffrage, real parliamentary institutions, the abolition of capital punishment, a political amnesty, the suppression of the Imperial Council, and the expropriation of the large land-owners. Goremykin, a tool of the palace-clique which had put him in the place of Count de Witte, refused to comply, and on July 23rd the Tsar dissolved the Duma. The measure was a failure, and Goremykin had to surrender his place to Stolypin. The ejected Cadets retired to Finland, and appealed to the people to refuse to pay taxes or render military service: for which, three years later, they were condemned to imprisonment and the loss of their civil rights.

Stolypin had the ingenious idea of severing the great mass of the peasants from the radicals by separate concessions, and in October and November the Tsar appealed for their support. They were put on the same footing as other classes in regard to the right of entering the public service or schools, the issue of passports, and in rural elections. They were released from obligatory residence in the district in which they were registered, permitted to take away their share of the communal property, and protected from punishment without trial. By these means, and by tampering with the electoral law (which he dare not yet alter) Stolypin secured a second Duma in which the Cadets were greatly reduced. Instead of 185 seats they now had only 108. But they still formed the largest party, and their leader Golovkin was President of the Duma. In face of their demands the Tsar authorised Stolypin to offer the crown-lands and imperial estates to be shared amongst the peasants, but the radicals were not appeased, and on June 14th, three months after the opening of the Duma, Stolypin demanded a secret session in order to consider an indictment of the Social Democrats, whose number had increased to 77 at the last election. Almost the whole of them were charged with complicity in a plot to undermine the loyalty of the army and navy.

The Duma was still overwhelmingly radical—a sufficient commentary on the Tsar's claim that the mass of his people clung to the old traditions—and refused to lend itself to this manœuvre. Two days later, June 16th, Nicholas again asserted his power and dissolved the second Duma. It was, he declared, not representative of the "Russian spirit" and would not support his government in suppressing disorder. To make it more representative of this Russian spirit, which was supposed to animate the bulk of the population, he narrowed the electoral qualifications, in violation of his 1905 ukase, and reduced the membership from 524 to 442. The Cadets now sank from 108 to 45, the Socialists from 77 to 17. The conservatives rose from 60 to 100, and the Octobrists from 31 to 110. Liberalism, of one shade or another, still greatly outweighed conservatism even in this mangled representation of the Russian people; and assassinations, strikes, and fiery rhetoric impressed upon Europe the grievances of those who were excluded from representation. In the year 1907 there were 627 executions, and about 70,000 were sent into exile. In 1908 there were 786 executions, and the number

THE ROMANCE OF THE ROMANOFFS

of exiles rose to 180,000. The population of the jails of Russia rose from 91,000 in the year 1904 to 174,000 in the year 1910.

This was the "comparative tranquillity" which the chroniclers of Russian events ascribe to the country between 1907 and 1917. Quarterly notices of the number of political executions were put into small type in English and American journals, and from the sombre silence that brooded over the land there issued at times the lurid message of assassination. In 1909 occurred the astounding revelation of the secret-police spy and professed Socialist Azeff, and it became known that outrages were instigated by the police in order to strengthen their system. The former head of the police had to be sentenced to five years' imprisonment; the head of the secret police of St. Petersburg was assassinated. In 1911 Stolypin was permitted by the Tsar to suspend the Imperial Council and the Duma, so that he could avail himself of the clause of the constitution which enabled him to pass laws while the councils were not sitting; and on September 14th, while Nicholas sat in his box in the opera at Kieff, he had the horror of witnessing the murder of his complaisant minister. Still he clung to his poor rags of autocracy. Still religious adventurers and spiritist mediums plied their lucratic charlatanry in the palaces. Still the flower of the young generation rotted in the overcrowded jails or lan-

THE LAST OF THE ROMANOFFS

guished in Siberia. The jails had a "maximum accommodation" for 107,000 prisoners, and in 1910 about 180,000 men and women were crowded into them. Typhus flourished in them. Suicides of prisoners rose to 160 in a single month. The most brutal outrages were committed on young women and men.

These facts one learned, as I experienced at the time, by a laborious comparison of the statements of little-read writers and statistics. To the world at large a different picture was offered. Men were told how, in 1906, a group of affrighted Polish peasants, headed by an abbess, came to St. Petersburg to inquire if it was really true that (as zealous Roman Catholic proselytisers had told them) the Tsar had made his submission to the Pope. They saw a minister, on Easter morn, and to their solemn salutation, "Christ is risen," he blunderingly replied, "Good Day"; and their hearts sank. But they also saw Nicholas, and to their faltering religious salute he replied cheerfully, "In truth He is risen," and they fell sobbing at his feet. Or it was the festival of Poltava in 1909, when Nicholas, seeing his carriage surrounded by a dense throng of peasants, alighted and talked familiarly with them for two hours. And there was the story of how at Christmas, 1912, when the members of the Duma were presented to him, he summoned the shrinking peasant-deputies from the last row and honoured them above the others. Nicholas II knew quite well what was happening in Russia. His small mind thought that tasting the food of soldiers and sailors—before a camera—visiting the hospitals, and embracing carefully-selected peasants would save the autocracy in the twentieth century.

The five-year period of the third Duma expired in 1912, and the new election proved a victory for the conservatives. The Octobrists had ventured to resist the demand of the clergy that the elementary schools should be handed over to them, and the popes had fiercely and unscrupulously canvassed the peasant-electors. Still, however, 285 Octobrists and other radicals faced the 155 members of the Right, and small measures of reform had to be passed. They were inadequate, and the year 1913 saw another great wave of disturbance. The number of strikers rose to 460,000. At Kieff a great gathering of representatives of all the towns of the Empire condemned the Government. The Octobrists united with the other radicals of the Duma and, by 146 votes to 113 (many abstaining) condemned the ministers for not proceeding in the path of reform. But I need not run in detail over events which are still fresh in the general memory. These brief notices will suffice to indicate that the spirit of progress lived and grew in spite of every effort of Nicholas II to strangle it.

The conflict entered upon its last stage. That

THE LAST OF THE ROMANOFFS

Nicholas II wanted war, however much he may have hoped to profit by the aid of France and England, we have no reason whatever to believe. Nor is it possible as yet to pass a sober opinion upon the charge that he intended, when the war dragged, to make a separate peace with Germany. That his German wife was won by the miserable adventurer Rasputin, and some of his ministers by German bribery, seems clear enough; and, although he had been second only to the Kaiser in the vigorous lead of his nation until the end of 1916, there is grave reason to think that he was then won by the prayers of his family and intrigues of his ministers. But the Russian revolution was not based on this theory as much as is generally believed. The mass of the people were bewildered by the war, and have not since shown any great zeal to prosecute it. The educated malcontents were, as we saw, thoroughly organised and ready to grasp any pretext for a successful revolution. Only a minority of military men and liberal politicians were essentially moved by the failure of the dynasty to arm Russia efficiently and prosecute the war.

The food-supply was the immediate ground of the revolution. On February 8th, when the five-year period of the Duma of 1912 approached its term, the Tsar was urged to extend its life, as was done in other countries. The Tsar refused, and he spoke of elections in the coming fall. The suspicion that he was going to proceed irregularly coincided with a shortage of grain in the large cities, especially Petrograd (as the capital was now named), which was gradually stirring the anger of the people. We may assume that the revolutionary organisation exploited this anger with all their power, and especially undermined the loyalty of the few regiments which were left at Petrograd.

On March 8th the people of Petrograd, especially the women, began to throng the streets, and the workers to quit the factories. Rodzianko, the President of the Duma, summoned a conference on the food-question, and he and Professor Milyukoff, the second hero of the revolution, strongly criticised the incompetence of the ministers. Rodzianko, a former officer of the Guards and husband of a Golitzin princess, was a noble of distinction, but he was an Octobrist and a friend of the people. The crowds were still larger in the streets on March 9th; and on Sunday, the 11th, they turned out in immense numbers and fraternised with the few troops who were visible. The guards, however, were imperfectly won, and on the Sunday afternoon they fired a volley into the crowd and about a hundred were killed or wounded. It is one of the strangest testimonies to the amazing condition of Russia that the crowds remained on the streets and said, sympathetically, to the soldiers: "We are sorry for you, brothers, you had to do your duty."

On the Monday morning it became known that the Tsar had suspended for two months the sittings of the Duma and the Imperial Council, and the revolution was inaugurated. Troops to the number of about 30,000 marched upon the arsenal, distributed arms to the people, and fought the police and the loyal troops. The Progressives and the Socialists formed a committee of twelve of their ablest representatives, including Rodzianko, Milyukoff, and Kerenski; and Rodzianko telegraphed to the Tsar a peremptory demand for a new government. The fight with the police, who mounted the roofs with rifles and machine-guns, was continued on the following day, but the public buildings fell one by one into the hands of the revolutionaries, and about midnight of the 13-14th the enterprise was crowned by the submission to the Provisional Government of the Preobrajensky Guards. Moscow soon sent its adhesion, and the troops in the field gradually assured the new government of their allegiance.

Nicholas II was with the army, at the headquarters of General Russky, when the alarming news from Petrograd reached him. He would return to the capital, he said; but at Bolgoe station he was quietly persuaded to return to Pskoff. There, in a small, dimly lighted room, the last of the

THE ROMANCE OF THE ROMANOFFS

Romanoffs received the delegates of the people—M. Gutchkoff and a conservative member of the Duma. It is said that Nicholas asked calmly what was required of him, and, when he was told that he must abdicate, he at once demanded a piece of paper. He would not, however, resign the crown to his son, as they wished. He would not be parted from his son, he said: and it is probable that he was moved by his deep affection for the boy. He would leave the throne to his brother Michael. The fateful document was there and then composed, and Nicholas II signed away his power: signed, as it proved, the death-warrant of the Romanoff dynasty. He remains ambiguous in his last imperial pronouncement. In words of singular dignity and detachment he answers the call of the Russian people to lay down his autocracy, and he prays for a speedy victory over Germany. But for the ghastly, unforgettable horrors which stain his reign we could find words of admiration for the last weak descendant of Michael Romanoff.

INDEX

Adacheff, 55
Adrianople, Treaty of, 296
Alexander I, 261-283
Alexander II, 306-337
Alexander III, 338-356
Alexandra, the Empress, 362
Alexis I, 82-88
Alexis II, 152, 156-159
Anne of Mecklenburg, 191, 197, 200-202, 214
Anne, the Empress, 187-200, 206-210
Anthony of Brunswick, 200-201, 209
Arakcheef, 278, 280, 292
Arsenieff, Daria, 152, 164, 183
Arsenieff, Marie, 152, 164
Askold, 14
Astrakhan, Expedition to, 148
Augustus II, 134, 142, 193
Austerlitz, 264
Azeff, 380

Bakunin, 327
Batu, 31
Beard prohibited, 136-7
Beketoff, 223
Bennigsen, 261
Bestuzheff, Alexis, 215, 220, 222
Bestuzheff, Mickael, 215, 217, 219, 220, 223
Bestuzheva, Countess, 219

Bible Society at Petrograd, 275, 292
Bielinsky, 327
Biren, Count, 189-203
Bismarck, 332, 333, 353
Bobrinski, 251
Bogolyubski, Andrew, 26-28
Bulgaria created, 333
Bulygin, 374
Byzantine Empire, the, 10, 34

Cadets, the, 376, 377, 378
Calendar, reform of the, 139-140
Castlereagh, 267, 270
Catherine I, 145-6, 155, 161-176
Catherine II, 221, 223-227, 228-257
Catherine II, character of, 246, 248-254
Charles Frederick of Holstein, 171, 172
Charles of Sweden, 135, 144, 145
Charlotte of Wolfenbüttel, 156
Chétardie, Marquis de la, 212, 213, 217, 222
Chino-Japanese War, the, 367
Chiuski, Andrew, 53
Chiuski, Vassili, 67
Christianity, entry of, 20
Church, reform of the, 136
Circassia, annexation of, 320

INDEX

Clothing, reform of, 137
Communism of the early Slavs, 6-7
Constantine, the Grand Duke, 271, 282, 285, 286, 287, 296
Constantinople, 10, 20, 21, 22, 24
Crimean War, the, 302, 303, 308, 309
Czartoryski, 262

Dagmar, the Empress, 339, 358, 361, 362
Dalny, 368
Danielovitch, George, 38
Dashkoff, Princess, 235, 236
Dchingis Khan, 30
Democracy of the early Slavs, 3, 17
Devier, Count, 177
Dmitri, Prince, 63
Dolgoruki, Alexis, 185, 186, 192
Dolgoruki, Catherine, 186, 192
Dolgoruki, George, 26, 37
Dolgoruki, Maria, 77
Dolgoruki, Prince, 103
Drunkenness in Russia, 85, 196
Duma, the First, 376, 377
Duma, the Second, 378, 379
Duma, the Third, 379, 382, 383

Elizabeth, Queen, 60, 64
Elizabeth, the Empress, 171, 174, 180, 187, 199-227
England and Medieval Russia, 60, 75
Erfurt, 265
Eudoxia, the Empress, 110, 152, 158, 164
Euphrosyne, 156

Feodor I, 61, 63
Feodor II, 98
Finns, the, 4
France, alliance with, 355
Frederick the Great, 222, 224, 228, 241

Gallitzin, Boris, 110, 112
Gallitzin, Vassili, 105, 106, 107, 108, 109, 110, 111
Gastavus Adolphus, 75
Gleboff, 158
Glinski, Helena, 52
Godunoff, Boris, 61, 62, 64, 65
Godunoff, Irene, 61
Golden Horde, the, 33
Golitzin, Prince, 275, 280
Golitzuin, Demetrius, 188, 190, 192
Golovkin, 152, 193
Gorchakoff, Prince, 317
Gordon, Patrick, 123, 151
Goremykin, 377
Greeks, Russia and the, 295
Grudzinski, Jeannette, 286
Gutchkoff, 386

Hague Congress, the, 366
Halturin, 335
Hastings, Mary, 60
Hertzen, 327
Holland, Peter the Great in, 118-120
Holy Alliance, the, 269
Holy League, the, 341
Holy Synod, founding of the, 141

Iaroslaf, 22, 23, 24
Ignatieff, General, 342
Ivan III, 39-46

INDEX

Ivan IV, 51-59
Ivan V, 238
Ivanovitch, Dmitri, 39

Japan, Russia and, 367-368
Jesuits, the, in Russia, 66, 67, 69
Jews, the, in Russia, 348-350, 365

Kantemir, Maria, 165, 167
Karakasoff, 330
Karamsin, 290
Kerenski, 385
Khazars, the, 9
Khlopoff, Maria, 76
Khodynski, 363
Khovanski, 106
Kieff, 12, 14, 15, 19
Kings, origin of, 3
Kisseleff, Count, 293
Kotchubey, 262
Krudener, Juliana von, 268, 269

Ladislas of Poland, 69, 71
Lambert, General, 318
Lamsdorff, Count, 370
Lanskoi, 250, 314
Lapukhin, Natalia, 218, 219, 220
Lefort, 114, 117, 151, 152, 153
Lescyznski, 194
Lestocq, 207, 208, 212, 219
Lieven, Prince, 290
Lithuanians, the, 35, 39
London, Peter the Great in, 119-120
Louis XV, 146
Luders, Count, 319

Magnitski, 280
Manchuria, 367
Marfa, 42, 72, 73

Marriage, 138
Maryna, 68, 69, 74
Matveef, Artaman, 93, 94, 97, 98, 103
Maurice, the Emperor, 17
Mazeppa, Ivan, 143, 144
Melikoff, Loris, 336, 341
Mengden, Julia, 203-205, 209
Menshikoff, Prince, 151, 162, 163, 168-177, 182, 183
Metternich, Prince, 267, 270 271, 280
Michael I, 72, 73
Mikhailoff, Peter, 117
Miloradovitch, General, 287
Miloslavski, Anna, 84
Milyukoff, Professor, 384, 385
Milyutin, 314
Mir, the, 4, 5, 11, 315
Mirovitch, 238
Mirski, Prince, 373
Mongols, the, 31-36, 42-44
Mons, Anna, 153, 166
Mons, Peter, 166
Morozoff, Boris, 83, 84, 88-90
Moscow, 34, 37, 41-44
Moscow, Patriarchate of, 62, 140
Moujik, 23
Münnick, Count, 201, 203, 204, 211, 233
Muravieff, 275

Napoleon I, 260, 262, 263, 264, 265, 266, 267
Narva, the battle of, 134, 143
Naryshkin, Natalia, 96, 97, 99, 100, 110
Nestor, 3, 17
Nevski, Alexander, 37
Nicholas I, 284-307

INDEX

Nicholas II, 357-386
Nihilism, 328
Nikititch, Ivan, 71
Nikon, 89, 90, 91, 92, 93
Norsemen, the, 12, 14, 15, 18-28
Novgorod, 12, 14, 27, 42, 43, 51, 58
Nystadt, the Peace of, 147

Octobrists, the, 98, 375, 379, 382
Oleg, 15, 19
Olga, 19
Oranienbaum, 234, 235
Orloff, Gregory, 234, 235, 248, 249
Ostermann, Count, 172, 174, 175, 182, 183, 184, 185, 207, 208, 209
Otrepieff, Gregory, 65

Pahlen, Count, 261
Palæologus, Sophia, 47
Panslavism, 332, 353
Paris, Peter the Great at, 146
Passek, Captain, 238
Paul I, 230, 253-262
Peacefulness of the Slavs, 11
Perovskaia, Sophia, 330, 334
Peter II, 169-187
Peter III, 214, 215, 228, 229, 230, 231, 233-7
Peter the Great, birth of, 97
  character of, 126
  education of, 112
  family of, 152, 162-164
  journey of, 117-121
  reforms of, 136-140, 148-150
  revels of, 126
  seizes power, 108-112
Petrograd, foundation of, 142-3
Philaret, 67, 72, 75, 76, 77, 78

Plehve, 372
Pobiedonostseff, 339, 340, 341, 342, 344, 362
Poles, the, 32, 35, 42, 45, 70, 134, 242, 248, 271, 296, 318, 350
Poltava, the battle of, 144, 145
Poniatovski, Count, 230, 231, 242
Port Arthur, 368
Potiamkin, 251
Prascovia, 153, 189
Preobrajenshots, 108, 109
Pruth, the battle of, 145
Pskoff, 29, 34, 43, 51, 58

Rasputin, 383
Razumovsky, Alexis, 208, 212
Regulation for Reinforced Protection, 366-368
Religion of the Early Slavs, 6
Revolution, the French, 254
Riazan, 51
Rodzianko, 384, 385
Romanoffs, beginning of the, 53-56, 72
Romanovna, Anastasia, 54, 58
Rumania, independence of, 333
Rumans, the, 7
Rurik, 14, 15
Rus, the, 13, 16
Russo-Japanese War the, 368-370
Russo-Turkish War, the, 301

Saardam, 119
Saltykoff, Daria, 240
Saltykoff, Sergius, 230
San Stefano Treaty, the, 333
Sarai, 32, 33
Sazonoff, 372
Scythians, the, 4
Serbia, independence of, 333

390

INDEX

Serfdom, growth of, 62, 240
Serfdom, suppression of, 276, 310-315
Sergius, Grand Duke, 362, 374
Seven Years' War, the, 225
Shein, General, 121
Sheremetieff, General, 151, 161, 162
Shishkoff, 281
Shuvaloff, Alexis, 244
Shuvaloff, Ivan, 222
Sigismund of Poland, 69, 75
Simeon the Proud, 38
Slavophile Creed, the, 291
Slavs, origin of the, 2-12
Socialism, beginning of, 310
Sophia, the Princess, 101-125
Sperenski, 272, 273, 274, 289
Stolypin, 378, 380
Strecknieff, Eudoxia, 77
Streltsui, the, 102, 123
Suvoroff, General, 260
Suzdal, 26, 27, 34
Swedes the, 34

Tatars, the, 30, 37, 39
Tcherkasky, Prince, 215
Telepnieff, Prince, 52
Terem, the, 49
Teutonic knights, the, 35
Theodosius, 171
Third Section, the, 330
Timur, 39, 44
Tolstoi, Anisia, 152, 164
Tolstoi, Dmitri, 351
Triple Alliance, the, 355
Troitsa, 106

Trubetskoi, Prince, 287
Tsar, title of, 48, 54
Tsikler, 117
Tzadovski, Count, 275

Ukraine, the, 43, 147
United States, the, and Russia, 273

Valdemar of Denmark, 80
Varangians, the, 13
Vassili, son of Ivan III, 51
Vassili the Blond, 39
Vassiltchikoff, 248
Véché, the, 11, 29, 36
Venning, Mr., 279
Viatka, 29
Vice in Russia, 85-7
Vienna Congress, the, 267
Vladimir, 27
Vladimir, St., 20-21
Voievolojski, Euphemia, 84
Volost, the, 6
Voltaire and Catherine, 244-5
Vorontsoff, Elizabeth, 231

Witte, Count de, 363, 370, 375, 377
Woman in Russia, 49, 85, 137, 329

Yaguzhinsky, 172, 190

Zarutski, 74
Zemstvo, the, 321, 344
Zotoff, 127
Zuboff, Plato, 250, 256, 261

www.ingramcontent.com/pod-product-compliance
Lightning Source LLC
Chambersburg PA
CBHW020827160426
43192CB00007B/548